KINGDOM
EXPOSED

NATHAN VAUGHN

KINGDOM EXPOSED

Edited by Caron Davis

NATHAN VAUGHN

Whosoever Press

Whosoever Press books may be ordered through booksellers or by contacting:

Whosoever Press
10749 AL Hwy 168

Boaz, AL. 35957

www.whosoeverpress.com
256-706-3315

Because of the dynamic nature of the Internet, any web addresses or links contained in this book may have changed since publication and may no longer valid. The views expressed in this work are solely those of the author and do not necessarily reflect the views of the publisher, and the publisher hereby disclaims any responsibility for them.

ISBN-13:978-1790875931

Library of Congress Control Number: Applied For

Printed in the United States of America

Whosoever Press Date: 8/24/2018

Whosoever Press adamantly supports the nation of Israel.

Table of Contents

Introduction

For the last 30 years, I have worked as a computer and robotics technician where I have had to understand the entire inner-workings of computers interfaced with mechanical equipment. I have had to understand it to the point that I could not only troubleshoot and repair it, but also understand every movement it made or why it didn't move as designed. I had to understand the strength and weakness of every part, its weight limit, every adjustment to the millimeter, understand how every sensor and photo eye worked, as well as how to adjust the software to make every part move as designed. Not only understand it well enough to repair it, but also understand it to the point where I could tear it down, rebuild it, and put it back together again, fully operational.

This is how my brain operates, in detail. Therefore I must understand every detail of how the spirit realm and demonic spirits operate. Paul tells us in (2 Corinthians 2:11) that we do not need to be ignorant of Satan's devices so that he cannot get an advantage over us. With this knowledge, I can better fight the battle against these forces and win. Because I understand their every move, I know their strategies, tactics, weaknesses and strengths; I can adjust my strategies and tactics accordingly, so I can win.

Throughout history, since the beginning of time, there have been— as Jesus described in (Matthew 5:8)—a history of *wars and rumors of wars* that would take place in the natural world, but there is also a war going on in the spiritual world. In the spirit world, which is just as real as the one that we live in, there are two kingdoms: the kingdom of God and the kingdom of Satan. These kingdoms are at constant, never-ending, never-ceasing war against each other, and this war bleeds over into the natural world.

People have no problem believing that God has a kingdom, but many people do not believe that Satan has a kingdom as well, even though Jesus told us that Satan does in (Matthew 12:26). Satan offered Jesus the kingdoms of the satanic world in (Matthew 4) if He would only worship him. Both kingdoms operate with a delegated system of power, rank and authority, just as the earthly military and governmental earthly kingdom. Paul tells us this in the (1st, 3rd and 6th chapters of Ephesians). In the spirit realm there are territorial spirits that are ruling these kingdoms.

The earthly military forces have both basic and advanced training that teach the science of planning and directing. This is known as strategy and tactics of warfare. The soldiers must learn not only their weapons, maneuvers, tactics, hand to hand combat, and their own strategies, but also the strategies, weapons, maneuvers, and tactics of their enemies so they can fight an effective war and win. They must learn their enemy's strengths and weaknesses to make each attack count when they are mobilized for the invasion. Both offensive and defensive warfare encounters are taught in this training. Without this training an army is useless. Basic training is useless without training on how to use the available weapons.

Jesus said in (Luke 14:31): "Or what king, going out to engage in conflict with another king, will not first sit down and consider and take counsel whether he is able with ten thousand [men] to meet him who comes against him with twenty thousand?" This is where our training pays off in the spiritual war that we are fighting.

The information in this book, along with the wisdom that we gain from God with each spiritual battle experience, prepares us. But it is a step-by-step process. No one, regardless of what kind of spiritual strength they may have in God today, started out that way in the beginning. Like many of you, they may have started by wondering:

"What is going on?"
"How do I fight this?"
"Why am I going through this?"

"Why did God allow this?"
"I'll never make it through this one."

Satan has declared an offensive war on you. So, you declare a defensive war back on him. But we can also declare an offensive war on him through God, His authority, and His Word, using prayer and fasting as our weapons. This is where training in the tactical maneuvers of warfare is applied.

In an earthly military the soldiers learn how to apply the training they have been taught in actual combat training situations. My son told me when he was in the army they used real ammo, 50 caliber machine guns, grenades and other munitions. The Jeep he was in got blown off the road. Another time the place he was in was blown up around him, and he was injured. But he would have never known what real battle conditions would be like without training. He may have frozen in the real fight, not able to save himself and others without training.

Someone told me once, "Oh, I wish that I could face battles with the peace that you have, and the faith that you have that God will just take care of it."

I said, "Well, do you want to fight a spiritual battle?"

They replied, "Well, no."

"Do you want to get thrown into the middle of a spiritual battle?"

"Of course not!"

"Do you want to get bit by a copper head and have to pray for yourself?"

"NO!"

"Do you want to have to pray for a family member's life that the doctors say should not make it?"

"Of course not."

"Do you want to wake up at night and face a demon face to face that is haunting your house, or pray for someone who is demon possessed while they are rolling on the floor, foaming at the mouth and speaking with an ungodly voice?"

"No way!"

Well, not every Christian will face all that, but some do, and more. But, you will never grow your spiritual muscles without facing, dealing with, battling, and learning to win the war, one battle at a time. In these kinds of situations, believing and watching God will bring victory each time.

(Hosea 4:6) tells us that God's people are destroyed, meaning demolished, torn down and destroyed, due to a lack of knowledge. Paul told us not to be ignorant of Satan's devices; meaning his schemes, tricks, and tactics of deceit. By learning the devices, he uses, we can detect when demonic spirits are at work and which ones we are dealing with, even if it is a case of possession. Through the Holy Spirit we can recognize Satan's strategies that he uses against us. And only through God, by the blood of Jesus Christ, can we win.

Chapter 1
Warfare

(Isaiah 54:17) is one of my favorite verses on spiritual warfare. "No weapon that is formed against you shall prosper, every tongue that shall rise against you in judgment you shall condemn. This is the heritage of the servants of the Lord, and their righteousness is of me, says the Lord."

The weapon formed against us is the attack, or the strategy, that has been planned and orchestrated by Satan and the demonic forces to steal, kill, and destroy us, and to cause us pain and torment while they do it. They watch everything we do and say, and they keep record of it to use against us in an accusation to God in obtaining a legal cause to attack us. But when we are covered and forgiven by Jesus' blood whatever they have in accusation is forgiven, and we know our authority that He has given us, and then we have the victory. This authority and victory is our heritage. Heritage meaning a tradition that is passed down from one generation to another; our heritage is a generational blessing of forgiveness, power, authority, and victory. That is our legacy. Our righteousness is of God. Our authority comes through Him and His righteousness and is recognized by Satan and the demonic as God in us.

At 3 a.m., on a Friday morning, God gave me a dream of this verse. I was in the spirit realm, and it looked much like the setting of a sci-fi movie or video game, like nothing that could be found on earth. It was semi-dark, yet I could see everything that was happening. There were demonic spirits 50 to 100 yards from me who were firing what looked like missiles of attack at me. I thought of the fiery darts that Paul mentioned in Ephesians 6:16. With each one fired at me, God would drop a shield down between the spirits and where I was, keeping me protected. After this had gone on for some time, I realized that I was being surrounded by many demonic spirits in what seemed an unexpected sneak attack. Each one of them had an array of different medieval weapons in their hands. They were in a circle closing in on me. The leader of the group looked me in the eyes and said with a sinister voice "I am going to kill you." I looked him straight in the eyes and begin to say over and over without stopping, "In the name of Jesus, In the name of Jesus, In the name of Jesus." Then I would point my finger in the face of different demons and say, "God loves you, in the name of Jesus. In the name of Jesus."

As I continued this, without stopping, they became paralyzed and could not move; they couldn't raise their arms; their hands lost strength and they began to drop their weapons to the ground.

I then saw large beings (about twice the size of the spirits) that I knew were angels, although they were not like any angels I had seen in pictures or imagined. I can't even describe their appearance. They were holding the demonic spirits back behind their angelic arms. The demonic spirits did not have the slightest bit of strength to fight for their release. I pointed my finger in the face of one of them and then waved my arm and pointed to the rest and said, with a voice of authority, "And THIS is "MY HERITAGE."

One interesting fact about this dream is this: the only part of this verse that I knew was, "No weapon formed against me shall prosper." I knew it was (Isaiah 54:17), so I looked it up and read it. That's when I found the part about our heritage. God is just cool isn't He!

Spiritual warfare is simply our battle against Satan and his demonic forces. In (1 Peter 2:11), Peter warns us to abstain from the sensual urges, evil desires and passions of our fleshly lust because the demonic use them to wage "war" against our souls. The Greek word for war here is "Strateuomai" which means to make a military expedition and to lead soldiers to war or battle as a commander, and to fight in battle array to either kill or to take captive. The word "expedition" means to go on an "exploration," which means to travel, to examine, investigate, and to learn about.

So, let me explain this: Satan and his demonic forces examine us, they investigate us, and watch our reactions to their suggestions or temptations so they will know exactly where and how to hit us and defeat us. Then they carefully add more fuel to the fire as the warfare continues. Therefore, a person may start out light in drugs, pornography, or whatever their problem is, and, over time, it grows into full-blown bondage and addiction.

In (2 Corinthians 10:3-5), Paul used the same Greek word for "our" warfare against Satan and his strongholds, where "we" are to lead a military expedition into the enemy's territory, going to war and battle as a commander to fight and to win.

But the battles are not always simple. Our warfare begins in the heavens. In (Matthew 16:19), Jesus gave us the power to bind what is already bound in heaven, and to loose what is already loosed in the heavens. Our power and authority come from Jesus whom we must remember as we consider that there are two kinds of spiritual warfare: offensive and defensive.

The only way to keep from being beat up in this war is to know everything about the enemy's tactics and strategies of attack and how to fight offensively.

Paul tells us in (2 Corinthians 2:11) that we are not to be ignorant of Satan's devices, which means his plans, schemes, traps, and tricks. (Ephesians 6:11) uses the word "wiles" meaning a trick or a trap. (Psalms 91:3) uses the word "snare," meaning to be caught in a trap. In this book, we will study many different tactics and strategies used by Satan and the demonic as well as our own strategies which we can use to fight back.

The main tactics of Satan are deception, to create fear and defeat, and to work through other people. We face family members, coworkers, people we go to church with, who seem to cause us trials and tribulations every day because they are being influenced by the demonic and are not even aware of it. Jesus even had to rebuke Peter, his own trusted disciple, a saved-child of God, a minister of the gospel, a world changer, an anointed preacher with enough faith to see the lame stand up and walk. He said to Peter, "Get behind me Satan," because of a comment Peter had made. Did Peter mean to do this? No, I'm sure he didn't. He was just being Peter, a plain-spoken, talk-before-you-think kind of person. Just as many people in the church are today.

Satan can use this as spiritual warfare to injure and destroy because behind these natural enemies are the spiritual enemies who inspire their actions against us. This is how these people seem to know exactly how to push just the right buttons to set us off. These spirits know they have done their jobs when they hear someone say, "Well, I'll never go back to THAT church again."

In World War II, Hitler, whom I believe was one of the men in history Satan set up to be an antichrist if the time were to occur, was greatly influenced by, and introduced to, much of the occult by Dietrich Eckart. Eckart was an occultist to the highest degree, and a practitioner of black magic. He taught Hitler how to receive demonic visions and how to communicate with them. By doing this, Eckart bragged that he had influenced history more than any other German. When Hitler was at an all-time low, it was Eckart who told Hitler that in just 30 days Hitler's life would change. Thirty days later, to the day, he became chancellor of Germany.

Hitler was empowered and influenced demonically by the spirit of antichrist, the occult, and the German army. This led him to invade many countries, towns, cities, and communities as his army marched across Europe.

I believe Hitler was protected demonically because there were an estimated 42 assassination attempts on his life. He survived them all with barely a scratch. The German invasion left many dead, crippled, starving, unjustly imprisoned, alone, diseased and, over all, caused massive destruction and havoc. Just as Satan and his demonic forces do to the physical, mental, emotional, and spiritual of the human race that does not know how to fight against them. Many were in total fear of the German and the S.S. uniforms. Why? Because they had superiority in weapons and fire power. None of the civilians had the power, knowledge, weapons or authority to fight back. But when the United States and many other countries allied together, we had the power, knowledge, weapons, and authority to win. We, as Christians must do the same in prayer and intercession if we want to experience revival, healing, and deliverance.

During the American Revolutionary War of the late 1700's, America would have lost the war to the English if it had not been for the tactics of warfare colonialists had learned from fighting the Indians. In other words, the new Americans could not fight the way they had always fought before in Europe, lining up in a straight line, taking shots at the enemy. Instead, they hid behind trees, rocks, under bridges, camouflaged under leaves, and any other way they could use to mimic the way the Indians fought. They changed their tactics and weapons; they used and adapted them to the battle to fight offensively rather than waiting to fight back defensively. They intercepted messages and knew in advance where the English planned to attack. This way they could ambush and foil the attack of the enemy "before" they themselves were attacked.

It is the same way with Satan and spiritual warfare. Through the Holy Spirit we can receive warnings ahead of an attack through dreams, visions, and the gifts of the Spirit. Through the gifts of the Spirit such as discernment, word of knowledge, word of wisdom, and prophecy, we can know about the attacks ahead of time. We can be praying against Satan and the demonic forces before they strike. However, we must learn their strategies of warfare to do this. We must know their weapons, and we must know our weapons. If you

15

know God's power, and you know how to take up your spiritual weapons and armor, and you have knowledge in God's word, then you will know your authority. Then YOU will be destruction in Satan's path. And that will be your heritage.

Many Christians do not even know there is a war going on or that they are in it. They are going through life like those small robot vacuums; they go in one direction until they bump into something, then they bounce off in some other direction, erratic as it may seem. Many of these Christians do not have sound doctrinal teaching; some have never heard the term "spiritual warfare," and some would rather have a "head in the sand" mentality wherein they say, "If I ignore it then it will go away." Well, it won't go away, and it won't disappear unless we stand and fight it. It is these people who continue to have chronic relationship and family problems, financial problems, mental problems, emotional and spiritual problems. They continue to be under the bondage of addictions that they can't seem to get free from. These bondages may be in the form of sexual, drugs, alcohol, behavioral, mental, or emotional habits and hang-ups. I've heard people respond to these kinds of problems as, "Oh it's just life." NO! It is not just life. It's SPIRITUAL WARFARE. As long as you take it from Satan, and the demonic, they will continue to attack you with it.

Engage, Dominate, Own and Control

God told Joshua in (Deuteronomy 2:24) to use his authority and possess what He had given him. The word "authority" means having the right to command, having another's power of attorney to possess and control a situation. The word "possession" means complete ownership and complete domination. Jesus said in (Luke 10:19), "I give you power over ALL the power of the enemy and nothing from them shall harm you." The word "ALL" means the whole quantity, the greatest possibility, everything, one's whole property, and totality. In other words, God told Joshua to ENGAGE THE ENEMY, DOMINATE, OWN and CONTROL everything, with the

16

whole quantity and authority that Jesus Himself walked in. Jesus said that He has given us the power to successfully engage, dominate, control, and own the enemy with victory. The word "engage" means to enter into conflict with the enemy. Many Christians are afraid of a conflict, or, as they say it where I live, they're plain "scared' to engage the enemy. Many Christians are not willing to do the fasting and praying that it takes to have this kind of authority. Many Christians who do not know, or do not use their authority, suffer many unnecessary attacks just like the little kid on the playground receives from the bully.

Chapter 2

The War Begins

The first spiritual war begins sometime in the dateless past, before Adam and the Garden of Eden were created. Some say it happened at the time of (Genesis 3) and the temptation of Eve, but since archaeologists have found idols that date back as far as 29000 BC, I would think this to be long before Adam.

In (Ezekiel 28:11-19), we find how God created Lucifer. He was totally perfect in every way, he was the anointed cherub, he was full of wisdom, and he was on the holy mountain with God. This is very important to know, because almost all the idol worship of that time was performed in temples on what the Old Testament called "high places," They were named such because they were usually on top of a hill or on top of a mountain.

Paul tells us in (Ephesians 6:12) that one of the places that we fight the enemy is spiritual wickedness in "high places." Other references say that Satan was ruling over planet Earth during the Pre-Adamite earth where he led worship to God. I know many people do not believe the Pre-Adamite story, while others do. I am one who does. I believe scripture can back this up.

It was during this time that Lucifer began to exalt himself because of his beauty and wisdom according to (Ezekiel 28). Verse 18 says that he defiled the sanctuaries where he and the other angels worshipped God by the multitude of his sins and slander against God. (Isaiah 14:12) says he had already weakened the nations over which he ruled "before" the fall with this slander against God, turning the Pre-Adamite inhabitants on the earth against God. This made it very easy for the fall and betrayal of one-third of the angels in a rebellion against God to take place.

(Isaiah 14:12-14) tells of the fall of Lucifer. He (Lucifer) said, "I will ascend into heaven. I will exalt my throne above the stars of God." To have a throne one must have a kingdom to rule over, which proves the rank and power of authority positions in the spirit realm. "I will sit also upon the mount of the congregation in the side of the north." God and heaven are in the sides of the north according to the book of Psalms, which says that promotion comes from the north. "I will ascend above the heights of the clouds." This proves the kingdom where he ruled was on earth under the clouds—how else to ascend "above" the clouds? "I will be LIKE THE MOST HIGH." Or "I will be "worshipped" AS the most High." "I will be the most high." This was Lucifer's plan to be worshipped as a God. This was the beginning of idolatry as we know it today.

Every demonic idol from the beginning of time was created to be worshipped in the place of God. Every world dictator throughout history who was set on world domination was empowered by these demonic spirits. This includes those who were set up throughout history as the antichrists. It will also include the man who will be the end-time antichrist, whose image will be worshipped (remember idols can be images).

Lucifer and the angels who followed him, invaded heaven and Jesus said in (Luke 10:18), in reference to this battle, that He saw Satan fall from heaven as lightning when he was cast back down to earth. (2 Peter 2:4): "…for if God spare not the angels that sinned but cast them down to hell." And this was the fall of Satan and the angels.

Because of this, Satan hates God and determines to make spiritual warfare with Him and His creation. The (3rd chapter of Genesis) tells of the temptation of Eve. Satan through his deception was able to bring Eve into agreement and covenant with him, and to rebel against God's commands. This was spiritual warfare plain and simple.

Myths, Legends or Warfare

From the beginning of time we have had stories of super-human beings, god-like men and women, mystical creatures, all possessing immorality, and super strength and abilities. We call this "mythology."

According to the Webster's dictionary, the word "mythology" can mean a fictitious story, but it can also mean a traditional story explaining a phenomenon. The word "phenomenon" means any observable fact, or event, that can be scientifically described or explained, or is very unusual; also, an extraordinary person or situation.

The word "tradition" means the beliefs and customs of convictions that certain things are true and trusted in confidence and are handed down from generation to generation. The word "legend" means a story, or body of stories, handed down from generation to generation that is popularly believed to have an actual historical basis. These stories began from the ancient cradle of civilizations of the world today. Where did these fantastic imaginations come from? Did someone just think it all up one day? Or did it have a beginning in reality? I believe the Bible tells us where these stories began, and I also believe it was all a design of Satan to further create even more spiritual warfare upon the human race for its defeat.

The reason that we should educate ourselves on this subject is so that we can understand how and where this war begins, and understand the enemy that we are fighting. By this we can understand where and how idol worship began, how it has filtered through the entire history of the earth, in every culture and civilization, to gain world domination. We must also understand and know that idol, god, and goddess worship has never died and gone away. It still exists very strongly today. By knowing and understanding how this scheme operates, we can see Satan and the demonic at work today in our society and world government, as well as down to our local communities.

In (Genesis: 6), in the Amplified Bible, it says: "When Men began to multiply on the face of the land daughters were born to them. The sons of God saw the daughters of men were fair, and they took wives of all they desired to take." In verses 4 and 5: "There were giants on the earth in those days and also afterward when the sons of God lived with the daughters of men, and they bore children to them. These were the mighty men who were of old, men of renown. The Lord saw that the wickedness of man was great in the earth, and that every imagination and intention of his heart was only evil continually."

Being purely evil, they would have had no inculcation (instillation) of God in them to restrain them. I teach only God's word as fact. But being interested in history as I am, I research many historical documents to sometimes find deeper views. The book of Enoch is one of those documents. Again, not teaching it as scripture, but it is interesting that it states these giants were so evil and corrupt they resorted to cannibalism, even with each other, and performed perverted sexual acts with animals. This is how Satan taught corruption to the human race that brought God's judgment against them.

Satan, using what God had already created, perverted it and introduced another race onto the earth to worship him, to kill and destroy what God had created. It was the race of the giant's half-human and half-spirit, and they were extremely evil. Some early texts and the Bible called them "Anunaki" which means "those who came from heaven to earth." The book of Enoch, the book of Jubilees, the King James Bible, and many other Jewish writings call these the "Holy Watchers" who were sent by God to watch over man and the earth. (Daniel 4:13, 17, 23) all mention the Holy Watchers; the Hebrew is "nun resh" which means "those who watch." Their offspring are called the "Nephilim," which according to Jewish tradition means "the fallen ones." In the Greek, Nephilim is translated "giants." Many believe this is where the legends of Greek mythology, half-man and half-animal creatures, and beings of superhuman strength, came from.

There are many similarities between the giants described in the Bible and Greek mythology. The Jewish historian Josephus says the appearance of these giant's features were terrifying in both sight and sound. The bones of these giants were on display in his day. And it is suggested that they resented God for destroying their ancestors.

In many countries and different cultures around the world, archaeologists have found proof of giants in mummies, bones, and weapons. These weapons would be too large for a normal sized man to be able to use. (Deuteronomy 3:11), "For only OG king of Bashan remained of the remnant of the giants; behold his bedstead was a bedstead of iron 18'9" long and 8'4" wide."

Most giants were from 9 feet to about 13 feet tall.

This represented more spiritual warfare against the human race. There is a very clear and distinct difference between the daughters of men and the sons of God. The phrase "sons of God" is mentioned five times in Scripture, and all five times it refers to angels. Some people do not believe that angels have the sexual ability when they appear as a human because of what Jesus said, that in the resurrection we will be as the angels of God, who do not give into marriage. Jesus did not say they did not have the ability, he just said they would not marry. This is because there will be no need for us to have offspring after we get to heaven. There, all the angels are already created that will ever be created and there is no need for any more.

When the angels came to Lot's house in human form, they were tired, thirsty, and hungry. They were able to talk, rest, drink, and eat. This sounds like they were functioning as humans in human form. So why not be able to function in every way as a human, even sexually?

(Jude, verse 6), says the angels which did not keep their first estate, but left their own habitation, God has reserved in punishment in eternal chains in darkness. In the Greek, the word "habitation" means they did not retain their own or original "principality," which means "rank." They did not remain in their realm as God's angels and fell and entered the human realm to marry the daughters of men. The Greek word for habitation in this verse is used one other time and is referring to the state that believers will be in after they get to heaven. So, this proves that the angels did voluntarily fall from their perfect angelic state to take on the form of earthly men.

Most people believe the demonic spirits are the fallen angels which fell with Lucifer, of which at least some are in hell in chains and are different from "evil spirits." Some people, Jewish tradition, and the book of Enoch in the lost books of the Bible believe and state that the evil spirits are the departed spirits of the spirit side of the dead giants from the spirit angel fathers in (Genesis: 6). Now, again, I do not teach the lost books of the Bible as scripture, but I do love history, and as an ancient historical document, in Enoch 15:8, we see: "And now the giants who are produced from the spirits and flesh, shall be called evil spirits upon the earth, and upon the earth, shall be their dwelling." Verse 9, "Evil spirits have proceeded from their bodies because they are born from men and from the holy Watchers." Verse 10, "As for the spirits of heaven, in heaven shall be their dwelling, but as for the spirits of the earth, which were born upon the earth, on earth shall be their dwelling."

Jesus said in (Matthew 12:43) and (Luke 11:24) that when an evil spirit is gone out of a person that they (the demon) will "walk" through dry places, and anyone who "walks" is earth bound as Enoch suggests, not being able to travel instantly from place to place as angels and the fallen angels who are the demonic spirits.

Verse 11, "And the spirits of the giants afflict, oppress, destroy, attack, do battle, and work destruction on the earth, and cause trouble: they take no food, but nevertheless they hunger, and thirst, and cause offenses. And these spirits shall rise up against the children of men and against the women, because they have proceeded from them."

In other words, according to this, they were half-human and half-spirit beings, so when they died, the human part was gone, but the spirit was then loosed and freed from the body and became the evil spirits to attack the human race. And it also states that having lived in a body they know and understand the appetites of human lust. This describes the exact nature of what we see evil spirits doing today. Satan does not have the power to create but both factors were already there: the daughters of man, to whom God had given the law of reproduction, and the sons of God, who in the human form, are believed to have the same capability as a normal human being. Satan will use and pervert what is at his disposal.

In the (first 4 chapters of Deuteronomy), we find that Satan had placed these Giants in the exact Promised Land that God had intended for His people. This was to keep them from reaching God's purpose for their lives. God equipped the Israelite army, who otherwise could not have won the battle, to drive the giants out of sixty cities and towns, and killed every one of them.

Chapter 3

The Spiritual Warfare From Nimrod

After the flood in (Genesis 6), as the earth began to be populated again, we find evil once again beginning to rise. Noah had placed a curse on his son Ham for his sin, and a curse was also placed on Canaan, whose descendants the Israelites would have to fight to win the Promised Land from. This leads some teachers to speculate that Noah's lineage may have contained giant DNA in the blood line because of this connection. Ham's grandson, Cush's son, was the legendary character Nimrod, some writings spell it Ninus.

Nimrod did more to help Satan create Spiritual Warfare on earth and the saints than anyone else in history. The name "Nimrod" in Hebrew means "let us revolt" and "rebel." As a mighty hunter, his name also meant the "subduer of the leopard." According to Jewish tradition, Nimrod initiated open rebellion against God. History records him as a despot, a tyrant king. He deceived, manipulated, intimidated, dominated, and controlled the people by fear, intimidation, and cruelty under his rule, which was a form of witchcraft. The Bible and history both say that Nimrod forced the people by his own law and taught them to be rebellious against God. He proclaimed that he was the promised seed of the woman. This was putting himself in the place of Jesus Christ as the first false Messiah or antichrist. He founded many cities, including the great Babylonian empire, and built the tower of Babel.

Nimrod, who was also King Amraphel of Shinar, with the help of his wife, who was also his mother, Shemiramis, or as some writings spells Semiramis, who Satan used to bring god and goddess worship to the world. Talk about having sick emotional problems separating from your mother; this is the first recorded in history.

This demented couple was used by Satan when they founded the first occult religion in history. This would become idol worship, satanic worship, and witchcraft, where infants were often sacrificed to demons. Scripture says he did not want the people to ascribe their happiness to God but rather to ascribe their happiness to their own means and wisdom; because of their own efforts and devices that their happiness was achieved. Sounds a little like the modern day New Age religion to me. He wanted the people to say it was by their own means and power that they had what they had.

This occult religion, along with astrology, grew with the worship of idols, images, rituals, ceremonies and statues. Nimrod later made this a law. If you refused to obey and worship his gods, you were killed. Parts of his rituals were human sacrifices and the drinking of menstrual blood which they believed to be a life-giving force. The human sacrifice was a counterfeit to the sin-sacrifice that God commanded for the forgiveness of sin under the law. The drinking of the menstrual blood was a counterfeit and blasphemy to the future Holy Communion, the last supper, and the shedding of Jesus' blood for the ultimate sacrifice for sin. The menstrual blood is why the color red is still important to the Satanist today.

Shemiramis began to teach secret occult rituals and ceremonies to those under her authority. After Nimrod's (King Amraphel's) death by Esau, who according to historical accounts cut off his head, Nimrod's wife, Shemiramis, took over the occult religion that would later became known as Satan worship. She was so overwhelmed with grief by the death of Nimrod that she had images made honoring and immortalizing him and taught the people to worship him. She had Nimrod proclaimed as an immortal God, and herself proclaimed as a Goddess, known as the "Queen of Heaven," being symbolized by the figure of the crescent moon. There are cults today that worship a goddess known as the queen of heaven. The Catholics refer to the Virgin Mary as the "queen of heaven." Shemiramis later made worship of them both law, usually death being the penalty of refusal.

The modern-day cult known as the "Children of God" believe that the Holy Spirit is a voluptuous woman they call the Queen of Heaven. There were many other civilizations throughout history that had fertility goddesses with the same characteristics as Shemiramis, whose symbols were also the crescent moon; this was not just coincidence. The Children of God, as with Shemiramis, were into astrology; they used spirit guides and mediums, and they had sexual intercourse with these spirits. This is an example of the same practices being adapted into modern-day cults, occult practices, Satanism, and witches, who perform the same practices at Halloween, and they are still worshipping the same demonic spirits as they did thousands of years ago.

Satan knew the entire plan of God from beginning to end as far as the sacrifices that would be required for the forgiveness of sin, the sending of Jesus through virgin birth as our savior, the plan of salvation, and I believe even the gifts of Holy Spirit that empowers believers. So being the deceiver that he is, Satan's plan was to counterfeit everything that God was going to do in an effort to deceive the human race so that God's plan would be lost in the mix.

So, in this effort, the demonic spirits of the fallen angels began to plant thoughts and delusions in the mind of Nimrod for the hunger of power, influence, to be worshipped, and exalted. Nimrod became known and worshipped as Bel, the sun god, and the "Divine son of Heaven."

Bel, the sun god, is the personification of Satan. "Bel" means "lord and master." There is only one Lord and Master and that is God our Father. This was placing Nimrod as the first counterfeit to our God. The idea of Bel as the "sun god" was to place him as being as important as the Sun for our existence. (Revelation 21:23) says the glory of God and the Lamb who is Jesus is the light of the heavenly city, not the "Sun," and not the sun god Nimrod.

The Babylonians dedicated the first day of each week as the day they worshipped Bel the "sun" god. This is a counterfeit to the Sabbath day that God commanded to be Holy in our worship to Him. This is where we get Sunday as the first day of our week to worship our God. Therefore, God gave the command to "Honor the Sabbath day and keep it holy." Again, this is placing Nimrod as the Satanic counterfeit to our God the Father.

These first occult religions grew in Egypt, Pergamos, and other countries where Shemiramis became known as Ishtar to the Babylonians, and mother figure Isis to the Egyptians. The Greek meaning of Isis is "the woman," always depicted as a "mother" and fertility goddess, who also became wife to her own son, sound familiar?

It was after the death of Horus that he arose from the dead as the Egyptian god Osiris, the god of the underworld. When Osiris was born, a man from Thebes, whose name was Pamyle, while in the temple at Karnak, said he heard a voice telling him to announce to the world that Osiris the great king and the savior of all mankind had been born. Another account states that a loud voice was heard all over the world saying, "The lord who will bring joy to all the earth is born." It was believed that Osiris had no evil in him and that he was the great law-giver who taught the Egyptians how to worship the other gods. This sounds like what (Deuteronomy 13:13) says about the sons of Beliel, that they drew the inhabitants of their city away from worshipping God, and taught them to worship other gods. The Egyptians believed that Osiris left Egypt to carry his teachings to other lands; this is further reason that we see the spread of the occult in history.

Where Jesus arose, and became the Lord of Heaven, and we look to Jesus to be saved, the Egyptians looked to Osiris to be saved, in yet another counterfeit attempt to replace Jesus as the savior of the world. The Egyptians believed Osiris to be their reconciler, where we know that Jesus Christ is the one and only reconciler. Many Egyptian writings depict Osiris as "the seed." I believe this was another attempt to counterfeit the virgin birth of Jesus Christ, going back to (Genesis 3:15) to place Nimrod and Shemiramis in their place. History also shows that Osiris was represented as both husband and son to his mother Isis, because spiritually they believed he became the god of the underworld, but being reborn physically as Horus through Isis without the aid of a man. This is another similarity of Nimrod and Shemiramis being passed down through different civilizations. Yet another counterfeit to the virgin birth designed by Satan.

As I stated before, one of the meanings of Nimrod's name is "subduer of the leopard," "nimr" meaning leopard and "rad" meaning to subdue. So, the name Nimrod strongly implies, as does historical fact and the Bible that he was a great and mighty hunter, but possibly also that he had been able to train leopards to assist in hunting other animals. History shows that one of the territories conquered by Nimrod was Egypt. The Egyptian priests of Osiris are depicted wearing leopard skins in representation of the god Osiris, proving that Nimrod had an influence upon the Egyptians, and some even believe that Nimrod became known as Horus or Osiris. Some historical records also place Nimrod in the constellation Orion as "the mighty hunter placed among the stars."

Where Shemiramis became Isis the Egyptian Goddess, she was Ishtar to the Babylonians, and is identified with the gods of Assyria who are most likely Astoreth of the Old Testament and Astarte of the Greeks and Romans, and Athena and Minerva in Greece. In China, Shemiramis was known as "Song Moo" (Holy Mother). In ancient Canaan she was called Ashtoreth, and in Asia Minor she was Diana. The Roman goddess Diana was a huntress with a quiver of arrows; she was the cohort of Nimrod the mighty hunter. It's very clear this refers to Nimrod and Shemiramis, the sick mother-son-husband couple.

Going back to after Nimrod's death, Shemiramis claimed that she had been visited by the spirit of Nimrod who over-shadowed her one night and left her pregnant with a son named Tammuz. This is the Satanic counterfeit to the virgin birth of Jesus when the Holy Spirit over-shadowed Mary in the gospel of Matthew, depicting the birth of Jesus Christ. She said that Tammuz was Nimrod reincarnated and was to be worshipped as a God. This places her son as the counterfeit of Jesus Christ, or the first actual antichrist in the line of many more to follow.

Now I know that we don't go by the lost books of the Bible, but look at what Jasher 7:47 says, "Shortly after Nimrod rose to power, he made Gods of wood and stone, and he bowed down to them, and he rebelled against the Lord and taught all his subjects and the people of the earth his wicked ways; and Tammuz his son was more wicked than his father." This backs up what the King James Bible says.

When you consider that the occult is empowered by the spirit of antichrist, who is the counterfeit to the Holy Spirit, then this is the first counterfeit of the Holy Trinity. One difference is the Satanists and witches worship the demonic trinity at Halloween with Beliel as the false son. Nimrod, who is worshipped as Bel the son god, is in the place of Satan as the false father god. This was another effort to place Nimrod as a counterfeit to God.

Shemiramis and her son were worshipped in Greece, China, Japan, and Tibet as the "Madonna and child," again a counterfeit to the Virgin Mary and Jesus. I have found, so far, about 38 times throughout history of counterfeit virgin births, in Satan's effort to get Jesus lost in the middle as just another myth. They became worshipped in other countries as Fortuna and Jupiter in Rome and Venus (Aphrodite) and Adonis in Greece. In Asia, they were worshipped as Cybele and Deoius. Even the Egyptians, Aztecs and Mayan Indians worshipped a fertility goddess whose symbol was a crescent moon, the same as Shemiramis the queen of heaven. They believe she gave virgin birth and created everything in existence.

This proves that the main focus of Satan's warfare is to displace God in worship by putting himself in that place. And having a long line of men that he has had in every generation, throughout history, up to the end time, who could be the antichrist of the book of Revelation. Who will be worshipped as a god during the tribulation. And proves that occult, demonic idol worship has continued throughout history, by the same demons, using different names, in different civilizations, to promote the same sins, the same sexual perversions and immoralities, the same rituals and ceremonies, and the same blood sacrifices adapting to the times to carry it from generation to generation.

I have followed many of these throughout world history and demonology all the way up to our modern time. In demonology, many of them carry the same attributes and characteristics they do in the Bible. Today, there are many of them who are protected by freedom of religion as churches.

When we study idolatry and god and goddess worship from ancient biblical time up to our modern times, we can see where every pagan civilization, all around the world, had gods of war, prosperity, fertility, sexual perversion, human sacrifice and the list goes on and on. As I stated before, in my study, I have found that the same attributes keep occurring in all these civilizations; they just go by different names. They are the same demonic spirits carrying out the same jobs in each of these civilizations, throughout the centuries. Many of these civilizations had no contact with each other. Therefore there is no way they could have known that another civilization 500 years before, on another continent was conducting the same exact worship ceremonies and rituals of a god or goddess represented by the same symbols. Many of these gods are the territorial spirits over war, sexual perversion, deceit, sacrifice, death and so on in that particular geographic area of the world. Some of the demon names that are mentioned in Scripture are found in demonology and have many of the same characteristics in demonology as they do in the Bible and history. And we will explore some of them.

All of this is spiritual warfare designed to kill, steal the truth, and destroy the human race from worshipping God so Satan can be worshipped as a god, and to stomp out all existence of God from the face of the earth. But God is much more powerful than this, and we are His children. (1 John 4:4) says "Greater is he (God) that is within us than he (Satan) that is in the world." (Romans 8:37) says that, "WE are more than a conqueror through Jesus Christ."

Chapter 4

Idol Worship

Now I will be only teaching what the Bible says as fact. But being interested in history as I am, in this chapter we will see what some historic writings have to say about idol worship, as well as what the Bible has to say. I do not teach this as Bible, but as a historical tool such as those who teach about the writings of the Jewish historian Josephus. It is very interesting that they all seem to agree very closely with what the Bible says.

When the Bible talks about gods and idols, these were not just inanimate objects made of wood, stone, or metal that represented no spirit; they were inspired by, and were possessed by, actual demonic spirits. (1 Samuel 17:43) says Goliath cursed David by his gods, so what did this mean? These were the demonic spirits that are still at work today, affecting and tormenting the human race, trying to keep us ignorant of how to be free. They are also leading people away from God into vile, wicked sins to destroy the human race as we find in (Genesis 6:3).

God created the human race for his worship. These spirits, or gods, are at work to turn the worship of the one true God into an evil worship of Satan. This was an attempt to doom the human race so Jesus the savior could not come through a woman in (Genesis 3:15) to destroy Satan and his rebellion.

When we talk about idols, remember an idol can be anything that we put more undeserved time, finances, affections and attention into than what we spend on God. Any addiction, whether it is drugs, alcohol, or any obsession like, gambling, sex, porn, co-dependence, money or whatever, can become an idol to us. When we give our affection and ourselves to its control then demonic spirits can get invoked and create bondage. Idol worship has never died. Today in modern times people still worship actual demonic idols. The same demonic spirits that were worshipped thousands of years ago are still alive and being worshipped today. Even many Christians unknowingly take part in this. That is why Paul tells us in (2 Corinthians) that we are not to be ignorant of Satan's devices. These devices can come in the form of the occult, witchcraft, Harry Potter books, demonic video games and movies.

Paul said in (Romans 6:16), "To whom you surrender yourselves to you are his slaves" which is the purpose Satan has for idols, whether they are gods worshipped as in the OT or those seen in modern times. What's really bad is you can watch people and you can plainly see what their idols are and what gods they serve. What they have allowed to be their substitute for God.

(Hosea 9:10) says, "Their abominations were according as they loved." The word "abomination" means to hate, to loathe, having intense dislike or disgust for. So as the people worshipped the demonic idols, the people began to take on the same sinful characteristic, or began to love the same sins that particular demon is in charge of promoting.

Satan is not always going to make known what he is doing since he is the father of lies and the master deceiver. (Joshua 6:18) tells us to keep ourselves from accursed objects or we ourselves will be accursed by allowing them into our lives and homes. Many times, people are tricked innocently into bondage by allowing accursed objects into their homes that can open the doors to demonic spirits, even spirits that are worshipped as idols. This can be through objects brought home from different parts of the world that may have been used in voodoo, prayed over by pagan priests, religious objects, and can even be children's toys that represent demonically inspired superheroes and occult items. By welcoming these objects into your home, you can open a permanent doorway, giving legal access to you and your children to be attacked by generational curses, accidents, depression, sickness, and fear; with your home being haunted by spirit manifestations, and even death.

Idolatry

The word "idolatry" means not only the worship of idols, but also an excessive reverence, love, devotion, loyalty, and deep affection for someone or something. In this case, it would be for the sins that become the bondage which enslaves a person who yields and obeys the demonic spirits bringing the temptation.

Many demons were, and still are, worshipped as idol gods today. The names of the idols mentioned in the Old Testament are the actual, legal names of the demons. The main satanic themes seen throughout the Bible are idolatry and the occult, both working together, being fueled by the spirit of antichrist. Let's see what the Bible has to say about idolatry.

The Greek word for idolatry is "eidololatria." "Eidolon" means idol and "latreia" means worship. Idolatry totally denies the existence of the one true creator God. It is absurd for someone to carve an idol out of a piece of wood or stone and then worship it, fear it, make devotion to it, make sacrifice to it, if it is not possessed by a demonic spirit. Otherwise, it would be total stupidity, which it is anyway. But either way, it is the worship of an object as a god, as a spiritual being or the spirit represented by the idol, instead of God. All demonic worship is witchcraft because it is not centered on God and is in direct disobedience to His word.

Because of the total commitment to idol worship by the Canaanites, God gave commands for their destruction. The Egyptians, Philistines, Canaanites and Syrians were some of the most idolatrous nations in history. This gave the children of Israel 400 years to become indoctrinated with these idols and their evil practices. Their involvement, some involuntary and some voluntary, brought generational curses upon them as a nation, although they were God's chosen people. We see Israel having a continual attraction to, yet never being able to get free from, idolatry. When they left Egypt, Egypt never left them. This is also why people have a problem breaking free from sin bondage today.

What you devote yourself to, and obey, the lust, passion and appetite is what you worship and come into agreement and covenant with. What you worship, obey, and have an intense love for will control your soul, your mind, your will, and your emotions. This is putting Satan and the demonic first in your life instead of God, and this constitutes idolatry. In many cases this is from generational curses where ancestors went into agreement and covenant with the demonic.

Idolatry worships the things that are created, and not the Creator, as Paul taught in (Romans 1). By worshipping statues, objects, religious titles, etc., Satan gets the honor.

The Romans believed in many gods and goddesses. They built temples to them where they offered animals as sacrifice. The animal had to be healthy and with no physical defects. They gave the animal to the priest, they cooked the meat, and it was eaten. This is a counterfeit to the sin offerings that were made by God's priests for the forgiveness of sin in the Old Testament.

The nature of the occult is giving submission and obedience to sorcery which is condemned in Scripture. All occult practices such as astrology, fortune telling, horoscopes, hypnotism, water witching which the Bible describes as divining rods, spiritualism, Ouija boards, lucky charms and anything like this is to worship the demon behind it and Satan himself.

Back in the Old Testament the idol worship was done inside a temple dedicated to that protector god. Today we may not necessarily have temples dedicated to these gods on the street corner, but in (1 Corinthians 6:19) Paul said, "do you not know that your "bodies" are the "temples" of the Holy Spirit? This is a person

36

who has given themselves to God and is His child, or those in the body of Christ. In the spirit realm there is always a counter effect, or a balance, from one side of the spirit realm to the other side. So, when a person gives himself over to Satan and the demonic to obey and yields to their temptations as in (Romans 6:16) where he becomes a servant and a slave through obedience, then his body becomes the temple of Satan and the spirit of antichrist. This is true even though they may not be in full idol worship, or even know what it is.

Idolatry Today?

Yes, there are many people, even Christians, who are involved in idolatry today and are not even aware of it. In Christian worship service you have several different things. You have singing praises to God, Bible reading, preaching, praying for people, giving tithes and offerings, etc., If you take part in any of this outside of the church building and the worship service; reading your Bible at home, singing praises to God while you're driving down the highway, praying for someone at the grocery store, then you are still taking part in the same worship and you're coming into agreement and covenant with God.

It is the same with idolatry. As you will see in reading this book there are many different rites that took place in idol or demon worship. Sexual perversion and immorality, homosexuality, involvement in the occult, magic, anything that falls under the description of fortune telling, divination, and to where your money goes.

For example, financially supporting organizations that seem innocent, appearing on the outside as if they are doing great work, but they support the abortion industry, or gay rights. Even going to see a fortune teller may seem harmless, but it is not. I believe the gay movement and even strip clubs can be traced back to the origins of idolatry.

This is taking part in the worship of Molech and other demonic idols without even knowing it. And even the extreme of animal and human sacrifice can be traced back to idolatry. Allowing demonic and occult movies, video games, and objects into your home, is also taking a part in it.

But taking any part, no matter how small, in the same rites that are contrary to what God teaches, is taking part in the same idolatry, and the same demon worship, as in the Old Testament. (James 2:10) says "for whosoever shall keep the whole law, and yet offend in one point, he is guilty of all." You are still coming into agreement and covenant with the same demons that are still in operation today, promoting the same sins and opening many doors of legal access to attack you from them and the demons who work in collusion with them. And you are allowing your body to become the temple of Satan and the spirit of antichrist.

In (Isaiah 14:13-14) Satan said: "I will ascend into heaven, I will exalt my throne above the stars of God, and I will be like the most high."

To engage in the New Age practices, humanism, and the eastern mysticism where they are taught that "you are Gods" is a sin. They are trying to remove God and to make themselves gods; they are following and worshipping the one who first said, "I will be like God." Guess what? He was wrong, too.

Artemis

According to the Greeks Artemis who was a goddess and twin sister of Apollon, and among other things were the bringers of sudden death, plague, and disease and who was believed to work heavily with children and childbirth. In Rome she was Diana who was mentioned in the book of Acts.

Can you say, "blow out the candles and make a wish?" How many times as parents have we said that to our children? Not understanding or knowing where it came from. And not understanding the consequence of it or the doors that it can open. The Webster's dictionary says a wish is to make a request. Paul tells us in (Philippians 4:6) to let us make our request known to God. So, a request is a prayer. To make this request to anyone other than God is to make it to Satan. When you make the wish blowing out the candles you're not making the wish to God but to the demon Artemis.

Many take part, in the worship of Artemis today and do not even know it. In the worship of Artemis of the ancient Greeks, as a sacrifice they would bake a round cake representing the full moon. Next they would light candles on it representing the shinning of the moon. Finally, they would blow out the candles while making a prayer request to Artemis.

Oh, that's just a coincidence you may say. No, it isn't. Ask yourself, "where did this come from?" "Why are the details the same?" If you take part of a ritual of this kind in detail, you are taking part of the same ritual of worship and it will open doors giving demonic spirits legal access to attack your family. Maybe through sickness, the sudden death of a child, or disease.

Ashtoreth

The children of Israel were very familiar with all the gods of Egypt. From my study, I've found at least 39 different gods and goddesses that were worshipped by the Egyptians. When Israel reached the Promised Land, they found it filled with shrines dedicated to Baal and Ashtoreth, Baal's cohort. Ashtoreth, also referred to by the Egyptians as Ishtar, was known as the mother Goddess, and as the queen of heaven. The name Ishtar, queen of heaven, has been found in Egyptians writings. She was known to the Greeks as Aphrodite, and as Astarte to the Phoenicians. Intense sexual immorality, prostitution and ancient depictions of pornographic nudity have been found in Egypt showing these were involved in her worship and became a part in many other eastern cultures. Involved in this worship were many small idols of Ashtoreth that have been found dating to the Paleolithic period. Very important to remember is this idol was a female with a crescent moon on her brow. Throughout history we see this many times in female fertility goddesses in cultures that never had any geological or chronological contact with each other. Israel knew them because of Egypt.

Baal

Baal, whose name literally means "lord," was one of the main Canaanite gods. He was the male sun god worshipped in western Asia as a chief deity. There were altars and temples built on high mountains to get the first view of the rising sun and the last view of the setting sun, as the sun was believed to be the source of all life and power of nature. Baal went by the titles of "rider of the clouds," "almighty," "lord of the earth" and the "divine king." The Canaanites believed that Baal was the source of all life and fertility, the mighty hero, and the god of war, and they celebrated his death, burial, and resurrection annually. As a counterfeit to our Christian beliefs of Jesus. These rituals included human sacrifice and temple prostitution. Baal was believed to be the son of "El" who was also known as Dagon, whom they believed to be the highest God. Since Baal was believed to be responsible for droughts, plagues, and other chaos, human sacrifices were made to him to bring favor and appease him for a blessing. I believe this was one of Satan's counterfeits to Jesus, the son of God, as being the source of everything we need in our life.

His name means owner, master, lord, and husband. Baal was first worshipped as the god of weather and the one who made life possible because in a dry area like Canaan this put him in the place of God as one of Satan's counterfeits for God. The Canaanites believed Baal and his other gods Ashtoreth, Anath or Anat controlled agriculture and fertility which controls life, which was Satan's way of trying to turn the focus off, God.

Anath was also known as the virgin; does that sound familiar? Anath was supposed to be both wife and sister to Baal, promoting incest and polygamy orgies and child sacrifice. This created soul ties, spirit ties, and generational curses bringing them into agreement and covenant with Satan. All of this was condemned by God. And you can understand why.

Molech

Molech, Moloch, or Milcom are just a few of the names given this god; there are about 16 different spellings of the name depending on the country where he was worshipped. But Molech, as the national god of Ammon, the same as Chemosh of Moab, was worshipped by the Egyptians as Amun or Amun-ra meaning "the king of the Gods." His name means "king" and was also known as the fire god. It was he who was represented as a statue of brass, sitting on a throne of brass, he had a head of a calf or bull with a crown, with outstretched arms. The entire statue was red-hot by fire. Children were placed in the red-hot arms which sloped downward so the child would roll down into the fire. Loud music and singing were used to drown out the screams and wails of the children, so the people would not hear them.

In many cultures throughout history, that had no connection geographically or chronologically, children were burned alive in sacrifice to him. He required newborn babies (sometimes up to six years old) to be sacrificed and burned to death in his arms. I believe that he is responsible for the abortion industry today.

Also, throughout history, even today, this happens in Satanism, cults, and sometimes in witchcraft. I believe this is another demonic effort to kill the human race that God created to worship Him. In just one instance alone, an ancient cemetery was excavated in Carthage between 54,000 and 64,000 square feet containing around 20,000 vessels filled with the charred remains of 2-3 children each, aged from 0-6 years, that were sacrificed by fire. This is in addition to thousands of vessels that were destroyed by the Romans. This continued there for 600 years.

In Leviticus and in Deuteronomy, we find that all this carries curses that open doors to the demonic, giving them free, legal access to continue afflicting future generations. Paul said in (1 Corinthians 10:20) that anything offered or sacrificed to idols were to demons and not to God. Evidence of this is found in many other cultures. This is something to think about because you will find all these same sins have continued throughout history, from then until today, because the same demonic forces are still at work afflicting people today.

Some Scripture references to this include: (Deuteronomy 12:31, Jeremiah 7:31, 32:35, 2 Kings 3:27, 16:3, 17:17 & 31, 19:51, 23:10, 21:6, Ezekiel 20:26 & 31, 23:37; and Judges 11:31) talk about "passing through the fire," and "burnt offerings." This was also counterfeiting the burnt offerings to God for sin. Some of these scriptures show that children became involved in this practice.

(Jeremiah 32:35) and (2 Kings 23:10) directly connect Baal and Molech as working together. Baal and Ashtoreth worked together, along with Beliel, who also works with Jezebel in Scripture. By working together, I mean in collusion. The word "collusion" means a secret agreement between 2 or more for the purpose to trick or deceive another out of his or her legal rights. Are you beginning to see the inter-twining of these demonic spirits working together to bring all the areas of sin they promote together to infiltrate and defile all the cultures of the human race around the world throughout history? And when people give into obeying them, the people are coming into agreement and covenant with them.

42

Baal-berith

Baal-berith in Hebrew means god or lord of the covenant, and means also "to cut until blood appears." In (1 Kings 18:28), the prophets of Baal in worship would get into an emotional state where they were cutting themselves "until the blood gushed out upon them." Sounds like the emotional cutting many people are involved in today. This creates a blood covenant between them, others, and this demon.

He was the same as Jupiter and Mercury to the Romans and Greeks. Mercury was considered the god of abundance, financial, material, and commercial success. That is making this god a demonic counterfeit to God, our Jehovah Jireh as our abundant supplier. Satan tempts Christians with a wrong balance of money, success, social status, pleasure, and material things; what (2 Timothy 3:4) calls "lovers of pleasures more than lovers of God."

He was called the god of the covenants because he was supposed to preside over pacts, covenants, and leagues. The word "league" here means an association of nations for promoting a common interest. This is an act of collusion of many demonic rulers all around the earth to increase the bondage of generational curses, and they all work under the authority of the territorial demonic spirit Baal-berith.

Now think for a moment, we have the god of covenants and agreements; also we have the same god who is worshipped as the god of financial and material abundance, pleasure and prosperity, who is also over agreements and covenants, for the entire planet earth and bound by a blood covenant. We live in an age where people think they must have the largest and fanciest home and automobile, the newest and most expensive designer clothes, all for keeping up with a social status in a society where you are looked down on if you can't provide these status symbols. The only way for most people to accomplish this is through second and third mortgages, credit and credit cards.

I understand most of us cannot pay cash for a home or automobile, so it must be financed and God knows that's not what I'm talking about here. Could it be that keeping up with the social status through credit cards we cannot afford, which is an agreement that we have signed, coming into covenant with the company that we will pay what we have agreed to, is putting us into bondage and is also against God's word that we should "owe no man anything." Is this, this demon's way of continuing the same thing that he did thousands of years ago, just adapting the plan to fit a modern world?

Also think about this: Jesus said it was possible the very elect would be deceived. That tells me it is not coming as a roaring lion, but as the thing that would deceive people here and now subtlety and innocently. After all, everyone else is doing it, so it must be ok.

The book of Revelation says the mark of the beast will be on the right hand or on the forehead. Could it be that all this ties in together, the credit card in the hand, having the numbers memorized in your head, and is it a coincidence that the part of the brain used in memorization is the frontal lobe? If a first-century man was seeing this take place without having the 21st century vocabulary to explain it, he would probably say the forehead. Now I do believe there will be a definite thing that will be the actual mark, but I do believe this is a forerunner of it. Something to think about.

In (Deuteronomy 30:19) God said: "I call heaven and earth to record this day against you that I have set before your life and death, blessing and cursing: therefore, choose life that both you and thy seed may live." Now look at what Jesus said in (Matthew 12:36-37), "that every idle word that men shall speak, they shall give account therefore in the day of judgment. For by thy words thou shalt be justified, and by thy words thou shalt be condemned." If you read the chapter "Agreement and Covenant" and you understand that yielding to the temptation is coming into agreement and covenant with the demonic spirit bringing the temptation, you will see what I am talking about. Also, Satan and these spirits being, the "accuser" of God's children as Satan did with Job, you can begin to understand how they keep records of our words and actions to use against us by our opening doors allowing them access into our lives.

Now we know that God also keeps a record of our lives, our words, and our actions. But the choices that we make in life are as serious as life and death, blessing and cursing, because we can allow the demonic access by those choices, or we can allow God access. And those choices are being recorded on both sides, according to what I see in Scripture.

Remember the Satanic-demonic kingdom is set up as we see kingdoms in the physical world where we live. He was accepted by many of the Israelites as their god. He was worshipped in the place of Jehovah God, making him a Satanic counterfeit for God. (Judges 8:33) says: "the children of Israel turned again, and went a whoring after Baalim, and made Baal-berith their God." The word "turn" means to change directions, to reverse sides, to change beliefs, to reverse course, to make a sudden attack, to change all and a change of one's duty, devotion and loyalty. To go "a whoring" refers to selling one's self, in this case, selling your soul, and refers to the immoral rites that took place in idol worship. We see from the last part of (Deuteronomy 30:19) God said, "choose life that you and your seed, (your descendants) may live." This means that your choices will create soul ties, spirit ties, and generational curses or generational blessings.

Succoth-benoth

Succoth-benoth was an idol and a Babylonian god of the city of Samaria, mentioned in (2 Kings 17:30). In the temple of worship of this demon there were erotic seductive dances performed by the temple prostitutes, mostly in the nude. The name Succoth-benoth means "booths of the daughters." This refers to the booths inside the temple where women gave their bodies to men who were devoted worshipers and givers to these idols for immoral sexual acts and rites. In other words, you could get whatever sexual act you wanted. This describes the modern-day strip clubs and the booths where men can go with women to do different kinds of sexual acts for the men. I know this all too well from many years ago, having had an addiction to that lifestyle which God delivered me from. And again, this created soul ties, spirit ties and generational curses on the participants as well as it does today in the strip clubs with pornography and sexual immorality. Again, obeying this temptation is coming into agreement and covenant with these demonic spirits. I do not believe all this is just a big coincidence.

There are many, many more idols mentioned in the Old and New Testaments which were demonic spirits.

Many places in Scripture, for example, (1 Corinthians 10:20-21) and (Leviticus 17:7) mention idolatry. Pagan sacrifices and their worship are clearly made to devils or demons. (Leviticus 17:7b) says, "This shall be a statute for them" meaning an "established rule," to have an influence over and to govern. Even so far as to further establishing generational curses and coming into agreement and covenant with demons like Bel-berith. People wonder why a God of love would require an entire nation to be destroyed all the way down to the infants and animals. It's because of the demonic.

Idol worship did not die in the Old Testament as some people think. It continued throughout history, continuing even today in every civilization as the Greek gods, as the Egyptian gods and goddesses, and will continue up to the tribulation with worship of the antichrist as a one-world dictator.

Satan tried to make this happen in the book of Genesis. Satan wanted to bring the entire world under one world worship of himself as God as in (Isaiah 14). At the time of the flood of (Genesis in chapter 6) around 2500bc to 2300bc, the supercontinent of Pangaea was still intact. The continents had not yet separated. This is how the entire earth was able to be flooded. At this time Satan could bring the entire population of the world into one place, on one land mass, together in worship to him through idol worship. By an act of counter warfare called the continental shift theory, God was able to prevent this. About 100 years after the flood, (Genesis 10:25) says in the days of Peleg was the earth divided. The name "Peleg" in Hebrew means to shift, to split, and to divide. The Hebrew definition of the word earth means continent or land. This is plain to see to be the continental shift that scientists have discovered. By this the people could no longer come together as one. But in these last days, through computers and communication, he can make it happen worldwide. He will do this during the tribulation period with the worship of the antichrist, which is worshipping Satan in a man. But God will win this battle.

Chapter 5

Beliel

(Deuteronomy 13:13) Certain men, the children of Beliel, are gone out from among you, and have withdrawn the inhabitants of their city, saying, Let, us go and serve other gods, which you have not known. In this chapter we will explore the demonic spirit Beliel. Some say that Beliel is Satan, some writings say they are 2 separate spirits, this is what I believe, you decide for yourself.

In the Dead Sea scrolls, in the war of the "sons of light" against the sons of darkness, Beliel is the leader of the sons of darkness and the massive demonic troops working under him. His purpose is to bring about wickedness and guilt. All the spirits that are in rank below him are in association with him and are all spirits of destruction, and are all working together.

Isn't it interesting that Paul tells us in (Romans 13:12) that we are to put on the armor of light? In (Revelation 21:23), Jesus is the light. In (Ephesians 5:8), we are to walk as children of light. In Malachi, Jesus is described as having healing rays and beams of light emitting from Him. All through the Old Testament, God's glory is spoken of as being composed of light and that is because we are fighting the spirits of darkness. (Luke 22:53) tells us that we have power over darkness; (Romans13:12) says that we are to cast off the works of darkness. (1 Peter 2:9) says that we have been called out of darkness. We are beginning to see a battle between darkness and light.

I believe from the study I've done that in the spirit realm when Satan and the demonic spirits see us, if we are armored in God as we should be, they see us as bright shining lights, piercing through the darkness that they dwell in, so they have no problem distinguishing who we are.

The Book of Jubilees:

Again, not as scripture, but in one of the lost books of the Bible, the book of Jubilees, and in a writing called the Damascus document, it says that Beliel will be let loosed against Israel as God spoke through Isaiah. This writing says Beliel is responsible for fornication and the pollution of the worship of God. It was Beliel who inspired the Egyptian sorcerers to oppose Moses and Aaron. This book says anyone who follows Beliel and speaks of rebellion against God should be condemned to death as a necromancer or a wizard.

The Testament of the 12 Patriarchs:

Beliel is mentioned in this book also. Simeon 5:3 says fornication separates man from God and brings you near to Beliel. In this book, Levi tells his children to choose between God or the works of Beliel because when the soul is constantly disturbed by the works of Beliel, which are sexual perversions, fornication, worship of other gods, who are in association with him, lying, deceit, when given in to this, Beliel rules over that soul. Again, (Romans 6:16) says that whoever you continually obey you are the slaves of. Paul warns in the (6th chapter of Romans) to not let sin have domination over us. This book says that the Messiah will bind Beliel and give to His children the power to trample on Beliel and his spirits who are under his rule.

In the Satanic Bible:

Beliel is the one of 4 crown princes of hell below Satan, reigning over the northern reaches of hell. He controls earth, reigns over all the earthly demons, giving orders in sexual perversions, lies, deceit, deceiving the earth to worship other gods.

Remember what (Deuteronomy 13:13) says about worshipping and serving other gods. Other historical writings say he is the prince of trickery, the demon of sodomy, and sometimes referred to as the antichrist.

I believe that we can all agree from these writings of the Bible and ancient historical documents that Beliel is a high ranking demonic ruler, or prince, with others under his rule or command, setting out to ruin, control and to curse everyone that he can. Throughout this study you need to remember that the name "Beliel" means wicked, worthless, ungodly, and naughty, without profit, destruction, wickedness, evil and mostly "worthlessness" and good for nothing.

"Worthless" means valueless, useless, and "despicable," which means deserving to be despised. As you will see later, the works of Beliel are alive and strong today, bringing destructive sins that are clearly abominations in God's word that will bring intense judgments as the reward.

But the good news is that we will learn how to defeat Beliel and all the ranks of Satan in our lives. Jesus said in (Mark 3:27) and in (Matthew 12:29) that first we must bind the strongman then we "will" spoil and plunder his house. Beliel is a demonic strongman that is at work today, which means that we have the tools (knowledge in the Word) to have the authority to plunder the strongman's house.

First let's look at (Ephesians 6:12) where Paul said, "For we wrestle not against flesh and blood, but against principalities, against powers, against the rulers of darkness of this world, against spiritual wickedness in high places."

Everybody agrees that there is a kingdom of God with different ranks of authority of angels, but for some reason it just blows people's minds to tell them that Satan has a kingdom and that there are chief rulers with different ranks of demonic authority, known as a hierarchy. The highest title ever given to Satan in the Bible is prince. Every part of the surface of the earth is governed, or under the rule, of a different demonic spirit, broken down from top to bottom, including countries, cities, towns and communities, all controlled by bondage.

In these geographical areas, you can see through history, right up to our present time, what areas of sin the ruling demonic controls.

For instance, Sodom and Gomorrah, as well as San Francisco, are ruled by a spirit of sodomy. The country of India is ruled by a spirit of lust. The people who are under demonic control have access to technologies, giving them access to technologies to promote the sin and bondage they are ruling over. The internet can be a good thing, but you can be assured there are many demonic spirits who are working through this technology. Las Vegas is ruled by a spirit of gambling, lust, death and many others who are all working together, which goes back to (Matthew 12:26) which says they cannot be in division with each other or their kingdom will not stand.

These demons work in collusion together. The word "collusion" means to enter into a secret agreement, between two or more, for the illegal purpose to cheat (fraudulently) someone out of his or her legal rights. It means a conspiracy. The word "conspiracy" means the conspiring of one or more against another or a group; also, an unlawful plot. The word "plot" means a secret, usually evil, scheme.

They are bound together by agreement. Their own agreement is why they can be defeated together, from the top down, by our agreement. All through this study when I talk about Beliel it is because of this association or agreement. You should remember that Beliel is working under Satan's authority in this association. This makes them one in the same in agreement. (Matthew 12:26) says "and if Satan cast out Satan, then he is divided against himself and how shall his "kingdom" stand?" Jesus himself is saying that there is a demonic kingdom. And Jesus is telling us there are ranks of authority, that the demons respect that authority, that they are legalistic and held in their assigned places, not fighting against each other with internal wars for another's rank. I believe Jesus proved this because he said if Satan's kingdom is divided against itself how can his kingdom stand? For the people who do not believe that Satan has a kingdom, Jesus says it in (Matthew 12:26); also in (Matthew 4:8) when Satan tempted Jesus in the wilderness and offered him all the kingdoms of the world. He wasn't just offering Him the earthly kingdoms, but he was also offering Him the demonic kingdoms that are in the spiritual ranks of control around the earth.

Paul is also telling us that there are different ranks just as in our military and world government systems. One-on-one combat to the death; not our death, but theirs.

And you may say, "One-on-one combat"? I thought you said, "Start at the top and take them all out at one time." That's right; the Bible says that 2 or more can agree as 1. And Jesus said in (Matthew18:19) that, "If two of you shall agree on earth as touching anything that they shall ask it shall be done." (Leviticus 26:8) says, "Five of you shall chase a hundred, and a hundred of you shall put ten thousand to flight: and your enemies shall fall by the sword." And it keeps multiplying. Remember, what we see in the physical realm reflects what is in the spirit realm.

In (Ephesians 6:12) the Greek word "wrestle" is "pale" and means one on many; (Ephesians 6:17) tells us take the sword of the spirit which is the word of God. When God began to talk to me about this He said it was accelerated multiplication in prayer. I wanted the full revelation on this. He begins to remind me of the parable of the laborers. Some agreed to work all day at a certain wage. Some came in at the last hour and worked for the same wage. God begins to say to me that in the last days there would be those generals in his word and power that have been in his army for 20, 30, 40, years and are ready for war. But there would be those who are new Christians, who because they have spent time in his word with him, fasting and praying, they would be accelerated at a multiplied rate. By this, in a short period of time they would be ready to fight with his anointing beside the generals.

The word "principality" means a prince or a chief that rules over a territory. The Greek word for principalities is "archas" which refers to the top ranking demonic positions over geographic regions of the earth. (Ephesians 6:12) in the amplified Bible says "despotism" which is basically the same but explains it a little deeper. Despotism means a system or government with a ruler having absolute authority over others, a form of government system ruled by a tyrant dictator, and a master of slaves.

The word "powers" means one with influence over other "nations." A person or thing having influence, force or authority, legal authority and vigor, force and strength. Here it is referring to demonic spirits who are second in command below the principality, who would still be over geographic regions, broken down to smaller areas, with others under their authority to carry out commands and strategies against the saints.

The word "powers" in Greek is "exousia" and means delegated authority. The word "delegate" means, a person authorized to act under the rule of another's representation, to entrust power and authority to another of higher authority. They are given orders to be carried out for all kinds of evil.

When we think about the rulers of the darkness of this world, "ruler" means one who governs. It is taken from the Greek word "kosokrateros" and is made up of two other words: "kosmos" and "kratos." The word "kosmos" means "order" or "arrangement." "Kratos" means "raw power;" this means raw power that has been harnessed to put into an order. The word was also used by the Greek military to describe certain aspects of the military.

Look at it this way, what we see in the physical realm where we exist reflects what is going on in the spirit realm where the demonic kingdom exists. The Greek army had a lot of young, strong soldiers who had a lot of natural fighting ability, strength and energy, or (raw power). For that raw power to be harnessed and effectively used in battle, it had to be harnessed, trained and organized, by top ranking officers to form a strong military, instead of confusion and weakness.

We are on a battlefield also. The war that we're in does not have cease-fires. Even if you are not directly under fire at this moment, you are still a target, and are on the battlefield, because you are a threat to the enemy. That's why we must stay constantly in prayer and in God's word, learning and using it. We are an army and we need to join and fight as an army, instead of saying, "Oh, you're not of my denomination!" Oops! I shouldn't have said that, but getting forgiveness is easier than getting permission.

Let's look at the phrase: "spiritual wickedness in high places." The Greek word here is ponerias, the meaning comes down to fornication and pornography. It also means vicious, impious and "malignant" which can mean evil, malicious, very intense and forceful, all having an evil influence over, or likely to cause death, cancerous, and no reverence for God. This also refers to the idol worship that we have already been studying about. In this area we battle witchcraft and the occult.

In the Old Testament, "High places" were the place where the temples were located for worship. The Greek word here is epouranois which also means heavenlies. Paul said in (Ephesians 2:2) that Satan is the prince and the power of the air. We also see that all through the Old Testament high places refers to idol temples built on high mountains or in high places.

You will later see that I refer to Beliel as a strongman, and this is why. He's just one of many that are in demonic authority under Satan. Jesus said in (Matthew 12:29) and in (Mark 3:27) that if we want to spoil and plunder the strongman's house we must bind the strongman. Paul said do not be ignorant of Satan's devices. We must know everything there is to know about our enemy if we expect to win. Where he is, who he is, how he fights. His strengths, his weakness's, what we do that brings on his attacks, and how "we" fight. If we don't know these factors it's like sending a spiritual prayer-missile off into the darkness, just hoping that we hit something. Yes, we can get close; yes, we can hit something with the concussion of our misses, but it takes a lot more work in prayer this way. However, if we know all these factors, and exactly who and where the enemy is, then we can send the missiles of our prayers, and of the words that we speak, and make a direct hit, taking out and binding the demonic strongman.

Beliel: The Strongman

In (Deuteronomy 13:13), we read: "Certain men, the children of Beliel, are gone out from among you, and have withdrawn the inhabitants of their city, saying, let us go and serve other Gods which we have not known."

The children of Beliel were the people who worshipped and were under the control of Beliel. They were being used to draw God's people away from God to serve other gods, which are Satan and the demonic spirits.

This also goes into occultism, and we are seeing the same thing today in sorcery, witchcraft, spiritualism, divination, magic, casting spells, curses, and conjuring and contacting spirits of the dead, as well as astral beings and spirit projection. But this is nothing new, it happened all the way back in the Old Testament.

The Greek word "pharmakeia" is translated witchcraft and sorcery, referring to spells, and poisoning. It also means the medical use of drugs. In sorcery, various incantations, the casting of spells, using charms and amulets are often used in conjunction with drugs. Have you ever wondered how so early in history, so much was known about drugs? It would be impossible in the natural, or at least seem so. But when I studied demonology, I found there were two demonic spirits who were in control over this area. And they had many demonic troops working under them carrying out their plans.

[Nathan, you may want to give more detail here about who the 2 spirits are or what they do].

This drawing away of God's people also included contacting the spirit world through channeling, which is talking to spirits and the dead. It is often used to manipulate the spirit world to do what someone wants, such as putting curses on people for harm and torment, or to contact ghosts through séances, or to gain protection from evil malevolent spirits by coming into an agreement with "good" spirits. In (1 Corinthians 10:19-21) Paul condemned this.

To gain knowledge from the spirit world outside of the gifts of the Holy Spirit, or outside of God's word, is condemned. All of this represents making an agreement with the demonic, even if the terms are not clearly understood. Even if done in ignorance, it doesn't matter; you're still hooked.

I also believe from my study that the origins of Halloween can be traced back to Beliel in the book of Deuteronomy. This was long before the Druids. This is just my opinion.

"are gone out from among you." This part of the verse gives reference that some people had been deceived into turning their backs on God to worship Beliel. This is done by the spirits under the ruler ship of Beliel, which caused these people to go into bondage.

Some of the ways that Beliel is causing people to worship other gods are to make them think man is an independent, self-sufficient being, and that they don't need God. It is also caused through idolatry, the worshipping of false gods created by men.

(1 Timothy 4:1) says in the latter times some shall depart from the faith, giving heed to seducing spirits, and doctrines of devils. How much more clearly can it be to the people who do not believe what

I'm saying? Paul uses the words "seducing," "spirits" and "devils." The word "seduce" means to tempt or to "draw" away to wrongdoing. Verse 2 speaks of lies in hypocrisy, having their conscience seared with a hot iron. The Phillips translation says, "whose consciences are as dead as seared flesh." The amplified says "whose consciences are seared (cauterized)." To "cauterize" means "to deaden" in (1 Kings 21:13) in the Living Bible it says, "then two men who had no conscience accused him," talking about Naboth. These two men in verse 10 were sons of Beliel. Beliel causes men to act without conscience.

(Titus 1:15) says, "But unto them that are defiled, and unbelieving is nothing pure; but even their mind and conscience is defiled." The word "defiled" means to make filthy or profane, to contaminate, or to make unclean, and to tread underfoot. "Filthy" means obscenity, "profane" means total disrespect for Godly and sacred things. In verse16 they profess that they know God; but in works they deny him, being abominable and disobedient and unto every good work reprobate.

When the conscience is seared in this way, it gives legal access and opens people's lives up to all kinds of demonic attacks where in their minds they can commit these vile acts and not feel any remorse about it. The soul is made up of your mind, your will, and your emotions. I believe this proves the evil spirits of Beliel are working and controlling the conscience, controlling the mind, the will, and the emotions. This means there is no limit to what a person with no conscience can do.

The word "seduce" means "to lead away,, "to persuade to disobedience," and "disloyalty," to lead away by persuasion of false promises, to attract and to lure. This is known as "apostasy" which means a total falling away or desertion of the faith. This is different from being a backslider.

Apostasy is when a person totally and completely rejects Jesus as

Christ the savior and the work that He did for us on the cross, as the only sacrifice for sin. The Greek word "koinon" means to make common or unclean, to make as an unholy thing. They make the blood of Jesus a common thing, or of no value as atonement as they once did, regarding it to them as unfit to redeem.

This is what the spirit of Beliel attempts to do in (Deuteronomy 13:13) where it says: "Certain men, the children of Beliel, are gone out from among you, and have withdrawn the inhabitants of their city." It is showing ownership, leadership, and a bond by saying, "let us go and serve other gods which ye have not known." That is why we have to stand together as an army praying for our towns, cities, and our country and then the world.

Beliel: Demonic Strongman of Greed

In (Deuteronomy 15:9), the spirit of Beliel causes people to be selfish. It says, "beware that there be not a thought in thy wicked (remember one meaning of the name Beliel is translated "wicked") heart saying the 7th year of release is at hand: and thine eye be evil against thy poor brother and thou givest him naught; and he cry unto the lord against thee and it be sin unto thee." The Hebrew word for "heart" in this verse is Beliel.

Beliel: Demonic Strongman of Homosexuality and Sexual Immorality

(Judges 19:22) says, "Now as they were making their hearts merry, behold, the men of the city, certain of the sons of Beliel, beset the house round about, and beat at the door, and speak to the master of the house saying, Bring forth the man that came into thine house, that we may know him." In verse 23 he said to them, "No, my brethren, I pray you do not so wickedly; seeing that this man is come into mine house, do not this folly. verse 24: "Behold my daughter a maiden, and his concubine them I will bring out now, and do with them what seemth good to you."

In verse 25 they finally took the woman and the Bible says they abused her all night long until morning, when she was found dead.

Long story short, they literally raped her to death. A demonic spirit under the authority of Beliel was responsible for this. In verse 28 her master said to her "get out, let's go and there was no answer." The Amplified Bible says, "but there was no answer for she was dead."

In (Judges 19:29-30) when he reached home, he took a knife and cut her up limb by limb, into 12 parts and sent them into all areas of Israel. Everyone who saw it said, "such a thing has never been seen or done, not since the day the Israelite came up out of Egypt." And we still see the same thing happening all through history, until our present day. In movies, on TV, on the internet desensitizing our minds to the point that it is no longer shocking when we see or hear it.

Back a few years ago, before I had ever found this verse, God gave me a dream about a woman I had worked very closely with in ministry who was dynamic in her area of ministry. She decided to step down out of ministry, and I knew she was stepping out of God's will by doing this. In the dream, I saw her in a very rocky, distant terrain. Her entire body had been cut up into small pieces and lay there alone on the rocks. I began intercessory prayer for her for a long period of time after that. Sometime later I was told by a very reliable source that she had gotten completely out of church, no longer in ministry. She had gone through a very abusive marriage, the death of a child, and her life was a wreck. God was showing me what was going to happen to her spirituality.

As we read in (Deuteronomy 13:13), Beliel wants to draw the hearts of people away from God. As we saw in (1 Timothy 4:1) causing them to depart from the faith giving heed to seducing spirits and wanting to destroy ministries.

*Reminder: the name Beliel means worthless, wicked and good for nothing. *

In (Judges 20:6) it tells of the act of cutting her into pieces, that he had committed lewdness. The word "lewdness" means evil, wicked, sexually unchaste, and obscene. The word "obscene" means repulsive, disgusting. Beliel is responsible for these acts of sin.

Beliel, and the spirits working under him, are in control of and inflicting curses of rape, incest, molestation, sexual abuse, sexual immorality, sodomy, and obscenity. One reference I have found uses the Hebrew word "zana" meaning to have illicit intercourse. And refers to the temple prostitutes of the Canaanite pagan idol worship. This always begins generational curses on family lines. Generational curses will be discussed deeper in another chapter. The idol worshipers committed a double sin: sinning against God, and the sexual sins of the ceremonies.

But when someone is a victim of sexual and abusive crimes such as rape, incest, and sodomy, they are violated. A lot of times it's like something in them dies. It causes what is known as a soul wound which is simply a wound in their soul. Because the soul wound is created by sin, it gives the enemy the legal right, or an open door, to torment that person until the soul wound is healed. Soul wounds will be explained in a later chapter.

We also find in the Old Testament that perversions like homosexuality and lesbianism also work under the demonic strongman Beliel. "Pervert" and "perversion" means any sex act considered abnormal, to lead astray, to corrupt, to misuse, to distort from what is good, true or morally right. "Sodomy" means an act with someone of the same sex or with an animal. The term sodomite is mentioned 5 times in the Old Testament. Sodomites were temple prostitutes who were a part of idol worship to draw people to serve other gods.

Homosexuality is a strong demonic force because they "give" themselves to it. The word "give" means to hand over, to devote or sacrifice and to yield. The word "yield" means to surrender, to concede, to give away to lose precedence, and to be submissive. The word "submit" means to yield to the control or power of another, obedience, to yield and to give in. These demonic spirits get their legal access and authority into a person's life because the person gives yields, submits and hands over their control of themselves to it.

Now, listen to what (Romans 6:16) (King James Version) says, "Know ye not, that to whom ye yield yourselves servants to obey, his servants ye are to whom ye obey." Now, (Romans 6:16) (New KJV): "Do you not know that to whom you present yourselves slaves to obey, you are that one's slaves to whom you obey." Now, (Romans 6:16) amplified: "Do you not know that if you continually surrender yourselves to anyone to do his will you are slaves of whom you obey."

This comes from demonic spirits controlling their victims through lust. I just love the dictionary. The word "lust" means appetite, an excessive sexual desire, an overwhelming desire and a lust for power to feel an intense desire. The word "overwhelms" means to pour down and bury beneath, to crush and to overpower. You see not only in homosexuality, but also in sexual sin bondages of immorality, when you give your control and will over to obey the demonic, and that is what they want, they control your will because they own you.

Jesus said in (John 8:34) that if you commit sin then you are the servant of sin. (1 John 3:8) amplified says he that commits sin (who practices evildoing) is of the devil, (and takes his character from the evil one) for the devil has sinned (violated the divine law) from the beginning. The reason the son of God was made manifest (visible) was to undo, destroy, loosen, and dissolve the works the devil has done. This means Jesus came to tear down, demolish, to ruin, to do away with, to kill, to end, to cause to disappear what Satan has come to do.

(James 1:14-15) says every man is tempted, (when he is drawn away of his own lust, and "enticed," meaning to allure, to beguile, a burning, to tempt with a hope of reward or pleasure) then when lust hath "conceived" (meaning to take, to become pregnant with, to form in the mind) it bringeth forth sin: and sin when it is finished, bringeth forth death.

This involves your soul, which as I said before consists of your mind, your will and your emotions. Look at this:

Tempted – thought of evil, in your "mind."
Drawn away – strong imagination, more thoughts of evil, from your "mind."
Lust – delight in the imagination in your "mind."
Enticed – your "will," which by this point is getting weak. Inability to make sound judgments and to choose right and wrong.
Lust conceived – which is your "emotions;" it has become a part of your soul, giving into the sin. It has controlled your mind and your will.
Sin and death – the results of yielding to what you feel, instead of obeying God.

Let's look a little deeper into (James 1:14-15) and how sin is coming into agreement and covenant with a demonic spirit. Verse 14 says "But every man is tempted, when he is drawn away of his own lust and enticed."

Who draws you and entices you? The demonic spirit is speaking the temptation into your mind and is getting into your soul, your mind, your will and your emotions. According to (Romans 6:16), this makes you a slave and a servant to whomever you obey. When the demonic speaks to you, this is the opposite of the Holy Spirit speaking to you. Then James says, "and lust is conceived" meaning to become pregnant with, the thought that has been implanted inside of you waiting to give birth. It can't wait to get out; you feel like you just have to do it. Then James says when the lust has conceived that "it brings forth sin, and sin when it is finished it brings forth death."

(Isaiah 28:15) says "We have made a covenant with death, and with hell we are at agreement." This is a Satanic-Demonic agreement and a covenant is created.

In (1 Samuel 2:12) it says: "Now the sons of Eli were sons of Beliel, they knew not the Lord." Eli's sons committed some major sins and they were sons of Beliel, which means they chose to serve Satan. They committed adultery with women who gathered at the tabernacle of worship (verse 22). They robbed the offerings (1 Samuel 2:13-17). They refused to obey the truth and to quit even when they were found out in (1 Samuel 2:25). So we see Beliel is responsible for adultery and rebellion against authority and God. And it caused their deaths.

The works of Beliel is to bring not only sin but also sexual uncleanness into the temple of God, targeting ministries and ministers, drawing them who are greatly anointed by God into sin to bring a reproach to the church to destroy its reputation. Another reason Beliel wants to get Christians and ministers of God involved in sins that are an abomination to God is to bring them under a curse and into a place of judgment. (1 Samuel 3:13) is described in detail in (Romans 1:18-32). This proves Beliel is the demonic strongman that leads people into sins that are "vile," meaning shameful and dishonor. The spirits responsible for these sins mentioned in (Romans 1) work under him to carry this out. Because unclean sexual acts as these bring curses from evil spirits and judgments from God, the only way to be free is to repent and be delivered.

And we even see sexual immorality in churches today. Paul warned the Corinthian church about it. (Revelation 2:20) says, "Notwithstanding, I have a few things against thee, because thou sufferest that woman Jezebel (who, by the way, was a daughter of Beliel) who calls herself a prophetess, to teach and seduce my servants to commit sexual immorality and to eat things offered to idols."

This should remind us of (Deuteronomy 13:13), "to draw away to serve other Gods." This is a problem in many Christian churches. A few years ago, I was over a single's ministry. I had to deal with the singles sleeping with each other on a regular basis. It was like you take care of my needs, and I'll take care of yours. No big deal. Wrong! This is what God calls fornication, which we see from (Revelation 2:20) as giving into the seduction of a spirit who is working under Beliel.

Beliel: Demonic Strongman Behind Pornography

One of Satan's main areas of attacks against the human race is pornography. The Greek word is porne or porneia and means a prostitute and a harlot in the New Testament, referring to both male and female.

It is estimated that there are over 420 million pornographic web sites on the internet. Every hour over $185,000 is made from pornography. Every hour there is an estimated 1.7 million people viewing internet pornography, and another 23,000 using search engines for pornography, making it a $100 billion a year business. Every hour almost 2 new pornography internet web sites are created.

(Psalms 101:3) says: "I will set no thing wicked before my eyes: I hate the work of those who fall away; it shall not cling to me."

The word "cling" (the King James uses the word "cleave") but both words mean almost the same thing: to adhere to like glue, to be faithful to, to hold fast as by embracing, to be "emotionally" attached to. There it is again: the giving of your soul, your mind, your will and your emotions.

64

The word "adhere" means to give allegiance or to support. The word "embrace" means to take up or adapt, to clasp in the arms lovingly, and to accept. As I have said before, the word "wicked" means evil, morally bad, a wicked storm. The word "storm" means a strong emotional outburst, a sudden strong attack, to rage and rant violently, and to storm into a room to attack vigorously; to steal control of your soul, your mind, your will and your emotions.

Wow, if that does not explain what the curse and bondage of pornography does in a person's life then you've never fought it in your own life as I did. Pornography first begins with a glance at someone immodestly dressed and looked at too long. The more you do it, the easier it gets. It infiltrates the mind with false delusions of what all human bodies should look like. And let's be honest, not everyone looks like a perfect airbrushed #10.

The battleground is in the mind, the imagination, and the fantasy realm. The Greek word for "fantasy" is "phainein" which means to show, imagination, an illusion, fiction portraying highly imaginative characters and settings. "Imagine" means to conceive, and "conceive" means to become pregnant with something. Pregnant denotes intimacy, which denotes a soul union. Jesus said in (Matthew 5:28) that if a man looks on a woman to lust after her, he has committed adultery in his heart and it goes the same for women. Jesus did not say it was kind of like adultery. He said it was adultery. The same as committing the sexual act. That is why I believe soul ties and generational curses can be created through lust. Jesus did not say that it is a sin to look and acknowledge that a person is attractive, anyone with eyes can see that, but lustful thinking about him or her is a sin.

This can wreck the mental and emotional process of passion in a marriage. And, in some cases, may lead to divorce. This can occur because one spouse is not meeting the physical and emotional needs of the other spouse in the relationship. Why? Because the mental picture that is there is taking away from the spouse if they do not look like a perfect #10. You will get to the point where you think of the pictures that you have seen just to be able to make the mechanics of intimacy even happen. It keeps taking more and more mental and emotional energy, just so you can function. When this happens, there is no way intimacy can be what it should be, and your spouse will notice.

You have to allow the Holy Spirit to deliver you from this bondage, and then you can learn to turn and focus all that mental and emotional energy from lust into love and passion for your spouse, and they will notice. They may not know what has got into you, but they will know whatever it is, they like it. They will be happier, kinder, and nicer because now their needs are being met, physically and emotionally. There is a lot of truth to the old saying, "If momma ain't happy, ain't nobody happy."

Pornography and fantasy go hand in hand. Sexual fantasizing about someone that is not your spouse is a sin. If someone is fantasizing during intimacy, they are there physically, but their mind, their will, and their emotions are not; they are with the mental image that they are seeing. Wow, there it is again, their soul is not in it. This is also adultery.

In (Matthew 5:28) (amplified) Jesus said, "But I say to you that everyone who so much as looks at a woman with evil desire (the K.J. says to lust after her) for her has already committed adultery with her in his heart."

The word "lust" means an excessive, overwhelming appetite and desire. The word "overwhelms" means to pour down upon and to bury, overpower, and to crush beneath. "Appetite" means a strong desire and craving that you think you can't do without. And because it is making a connection with the mental image of someone in a picture, (looking and lusting) and because it is done with the mind, the will and the emotions, (the soul), it causes a soul tie.

I do not necessarily believe that any time you let the Bible fall open and let your finger fall to wherever that God is giving you a message. But sometimes he can use that method. When God was trying to get this message to me, I did exactly what I just described. My finger fell directly on (Matthew 5:28). I thought, "Well, that's odd." I put that Bible down and picked up another Bible and did the same thing again. You guessed it! My finger fell again on (Matthew 5:28). Knowing God doesn't work by coincidence I said ok God, I get it.

We read in (Genesis 6:5-6) what the Lord saw before the flood: "The wickedness of man. And that every intent of the thoughts of his heart was only on evil continually." Besides the fact that it is a demonic bondage that forms an addiction, it is also addictive because it uses endorphins and must constantly have more and more erotic images to increase the endorphins to achieve a greater high each time. This, combined with the demonic bondage, is why this is a bondage that continues to grow deeper into a worse condition as time goes on. Pornography can never maintain a constant point.

I've even seen way too much skin in church before. Once I thought: I sure hope she don't raise her hands very high today or bend over in front of anyone because she will be showing something if she does. Major wardrobe malfunction for sure. One friend said the women on the Sunday morning praise team wore skirts so short and tops so low that he couldn't even look toward the stage. In this church he spoke of many there who were sleeping around because of lust. Several, from this church went to a private swim party that turned into a skinny dipping party. All because of obeying lust.

In (Romans 12:9), Paul tells us to abhor that which is evil. "Abhor" means to hate, detest, loathe, shrinking from in disgust. Since we've already seen where Beliel and the spirits under him are leading their followers in sexual immorality, we must see where pornography is also a part of that same control. It opens the door to many other evil spirits of lust and perversion as we've already discussed like rape, homosexuality, prostitution, and many others.

Pornography is an addiction and bondage that is totally out of control. It is Satan's perversion trying to turn a legitimate human, God-given sex drive into an illegitimate drive. The Bible says a sexual relationship is to be only between a husband and wife, and not outside of that relationship. It is not to be fulfilled by looking at an erotic picture of someone other than a spouse. Think of it as a fire burning inside of you. The more fuel you throw on the fire, the bigger the fire gets. (Ecclesiastes 1:8) says, "The eye is not satisfied with seeing, or never satisfied at all." This is something that God delivered me from. You will say after this time I won't do it again. But then you can't stop, there's always the next time, and the next time. It's never enough to satisfy you.

(Galatians 5:17) says, "For the flesh sets its desire against the spirit, and the spirit against the flesh, for these are opposite to one another." You have to decide that you want freedom more than the bondage. The only way you can do this is through the power of the Holy Spirit. You cannot do it by yourself. I know because I tried.

Trying to stop the habit yourself won't work, you are not strong enough; I wasn't. I couldn't make it even a day. I finally said, God, 60 seconds at a time is all I can do, so with your help I'll make it 60 seconds at a time. I said, devil, listen up, from now on, when you tempt me I will read my Bible and pray, and then if you don't stop, I will memorize some scripture. Then if you don't stop I'll find someone to witness to.

Well, over the next few years I did a lot of Bible reading. I memorized a lot of scripture and even had to find a few people to witness to. Then one day, I realized I didn't have to fight that battle as I had in the past. God gave me a dream. I love dreams.

I saw myself walking down a long dirt road. There was swampy, murky looking water on the left of the road. There was a deep drop off on the right of the road, so deep I could not see the bottom. In front of me the road went almost straight up a high mountain. I climbed up to the top of the mountain, and I stood there looking back from where I had just come from. I could see beneath the water a huge "dead" snake coiled up, about the size of a house. God gave me a message as I stood there. He said, "As long as you choose to remain on top of the mountain you are delivered. But if you ever choose to go back down the mountain from where you came from, the snake will come back alive, and it will try to consume you." I have chosen to remain on the top of the mountain.

You have to cut off all opportunities to look at pornography ahead of time. TV, HBO, sin to the max or I mean Cinemax, the internet, magazines, strip clubs, even book stores. These were all the places that I went to. Temptation is an area you can put yourself into, or you can take yourself out of. You must choose to stay away from it.

One way is by praying and fasting, and, no, I didn't say to pray fast. Fasting and praying shows God you're serious. It is going without food, or limiting what you take in, while spending time with God in prayer. It is not a diet. As your hunger for food decreases, the more your hunger for God will increase, and He will begin to take the sinful desires away.

Then find an accountability partner (of your gender) that you can trust to hold you responsible to purity. And be honest to him or her about how your progress with your struggle is going.

As you stop throwing the fuel on the fire you begin to see the desire for the pornography die and go out, or at least get to a controllable point, but still that's only with God as your helper. So, long as you are involved with pornography, it is not possible to be, or to have, the relationship with your spouse, or with God, to its fullest. It will affect the intimidate moments. But when you begin to focus that energy totally on your spouse instead of the pictures, and your mind and energy is focused on your spouse during intimate times, instead of seeing the pictures in your mind of what you have looked at, you will be more passionate, and your spouse will notice it and will respond. Well, let's just say fireworks will go off. And your love for each other will increase. Wow. This is marriage-saving advice.

(1 Samuel 2:12) says that Eli's sons were supposed to be priests in the temple, but they were sons of Beliel. Eli's sons were deceived into becoming the sons of Beliel, leaving the law of God. I believe this is a clear indication of what we are seeing today as so many so-called church officials are allowing things into the church that are clearly stated in God's word as abominations to God. For instance, ordaining homosexuals, telling fornicators they are all right and much more.

I believe this is what Paul spoke of in (2 Timothy 3:5) as having a form of Godliness, but denying the power thereof, from such turn away. Now notice this verse does not say "Godlessness;" it says "Godliness." There is a difference, because one of the goals of the children of Beliel in (Deuteronomy 13:13) was to entice people to worship other "Gods." And Paul warns us to "turn away from them.. Turn means "about face" in the opposite direction. Verse 6 says they "creep" into houses; creep indicating being deceptive, sneaky, and to lead captive women laden with sins, led away with diverse lusts. All of which we have already seen are the works of Beliel and those working under him.

Beliel: The Demonic Strongman Behind Alcohol

In (1 Samuel 1:12-16), Eli thought Hannah was a daughter of Beliel, thinking she was drunk. This gives clear indication Beliel is also responsible for promoting alcoholism, if Eli thought drunkenness was an association with being children of Beliel.

The spirit of Beliel operates through alcohol and drunkenness because it is a prime way to destroy morals and open doors in people's lives to lust and perversion. It is also a proven fact that many children and spouses of alcoholics are often victims of incest, neglect, rape, verbal, sexual and physical abuse. This means the door of legal access has also been opened to these.

In (1 Samuel 10:27), we find that the children of Beliel were responsible for slander, false accusations, and leading rebellions against God's people. (Does that sound familiar, to people coming against the church and ministers today?). Here, he was trying to slander Saul's reputation as being king of Israel. God had called Saul to be king. Slander causes doubt in people about your ability, but it will also tear down your own confidence in yourself as it tries to stop you from reaching the purpose that God has called you to.

For instance, a person who has a calling to be a minister, to preach, or to teach, maybe even from childhood, and all through their lifetime, may experience people putting down their abilities in this area. This false slander comes from the spirit of Beliel. This becomes very frustrating to that person because they know the calling is real, but if they are not careful they will allow their purpose to be stolen and never fulfill it. This happens because they have believed a lie from Satan that has set up a stronghold of defeat in their mind, and that stronghold is controlling them.

In (1 Samuel 25), we find that Nabal, whose name means "fool," as verse 25 says was a son of Beliel and moved by greed and selfishness and refused to help David by not sharing his food with him. We see greediness everywhere today.

Again in (1 Samuel 30:22), we find where the "men of Beliel" were greedy, selfish, and not willing to help others.

In (2 Samuel 20:1), Sheba, a "man of Beliel," had come against David.   seems a pattern that there is always "men of Beliel" in every gathering of God's people to fight them by sowing slander, strife, and discord to promote their own evil desires.

71

In (2 Samuel 23:6-7), "But the sons of Beliel shall be all of them as thorns, thrust away, because they cannot be taken with hands. But the man that shall touch them must be fenced with iron and the staff of a spear; and they shall be utterly burned with fire in the same place."

The original text says, "But Beliel, all of these as thorns shall be thrust down." It also says that Beliel cannot be overcome by mere man on his (man's) own power, but by a person with God's anointing, protection, and power. Jesus said in (Luke 10:19), "Behold I give you power to tread on serpents and scorpions and over all the power of the enemy, and nothing shall by any means hurt you.

Jesus said this power was to all who believe, not to just the first disciples, but "to whosoever believeth." There is no chapter and verse that ever says that the power was ever taken back from us. Why would Jesus give His life on the cross, go to hell to take control of the keys of death, hell, and the grave, and then take the power away from us so that we would not have the power to defend ourselves? That would give Satan complete mastery over us. There is one word to describe this kind of thinking "stupid."

Ignorance is simply not knowing, a lack of knowledge. Stupidity, on the other hand, is not caring to know or to learn. And that is one of the works of Beliel.

Jesus gave us the power of attorney to use His name. The Greek word here is "exousia" which means "delegated authority," the right to use power to destroy Satan's works. To "tread upon" means absolute, total, complete mastery over serpents, scorpions and all the power of the enemy. Serpents and scorpions refer to the ranks of demonic power that we have been given mastery over through the name and authority of Jesus Christ.

In (Proverbs 6:12), a naughty person, a wicked man, walketh with a froward mouth. The Hebrew word here is "adam beliyaal" which means good for nothing, worthless, and a man of Beliel.

"Naughty" means disobedient and improper. "Wicked" means evil, immorality, and generally bad, and unpleasant. The word "storm" means, a strong emotional out-burst, a sudden and strong attack, to rage and rant, to rush violently, and to attack vigorously.

The word "froward" means not easily controlled and willfully contrary.

So, we see through this the nature of Beliel. We see how he attacks suddenly and violently. For this reason, we must be ready to attack with God's power. He's disobedient and contrary to God's truth. It says a strong emotional outburst, not easily controlled, and willfully contrary. As I said before, your soul is made up of three parts: your mind, your will, and your emotions. Read back over this description of Beliel and you will see that he is targeting your soul: your will, your mind and your emotions.

In (Proverbs 16:27), a scoundrel plots evil and his speech is like a scorching fire. This means Beliel causes his followers to bring up evil and set people against each other, by causing lies and strife in families and in our churches. In the book of Proverbs, one of the seven abominations that God hates is he that sows discord.

I've seen many families broken by divorce and many churches split and dissolved by division, and we can see in this verse that Beliel is at the root of this problem. Divorce in marriage is the norm today and almost expected. If the family is split, a lot of times, one or both parents may drop out of church. The children are no longer taught about God and the cycle that Beliel is working repeats.

Beliel's Curses Bring Physical Sickness:

(Deuteronomy 28) tells us of blessings that God will pour out on us if we serve and obey Him. But also in (Deuteronomy 28), He tells us of curses that will come upon us if we do not serve and obey Him. In (Deuteronomy 28:22), it says, "The Lord shall smite thee with consumption, and with a fever, and with an inflammation, and with the sword and with blasting, and with mildew and they shall pursue thee until thou perish."

The sins of perversion, immorality, and rebellion against God that Beliel brought on people carried a stiff judgment from God.

Beliel has many spirits of infirmity and sickness that are under him. Beliel wants to draw us into sin to bring these curses on us.

(Hebrews 13:4), says that God will judge the whoremongers and the adulterers. Because of the sin of homosexuality and fornication, AIDS has come, I believe, as one of those judgments for sin that God calls an abomination. AIDS is a fatal disease. (Psalms 41:8) says, "An evil disease say they, cleaveth fast unto him, and now that he lieth he shall raise no more."

In other words, he had a fatal disease, and he was going to die from it. In some translations this is referenced to Beliel. These spirits can also work through witchcraft. "Witchcraft" means the power or practices of a witch. "Witch" means one thought to have supernatural power because of a "compact" with evil spirits.

"Compact" means an agreement or a covenant. Don't you see Beliel has many demonic spirits working under him in compact, in agreement in covenant with him to bring curses on God's people, on ministers and churches? These curses often manifest through sickness. Our leaders need strong intercessory prayer over them against the strongman Beliel who hates them and wants to destroy ministry gifts. (Exodus 23:25): "And I will take sickness away from the midst of thee."

Beliel Promotes Rebellion:

The word "rebellion" means an armed resistance to one's government, and a defiance of any authority. Satan is the author of all rebellion and of anything to do with God. Satan wants total control of earth but because of "us" he can't have it. What we see happening in the sexual perversions that we've discussed here is nothing more than Satan's rebellion against what God set in place. Beliel wants immorality, and all forms of immorality, to be in full force. I believe that is why we see our judicial system falling short from what it was originally formed to be. Because of this rebellion, we have seen in the last several years abortion legalized, the laws removed against homosexual and lesbian lifestyles, prayer made illegal in public schools, and so much more. All in the name of removing God and His authority, and we are the only restraint on earth to keep Beliel's goal from being totally accomplished.

(Psalms 2:2-3) says, "The kings of the earth set themselves, and the rulers take counsel together, against the lord and against his anointed" (us, the children of God); saying in verse 3, "Let us break their bands asunder, and cast away their cords from us."

The Hebrew word for the "band" that Beliel wants to break is "mocerah" which means "restraint." The church is the restraining force against Beliel's ungodliness and immorality. 9Proverbs 29:18) in the Amplified Bible says, "Where there is no revelation, no vision, the people cast off restraint." The King James says, "Where there is no vision the people perish: but he that keepeth the law, happy is he."

I like what Dake says on this verse, "Where there is no vision or consciousness of responsibility regarding keeping the law, the people perish for its lack of enforcement, but the one who in such times keeps the law is blessed." It still says restraint to me.

Rebellion is an open door to demonic oppression, possession, and bondage. (1 Samuel 15:23) says for rebellion is as the sin of witchcraft and stubbornness is as iniquity and idolatry. The amplified Bible uses the same Hebrew word that you find in the K.J. which is "tereaphim." This verse is 1 of the 6 times that it is used in the Bible. It represents family idols and images that were believed to have the power to cure diseases, and ward off evil spirits. They believed that when these evil spirits saw these idols it would cause them to have mercy on the person. This was making an agreement, a covenant, and a contract with the demonic spirits involved. These idols could be of men, or of individual body parts such as hand, feet, eyes, ears, mouth etc., This is obeying demonic spirits, fearing them, and giving them control of your life, and is still in use today. And it is rebellion against God.

The Hebrew word for witchcraft is "qecem" which also means divination. Both are in rebellion of God and are also clearly demonic possession. (Acts 16:16) say, "And it came to pass, as we went up prayer, a certain damsel possessed with a spirit of divination met us."

(Ezekiel 12:2) says: "Son of man, thou dwellest in the midst of a rebellious house, which have eyes to see, and see not, they have ears to hear and hear not, for they are a rebellious house."

Rebellion can open a door to Satan and Beliel to blind the eyes and ears of those who are in rebellion, so they will not heed, nor have a desire, to understand God. Paul said in (2 Corinthians 4:4): "In whom the God of this world (Satan) hath blinded the minds of them which believe not, lest the light of the glorious gospel of Christ, who in the image of God should shine unto them."

We often wonder how people can be deceived by what seems to be the worst politicians. Those who stand for issues like abortion and other societal damaging issues that tear down family values. It is because their spiritual eyes have been blinded by Satan.

According to Scripture rebellion and disobedience are also

responsible for mental illness in some cases. Many of the people in the prison system, who have made a lifetime career in rebellion and disobedience, are diagnosed with many different mental illnesses, bipolar disorder being one of the main ones. One out of four in prison is diagnosed with these problems. That is about six times higher than people on the outside.

King Saul is never recorded as having mental problems until after his sin of rebellion and disobedience against God by going to the witch of Endor, which was condemned by God. Saul was supposed to have destroyed all the witches, by God's command, but he did not obey (rebellion). After that, the spirit of God departed from him and he did not know it. The Bible says an evil spirit came upon Saul. But it was afterwards that he began to apparently have severe mood swings, one minute wanting to kill David because he hated him, and the next minute not wanting to kill him because he loved him. This sounds a lot like bipolar disorder. It also sounds a lot like my ex-wife, I'm not kidding. Living with someone like that is difficult.

(Revelation 12:10) reveals that the accuser of the brethren is cast down which accused them before God day and night. We, as the children of God, having the spirit of Christ in us, are accused by Satan. But this is also a battle in our minds.

(2 Corinthians 10:4) tells us to pull down the stronghold which is incorrectly thinking about us and what the word of God says, and it is thinking contrary to God's word about us and our situations. Basically, it is defeated thinking to cause us to continue to be weak, lose out on God's promises to us, and to even lose out on salvation. Strongholds are formed by deceptions and lies, told to, us by Satan and his deceived teachers in dead churches. We come to believe these lies and deceptions, our spirit man becomes programmed with this wrong thinking, and we begin to operate as if it is normal operation. The only way to break the strongholds is to find out what God's word says, with fasting and prayer. I'll have an entire chapter on strongholds later.

(Proverbs 16:27) in the Amplified says a worthless man devises and digs up mischief, and in his lips, there is as a scorching fire. Remember Beliel's name means worthless. (Psalms 37:12) says the wicked plot against the uncompromising righteous, the upright in right standing with God, they gnash at them with their teeth. The word "plot" means a secret, usually, evil, scheme.

(Psalms 37:32) says the wicked lie in wait for the uncompromisingly righteous and seek to put them to death.

Beliel in his effort to destroy God's ministers will set them up for a fall with these plots. This would be in front of many. This will turn many away from God. Ministers are human; they face temptations like anyone else. We need to pray for our church leaders to be strong. Each time they resist Beliel's plots they become stronger in God.

There are satanic curses and spells of witchcraft that can be placed against churches, ministers and against their families to break them up in divorce. A group of witches can perform a ceremony against churches on the church's property to break the church up. They remind you of your past failures to cause depression, despair, to tear you down emotionally, to destroy your faith and tear you down spiritually, and to make you feel like you're not good enough for God to love you.

Beliel wants to discredit God's people:

Once God gave me a dream of this. I was in the church I attend, and I saw a group of witches come into the building. They were there to deceive people with teaching, sow confusion, and cause strife. Because of strong intercessory prayer the Holy Spirit was able to reveal this to the church. The witches were immediately met by people in the church who discerned who and what they were. They were literally manhandled in the spirit, physically overpowered and cast out the front door. I relayed this dream to the pastor. A short time later, and after much prayer I saw one of the people in the dream walk into the church. The pastor and the intercessors took authority over this, and it was overthrown.

I thank God for a pastor who listened to my dream and had the intercessors praying ahead of time; the attack was attempted but was defeated. Other pastors and Christians need to learn from this.

Chapter 6

The Great Outpouring of (Joel 2:28-29)

"And it shall come to pass afterward, that I will pour out my spirit upon all flesh; and your sons and your daughters shall prophesy, your old men shall dream dreams, and your young men shall see visions. And also upon the servants and upon the handmaids in those days will I pour out my spirit."

On Friday night, August 19th, I was in one of the deepest most intense times of prayer that I've experienced in a long time. God began to remind me of the following dreams he had given me, 2 and 3 years ago, and how they fit into the outpouring of the spirit of God in the last days. Then he began to speak to me about the outpouring, but first the dreams.

Dream of the Staff:

God gave me a dream in which I and a few others were moving through various battlefields. We came upon several fights, some were expected; others were not. In all cases, God was with us. The enemy's artillery was coming down close to us but not hitting us. We felt the concussions but were not harmed and moved forward. We knew where the enemy was, and we were able to return fire.

In one battle, we ended up in a river of rough water, and we were covered in mud. But, as we came out of the river, we had no mud on us. It reminded me of the 3 Hebrews who were in the furnace and did not have the smell of smoke on them. As dreams will do, I then saw us coming out of a cave and finding several other people there. These people were not concerned about the enemy. We tried to warn these people of the enemy, but no one would listen. Some of these people had wooden staffs. The Holy Spirit told me that these staffs represented the level of His anointing on these people. The level on their anointing was directly portioned to the amount of time they spent with God, his word, and prayer. Some of these staffs were thin and weak and I thought if the person leaned on the staff, it would break. However, that thought was wrong. Even though thin, the staffs would hold. Other staffs were thick and substantial. I then realized another difference between the two was caused through fasting. The enemy knew we were winning and they glared at us with pure hatred.

I saw the enemy as king cobras, but these were not normal cobras as they were much more intelligent. They looked at me with anger in their eyes, wanting to attack me, but I would hold my staff up at them and they could not come any closer. I felt no fear toward them. I could not understand why some of the people would not listen to us warning them as the enemy was getting to them. They continued on with what seemed to be a party.

Dream of the Storm

This is a dream God gave me shortly after the previous one about demonic activity around the world.

The words in this dream and results were very interesting. The word "storm" means a strong turbulence, a sudden and strong attack; to rage, and to rush violently. The word "turbulence" means wild and disorderly, full of violent commotion. The word "disturbance" means to break up, to disorder, to make uneasy, to interrupt, commotion.

Time is shorter than ever, and we are promised to be kept by God.

I and myself were in ships sailing through the open sea. The skies begin to grow very intense to the point where the storm was only about 25 feet off the side of the ship. I began to see the storm turbulence was demonic and occultic. The demonic disturbance was so severe the earth itself could not stand it and begin to quake from the pressure. I was reminded of the verse in Romans where the earth wanted to return to the point of creation. Then I was reminded of (Matthew 24:5-8), "For many shall come in my name saying I am Christ and shall deceive many. And you shall hear of wars and rumors of wars; see that you be not troubled: for all these things must come to pass, but the end is not yet. For nation shall rise against nation, and kingdom against kingdom, and there shall be famines and pestilences, and earthquakes in diverse places. All these things are the beginning of sorrows. I was then reminded of the (91st Psalm).

Then I was in a different unfamiliar place. I looked at the sky, and saw very dark storm clouds rolling in at a fast rate. I was then transported to a high point above the earth, from where I could see a large portion of the earth below. I could see more of the chaos and wide spread destruction that was going on. During the storm there was a huge tornado that seemed to be hiding in the middle of the chaos, as it created more widespread destruction. I knew this was a demonic and occultic storm that was growing with intensity. I was then transported back to the earth, where I tried to warn people to take cover, to get into their closets and pray. I would go up to them and point to the storm and say, "Look there it is; go into your closet, hide and pray." Some people would listen, but most people would ignore me and continue laughing and joking, not taking me seriously.

As I entered my own closet, I knelt and prayed. I could hear the tornado hitting as debris inside the building was thrown around and torn apart. I could hear people screaming and crying for help, but it was too late; they didn't heed the warning in time, they were unprotected and were being destroyed. Only those who knew God's word, and knew how to get into their prayer closets survived.

Then God showed me two armies in battle against each other. One was the satanic demonic army; the other was God's army, with both armies advancing toward each other. The worshippers were leading the front line of God's army into the battle. They were in every way armored and weaponed just as heavily as the other warriors. The praisers and the worshippers were plowing through the enemy line of the demonic, which was powered by the spirit of antichrist, working through Satanism, witchcraft, and the occult like a huge bull dozer. Because of the praise, the communication of the enemy was confused, and their battle plans were defeated, with many of their plans not even manifested at all, because of the power of prayer, praise, and worship.

The Holy Spirit begin to speak to me that this spiritual military advancement was the great pouring of the Holy Spirit spoken of in (Joel 2:28) and (Acts 2:17). The word that I received from the Holy Spirit was this: "I want to show you great and mighty things you cannot yet comprehend become reality. I want to put within your spirit what to begin to expect to see me do. And it will come about through prayer, praise, and worship. Through this you will see people saved, healed, and blessed. You will see the depressed lifted, and those that are bound by Satan, you will see them loosed and set free. And it will come by prayer, praise, and worship. And when this begins to happen it will not take you by surprise, it will happen because YOU WILL HAVE ALREADY BEEN EXPECTING TO SEE IT HAPPEN. AND IT WILL COME BY PRAYER, PRAISE, AND WORSHIP.I then realized this great outpouring would not happen without a battle.

The Attacks Begin:

Most people do not realize that the great outpouring of the spirit in the last days will be preceded by spiritual warfare. I've done a very lengthy study, and I've found throughout history that whenever there was an increase in the occult, witchcraft, and the Satanic-demonic worship, God would always bring a revival, or an outpouring of His spirit as a counter attack. I made a list of each time it is historically documented of a rise in Satanism, witchcraft, and the occult. Then I made a list of each time it is historically documented that God sent a great time of revival. It was back to back throughout history. Warfare and counter warfare. And the last days that the Bible speaks of in prophesy will certainly be no exception.

In the time we are living, we are seeing that increase now in Satan's work. In 1951 the U.S. legislature made it legal to be a witch. In 1961 Anton Levey founded the church of Satan. Since that time the increase has been rapidly growing. It started in the 1960's television shows with what seemed to be an innocent show like "Bewitched" for example. Now we see a large majority of television shows, movies, and video games are promoting Satanism, witchcraft, and the occult. Some do it in a way to look very alluring to younger viewers. After a while many are hooked because of Harry Potter, Charmed, and other shows that promote witchcraft. I've studied this, and I know many of the dangers. Even many of our school systems are promoting Harry Potter. As Christians we should stand up to the school systems and say, "NO!!! My child will not read this.

In the county in Alabama where I live, I know and have seen many places where satanic worship has taken place.

The Satanic symbols were in these places. I've talked to eye witnesses who have seen it also. I have been face-to-face twice with 2 witches' who tried to intimidate me. A minister friend and I battled a group of Satanists in prayer who were attacking a church in this area. We saw and heard many things in this battle that neither of us will ever forget. We fought in the name of Jesus and did not give up or back down.

As I stated in the previous chapter, idol worship is nothing but Satan and demon worship, and it began before the book of Genesis was written with the story of Nimrod and Babylon. We have the history of how it began to spread throughout many cultures. This has never died and gone away; it has continued throughout history in every civilization around the world. These demonic spirits have had to adapt to changing laws and society, but they are still there. Through the Old Testament, each time the idol worshippers would try to come against God and His prophets, God would always have an Elijah, an Elisha, David, or a Jehu, with the counter attack in the spiritual warfare.

During the time of the early first century church Christianity had grown and spread to Asia Minor, Egypt, Gaul, Ireland, Scotland, Germany and throughout Europe.

It continued until the Medieval Era when witchcraft and Satanism were drastically diminished through a strong rise in the Christian church. The Waldenses' revival in the 1100's saw many converts. There were missionaries preaching in houses, streets and the market places, often seeing great results. After the end of the Medieval Era, people began to grow cold and the revivals diminished. Satan used this opportunity, and witchcraft, the occult, and Satanism began to be revived and grow strong again. In England from the 1200's, up to the 1700's, Satanism, witchcraft, black magic, and occult practices were rampant.

Then the Bohemian revival came along in the 1300's through the 1700's. God used men like John Wickcliff, John Huss, John Calvin, John Knox, Jonathan Edwards and many others to bring great revivals, where many were brought to God.

During this time witchcraft, Satanism, and the occult seemed to go underground for a while, due to these revivals that God brought to Europe and the United States. God used these revivals to bring counter-warfare against Satan and his kingdom. Afterwards, people began to grow cold spiritually, not seeking God and not seeking revival. When this happens, it always leaves the door open for the other side of the spirit kingdom to advance in counter-warfare, and once again there was another rise in witchcraft, Satanism and the occult.

But God wasn't finished. He brought an outpouring of revival that was known as the first great awakening, and it took place in America during the 1730's and the 1740's, with great preachers like George Whitefield and Jonathan Edwards. During this powerful move of God's Holy Spirit, multitudes became believers. Remnants of these revivals lasted for many years, but, again, as people began to grow slack seeking God in the late 1800's and early 1900's, there was another increase in the occult, Satanism, and witchcraft. This was used as an offensive attack by Satan.

In 1830's and 1840's, the growth of spiritualism, using mediums, séances, and many of the counterfeit gifts of the spirit working through the occult, came out more openly on the scene. Most denomination Christian churches did not allow women the opportunity to work or teach in the church. The occult offered women the opportunity to become prominent religious leaders, which was very attractive to them, and lured many women in. Most were used as mediums, false prophets, seers, channels, witches and in many other areas. This created generational curses and spirit ties that are still in force today in many families around the world.

In the 1800's, on up until about 1870, the second great awakening took place with preachers like Charles Finney. Finney was saved in 1821. For 10 years, from 1824 to 1834, Finney led many powerful revivals. These revivals affected New England and the Appalachians, and down into Tennessee. Many of the churches that were started then are still in active service today.

After that, the third great awakening took place in the late 1800's. This was led partly by men of God like Dwight L. Moody. These revivals fought strongly against bondages like alcohol which was rampant at that time and stressed Christ's return.

In the late 1800's and into the 1900's, there was another revival of witchcraft, Satanism, and the occult. Aleister Crowley who lived from 1875 to 1947 was used in part of this satanic revival. He and his followers made a pact with Satan. They were heavily into demonism, sexual perversions, and orgies, mixing wine and blood in a drink as a mockery to the Holy Communion, divination, and drugs. The counterfeit gift was in operation, and many times a sacrifice was made of an animal or an infant. All this activity is also demonic idol worship. During this time men like Dwight L. Moody were used by God to bring more revival to the United States and to Europe.

About that time in 1906 the Azusa Street revival led by William J. Seymour broke out as a defensive attack to this rise in the occult. This revival lasted until around 1915. Many other great men and women of God came on the scene, many of them from the Azusa Street revival itself, turning many people to God, spiritually opening people's eyes and working many miracles.

The 9 gifts of the spirit were in strong operation in these revivals; this had to be due to the counterfeit gifts operating through the occult, used to deceive many people. This revival was a defensive attack that was launched to counter Satan's attack. In 1904 and 1905, a great revival broke out in Wales with a minister named Evan Roberts. Roberts saw more than 100,000 converts during these two years.

In the 1920's and 30's there was another increase in the occult as another Satan-demonic offensive attack. Then Smith Wigglesworth and other men and women of God who God used to counter this attack through many more great revivals. Many people turned to God during this time of another defensive combat. Then in the 1960's and 70's, there was another offensive counter attack by Satan and his demonic forces in the occult, witchcraft and Satanism, and the hippie movement where many new false religions, drugs and cults were formed.

As Paul said in (2 Corinthians 4:4), Satan, the god of this world, has blinded people's eyes from the truth but their eyes were opened to

Satan's plans through this movement. Those who remained blinded to Satan's plans became desensitized to immorality and perversion. And this created more turbulence in the spirit realm. Remember the word "storm" means a strong turbulence, a sudden and strong attack; to rage, and to rush violently. The word "turbulence" means wild and disorderly, full of violent commotion. The word "disturbance" means to break up, to disorder, to make uneasy, to interrupt, and commotion.

But, again, God brought great revivals to counter this warfare which began again in the 1950's and 60's. But this time I was there, I experienced it. I remember as a youth, growing up in Alabama in the late 1960's, 70's and 80's, and experiencing these revivals well. I saw with my own eyes the mighty moving of the Holy Spirit. I saw the miracles of healing take place. I saw people get up out of wheelchairs and walk. I saw broken bones healed right in front of me as crutches were thrown down, and the people began to run. I saw the strong conviction that would move over people in these revivals as they would run to the altar. I've seen people being "slain in the spirit" as they were no longer able to stand because of the powerful anointing of God's power that was present. I heard the messages in tongues, and the interpretation being given, remembering the holy reverence that seemed to engulf the congregation at that time total silence. I've been there as a prayer meeting would go until 2 and 3 am and be so drunk in the spirit as in (Acts 2) that we were unable to stand, and some would have to be carried home because they were unable to drive. I've been there, and I'm hungry to see it all happen again.

In the time when God was giving me this series of dreams, I had one dream that was like the previous one. I could see a spiritual storm was coming. I was in a large church building, and I know the actual church where I was. As I looked at the back wall of the building, I could see through it as if it were not there. I could see very dark, ominous skies; I could see 3 or 4 huge tornados that were headed straight toward the church. I was running from person to person, grabbing them, shaking them, and pointing at the tornados and yelling, "Look, there is a storm coming, get ready and take cover." Not one person would listen to me and heed the warning; they continued talking, laughing, and paying no attention to what I was saying. I know that it was a warning of a spiritual storm and people did not care. I realized later just how unconcerned people really are.

After this, God gave me two more dreams that were basically the same dream two times. I saw people, many of them who had been unconcerned, running in a large store like a Wal-Mart. In a total panic, they tried to find survival provisions like food and water, but without any hope at all, as the shelves were empty; there was nothing there. God's people, who were in covenant with Him and that trusted Him, calmly walked around the store in total peace, with full buggy loads of the provisions they needed. Two trains of thought began to fill my mind. First, God is going to totally take care of His people. I had the feeling things in the spirit realm are in so much turmoil and distress that it is affecting the physical world's economic problems as well as reflecting the physical world's spiritual status. I felt this was not going to get any better, and would continue to worsen, perhaps to the point as revealed in Revelation where a loaf of bread costs a day's wages. This would open the door for the antichrist to come as the counterfeit savior of the world, where by him many would be deceived.

Second, I thought of the spiritual battles people were going through in their lives, automatically accepting defeat as the first reaction, instead of automatically having confidence in God to handle the problem and supply their needs.

The next dream during this time involved our spiritual armor from (Ephesians 6:10-18). First, I saw people who were walking around, going about their lives; they did not have God in their lives. They had no armor at all. They looked like their bodies were all swiveled up and drained of all substance and life, like a dried-up orange. I remembered they were swiveled up so much their hair was too big for their heads. They were so weak and puny. They were totally being attacked by demonic spirits, at the will of the spirits who were attacking. They were all over these people, like wild animals on their prey and they had no recognition of it.

There was another group of people, some were in church; some were not. They had on various stages of armor. Some were ragged, tattered, and rusty, with pieces hanging loose, about to fall off. These people knew of God, but only from a distance. They had a weak and elementary knowledge of God and the Word because they had not been taught. Because of this, they had very little or no knowledge of how to use His word in battle. The condition of the armor that they did have was the result of the little they had heard. They did not have a life of fasting or prayer. They did not have enough spiritual knowledge to even realize spiritual warfare when they were being attacked. They thought it was "just life."

I could see cracks in their armor. The cracks were results of disobeying God's word, disobeying His commands, and, basically, because of their sins. I saw demonic spirits jumping on them at the cracks; working to make the cracks larger. As the crack would become larger, another spirit would jump on and begin crawling frantically also; then another, and another. Each brings its own different attack. As I watched, I realized this was creating sin bondages in their lives. The spirits speaking to them were putting their evil desires in them. And as it did, the person would obey, and they would lose more and more pieces of armor. They were totally unprotected from the attack that they did not even realize was happening.

But then I saw a group of people who were built like a cartoon super hero with huge muscles, massive shoulders, chest and arms. They had a full suit of armor, extremely bright and shiny and illuminating. I then remembered Paul in (Romans 8:12) talking about putting on the "armor of light." These were the Christians who knew God personally. They knew His word and knew how to use it in spiritual combat. The demonic spirits would try to attack, but the armored ones would defeat them by using the Word in prayer, praise, and worship.

Then on Friday night, August 19, while I was praying, God reminded me of (Joel 2:28-29), the outpouring of the spirit in the last days and these series of dreams I had. I believe God began to speak to me about the dream of the storm.

In the physical realm, we see a reflection of what is going on in the spirit realm. The spiritual affects the physical. Even in the spiritual realm, there is a counter-balance or counter-attack from one side to the other. In the dream of the storm, God was showing me the great outpouring of the demonic spirit which is already in effect and increasing now!! And I use that word "great" as the dictionary defines as "intense," "larger than ordinary," "something done or planned skillfully," even referring to generations of families linked together. In other words, "generational curses" and "spirit ties."

God began to say the great outpouring of His spirit was to counter-attack the great outpouring of the demonic spirit which is increasing and becoming "intense" on the earth, partly as an increase of the occult, which is Satan's counterfeit to the gifts of the spirit. We who are battle ready (ready to fight skillfully), breaking free from the "generational links," are not just little privates in rank, but are the officers who are responsible for leading the attacks and educating the rest of God's army, who are not yet ready under the leading of the Holy Spirit. At the time of the dream, God was speaking to me about something he called "accelerated multiplication in prayer and knowledge." I said, "God, I don't really understand what you're saying so you will have to explain this to me." There is "zero" information on the internet about it; it does not exist there. So, I knew the knowledge would have to come from God.

He began to remind me of the parable of the laborers. Some agreed to work all day for a certain amount of pay. Others came in at the

91

last hour, and they also agreed to work for the same amount of pay. God began to say that accelerated multiplication in prayer and knowledge is compared to the laborers; some have been in this for years and are ready for battle; others have been lazy for years, but understand what is going on, and there will be those who become believers in the last hour of the day and heed God's call. He said if they will jump in and began to fast, pray and study the Word, then God will begin to multiply them at an accelerated rate in their anointing and knowledge, up to where it would have been if they had been working at it for years, making up for the time lost, so they will be battle ready and equipped to fight. Their spiritual eyes will be opened so they can see in the spirit what is going on, and have understanding well beyond their years in order that they can teach others how to fight as well.

Chapter 7

Different Phases of Spiritual Warfare

Satan, and the demonic, can gain control by spiritual warfare through many different areas. They use the occult through New Age, transcendentalism, mystical religions, spiritual healings through channeling, shamanism, black magic, divinization, mediation, yoga, fortune telling, psychic powers, astral projection, hypnotists, parapsychology, black mass, astrology, and clairvoyance. Many of these, as already stated, are used by the false prophets to counterfeit gifts to start these new religions. This method of warfare also uses horoscopes, charms, amulets, chance, luck, and superstition to replace faith in God. And many Christians, unaware of the dangers, are guilty of using these. Satan and his kingdom are fighting strong in these areas. All these have their origins with Nimrod and Semerimais.

Another phase of spiritual warfare is between the biblical and church denominations. Where the churches are segregated because one does not believe in the filling of the Holy Spirit and tongues, and another church does believe. Both are allowing their beliefs to separate the army that is supposed to be fighting Satan, instead it is causing them to fight each other.

One church may believe in the gifts of the Spirit and the other one doesn't. Using people to challenge the inspiration and accuracy of God's word and its authors, saying it is not relevant today, that God no longer heals, that miracles no longer exist, and God no longer speaks to us. Often using criticism like evolution and atheism to turn people's beliefs against God. This also creates the warfare against Godly morals.

One battle that Satan has devised is the Christian's prejudice against the Christian Jews. As Christians, as God's children, we are all on the same team, in the same army, battling the same enemy; we shouldn't be fighting each other. All this is a great deception that Satan and the demonic have devised to divert our focus off them and to weaken our abilities in battle.

There is a "Physiological" phase of spiritual warfare also, where false religions like Modernism, Post Modernism, Secular Humanism and Christian Science use scientific research, facts and figures and mind over matter, that keeps them from going to God for answers. They rely on man's wisdom, mind control, altered states of consciousness, and the use of spirit guides, or demons, for their answers.

Also, I believe this covers the mental battles that we fight. Often, they are from the hurts and pains we have encountered from a lifetime of verbal and mental abuse from parents, siblings, and others who have attacked us with degrading words that cause low self-esteem and defeated attitudes, all of which can rule and dominate a life. This could be where we think that everyone hates us, or that they could not possibly like us; that we're stupid, ugly, and just complete losers. This will destroy your faith level and cause you to believe that God does not love you or that He will not do anything for you. And by accomplishing this, Satan and the demonic can easily get you into different kinds of bondages and addictions. This destroys any chance of you ever finding God's purpose for your life.

There is also a phase of spiritual warfare on the "social level" to destroy what God has created in the family and in marriage. Broken families, adultery, single parent homes, same sex marriages, homosexuality and lesbianism, feminism, pornography, drug and alcohol addictions have become normal. Satanists and witches can curse the marriages of Christians to try to cause a divorce. If these people are not under God's covering, if they do not know his Word, and if they do not know that they are in a battle, they will be destroyed. And it's really very sad because God loves these people so much. These are the ones that Jesus gave His life to set free.

Territorial spirits, being over different geographical areas, can use "political" warfare to bend society in the direction they want it to go by influencing politicians in government to pass laws to overthrow God's plans. With Satan blinding the minds of people, it becomes possible for individuals like Madelyn Murray O'Hare to remove prayer from schools. These spirits work to sabotage our educational and moral values in society. By this they can grow an entire generation of unbelievers who are against Godly values. They cause riots, walk-outs, stand-offs, and overall strife and confusion. Therefore, we can see that morals have gone down over the past several years, to the point where the shock factor is now gone. All this is why we have so many horrible school shootings. This attack is also the reason Jesus said in (Matthew 24) that the last days would be as the days of Noah, where (Genesis 6) says the thoughts of men were constantly on evil.

But another phase of this political warfare is "domination" in the setup of the man, the antichrist. The purpose is world domination under Satan's control. Satan has tried this tactic from the beginning of time. Throughout history, men like Napoleon, Nero, Julius Caesar, Adolph Hitler, Mussolini, Joseph Stalin, and many others have brought about spiritual warfare disguised as "military warfare." Satan used all these men to bring oppression, aggression, and death. All these men strived to be worshipped as a god. Also, the Jezebel spirit is seen to be in domination of many churches and pastors, designed to destroy the churches, and ministers, from the inside out.

Another phase of spiritual warfare is "economic." Many marriages, families, businesses, and churches have been torn apart because of finances. Debt is one of the largest bondages in the world today. The average credit card debt is about $40,000. People are building houses and churches they can't afford, driving automobiles they can't afford, all just to keep up with the people down the street.

This spiritual warfare in designed to steal the money so people cannot give tithes and offerings. In (Malachi 3:8), God said that you have robbed him in tithes and offerings and because of that you are cursed with a curse. Once Satan gets you under this curse, you are destroying your blessing, and you are in bondage and are being controlled.

Offensive and Defensive Warfare:

When Rome was at the peak of its power conquering the surrounding kingdoms, they had to set up military strongholds or fortresses to maintain their position of power. It took a well-trained army to accomplish this. In the same way, we, as God's army, with His authority can advance in an offensive attack against Satan's kingdom, claiming territory that he controls, taking away his domain. At that time, we must maintain that control and use fasting, prayer, and God's Word as our fortresses and strongholds. At this point, too, God's angels can take control and work more powerfully for God's army.

The earthly militaries have both basic and advanced training in the science of planning and directing the battle, which is the strategy and tactics of warfare. The soldiers must learn not only their weapons, maneuvers, tactics, hand to hand combat, and their own strategies, but also their enemy's, so they can fight an effective war. They must learn their enemy's strengths and weaknesses, where they are, where they attack, how they attack, and what brings on the attack. This is to make each attack count when they are mobilized for the invasion. Without all this an army is useless.

Basic training is useless without training on how to use the weapons. Without this spiritual foundation we can never be successful. When a new Roman soldier joined the Roman army, he had to go through a very rigorous training that lasted for six months, day and night. It is the same with a Christian; we must be willing and patient, to take time, learning scripture, praying, and learning to listen to the Holy Spirit.

The Roman army, like our own military, had soldiers specialized in different areas of warfare, using different kinds of weapons, hand to hand combat, vehicles, and armor. It is the same way in God's army. Paul said in (Ephesians 4:11-12): "And he gave some, apostles, and some prophets, and some evangelists, and some pastors, and some teachers. For the perfecting of the saints, for the work of the ministry, for the edifying of the body of Christ." Some that he didn't list are the many people with the servant's heart, like missionaries who risk their lives in the jungles to carry the gospel to an unreached group of people; the ones who make the Sunday service possible, the people who minister at the grocery store to someone in need, or a co-worker on the job. There is much ministry that takes place outside of the four walls of the church building that the pastor by himself could never accomplish. All this is defensive and sometimes offensive spiritual warfare on the enemy's territory.

Jesus said in (Luke 14:31): "What king, going out to engage in conflict with another king, will not first sit down and consider and take counsel whether he is able with ten thousand men to meet him who comes against him with twenty thousand men?" This is where our training pays off in the spiritual war that we are fighting. The information in this book, along with the wisdom that we gain from God with each experience in the spiritual battles that we face, is a growing, step-by-step process. No one, regardless of what kind of spiritual strength they may have in God today, started out that way.

Many of you may be wondering: "What is going on? How do I fight this? Why am I going through this? Why did God allow this? I'll never make it through this. What else is going to happen?"

Satan has declared an offensive war on you. Offensive spiritual warfare means going onto the enemy's territory. So, you declare a defensive war back on him, going onto his territory. Often this spiritual attack is originated by the territorial spirits. These attack plans are made by Satan and the demonic and are given to the demonic spirits of mid-and lower ranks, to be carried out against you and others. Sometimes it is personal; this is the "Ground Level" warfare. The attacks of fear, depression, discouragement, hopelessness, despair, rejection, word curses over your life, attacks of failure, and sickness.

Sometimes "occult level" warfare comes through Satanism and witchcraft. This can create an attack on our children, through such things as the Harry Potter books that teach witchcraft ever so alluring and innocently. This level can very easily lead to demonic possession.

Sometimes this is on a governmental level to create spiritual oppression and bondage. One example, as already stated before, happened in 1951 when it became legal to be a witch. I believe that in the not so far future we will see one of these territorial attacks against the church.

But if Satan and the demonic can declare a strategic level war on us then we can declare a strategic level offensive war on him through God, His authority, His Word, prayer and fasting. In (John 15:18-21) Jesus tells us that one phase of warfare that we are going to fight are the battles in our everyday social lives, at work, at church, our finances, and in our own families. In the 20th verse, Jesus said that we would be "persecuted." In the Greek this means to pursue with malignant intent, meaning having an evil influence, to wish evil, to be very harmful, to cause death, and it also means cancerous. Cancerous in the sense that this spiritual oppression and bondage can grow at an alarming rate if it is not dealt with spiritually.

In (Galatians 5:16-26), Paul tells us that one phase of our warfare is between our own selves, or the desires of our flesh, and the desires of the Holy Spirit for us. Another phase of our warfare that Paul describes in (Ephesians 6:10-18) is one-on-one combat with the demonic. Each one of these phases is where training in the tactical maneuvers of warfare is applied. In an earthly military the soldiers learn how to apply the training they have been taught in actual combat training situations. The only way that we will really learn is fighting through battles.

In training an army in tactical maneuvers, soldiers learn how to apply their training to real combat situations, so they will know what to expect in battle. My oldest son told me when he was in infantry training in the U.S. Army they learned to use real ammunition, tanks, trucks, 50 caliber machine guns, and grenades. He was injured in training while in the Army. Sometimes we may be spiritually injured in a battle, but we learn from that. Just like he would have never known what real battle conditions would have been like without it. He may have frozen in the real fight, not being able to save himself and others, without the training. As we learn, we will have fewer losses and more victories.

(Hosea 4:6) tells us that God's people are destroyed (meaning demolished, torn down and destroyed) due to a lack of knowledge. Paul told us in (2 Corinthians 2:11) not to be ignorant of Satan's devices, meaning his schemes, tricks, and tactics of deceit, because if we are ignorant (meaning that we are unaware and lack knowledge and experience) then we will fail. Satan will have an advantage over us. By learning his devices, we can detect when demonic spirits are at work, and which ones we are dealing with, even if it is a case of possession. We can recognize Satan's strategies that he uses against us. We can learn what counter warfare strategies and weapons to use against him in defensive warfare. Jesus said in (Luke 11:23) that if we are not with Him then we are against Him. Why? Because if we do not stand in agreement with Him and His word then we agree with Satan, the demonic, and their word.

You cannot understand spiritual warfare by using only your natural mind. You must seek knowledge with prayer, asking God to open your spiritual eyes and understanding as in (Luke 24:45). In

(Ephesians 1:17) Paul prayed that God would give the Ephesians the spirit of wisdom and revelation in God's knowledge. We must use this knowledge and spiritual discernment to understand the spirit realm, therefore learning how to fight.

(1 Corinthians 2:14) says, "But the natural man receiveth not the things of the spirit of God: for they are foolishness to him; neither can he know them, because they are spiritually discerned."

In (2 Kings, the 6th chapter), the town where Elisha and his servant Gehazi were located was surrounded by the Syrian army. Gehazi was afraid and doubted they had the ability to win. Elisha asked God to open Gehazi's spiritual eyes. When he did, Gehazi could then see God's angelic host who were surrounding them with protection. If we would pray and ask God for a revelation into the situation we're facing then we, too, could literally see in the spirit God's victory surrounding us. Will God allow us to see this today? The answer is YES, He will.

Chapter 8

David and Goliath

In (1 Samuel 17), we see that the story of David and Goliath is not just a child's story for children's church. It was a real event that happened, but it is also a representation of the spiritual warfare between Jesus and Satan, and between Satan, the demonic and us. David's battle with Goliath was the victory of God, (remembering that Jesus is the King of Kings and the Lord of Lords) over the enemies of a people that would otherwise be helpless without God's help.

One of the meanings of the name Goliath means "exile" which means to be banished, a forced prolonged removal of living in your own home country. Jewish traditions say Goliath is a representation of paganism, evil, and a representation of every demonic spirit.

Goliath had harassed Israel to the point they had lost their will to fight. He had them looking at the size of the situation they were facing instead of God. He was constantly reminding them of their defeat to him. He had them believing he would totally devour them in battle. He had verbally torn them down, where they were spiritually powerless by their own defeat, losing their faith, because they were listening to and allowing what Goliath said to enter their spirits. By this, they were coming into agreement and covenant with the demonic, and Goliath was not letting up with this attack. This is a great representation of how the demonic works in people's lives. They were being beat up mentally, emotionally, and spiritually, and were getting ready to be beat up physically. And they were just sitting there waiting to be destroyed. They were not even trying to fight back. Why? Because they were already defeated mentally and emotionally. Does this sound familiar? This is his strategy to kill, to steal, and to destroy us.

But we don't have to fight a 13-foot tall giant named Goliath on a battle field today. But what we do have is a battle with Satan and the demonic trying to steal our health and healing through sickness and disease; he is trying to steal our peace of mind, our emotional and mental health through depression, anxiety, fear and stress, and confusion. Trying to steal and destroy our marriages and families, to make it a little more personal our husbands, our wives, and our children that God has given to us. Through unfaithfulness, pornography, and strife he tries to destroy us. He wants to steal your ministry, your business, your job and your finances. Jesus said we would be persecuted because He was.

You are doing everything you know to do, living a Christian life, working in ministry and being faithful, and you wonder why coworkers, people you thought were friends, and even family, come against you to cause problems, to try to get you fired, say false accusations, try to split up your marriage and family. You think these people would never do something like this to you and it hurts you deeply when they do. This is spiritual warfare. You have to realize these people are influenced demonically, not necessarily demon possessed. But it's not really them. They are acting upon what is being spoken into their spirit, their coming into agreement with the demonic spirit by yielding to it.

What is sad is many Christians yield and become slaves to this and never realize it. What Satan is trying to achieve here is to cause you to have hatred, resentment, grudges, confusion, strife, slander, gossip, and broken relationships or just overall chaos. Because this opens the door for so many different spirits; for example, the spirits of jealousy, lying, heaviness, bondage, fear, error, infirmity, and the spirit of Jezebel. We will study them in more depth in the chapter "Functions of Demonic Spirits." Their involvement can lead to physical, mental, and emotional sickness, demonic bondage, because of spirit ties, word curses from word judgments that you have made, and generational curses that are passed on to your children.

You may have a serious situation and decision to make. Satan will try to cause all the confusion he can to steal your peace, joy, happiness, and the ability to make a good sound decision. He wants you to make the wrong decisions, so you can be in bondage financially.

With one wrong decision he can steal your money for several years, so you can't afford your tithes and offerings to God. This can lead to the curse mentioned in (Malachi 3:10-11).

With just one wrong decision he can have your life messed up with the wrong spouse, causing misery, instead of joy, allowing the right spouse to be lost.

This can create problems in churches, causing church splits, destroyed ministries, backsliding, where someone never comes back to God, and more hurt feelings.

I have heard Christians, when facing these kinds of battles say, "Oh, that's just life, its spiritual warfare." I've even had people tell me to stop blaming Satan for all these problems because it's not his fault. If you say that then Satan has you deceived. NO IT IS NOT JUST LIFE; IT IS SPIRTUAL WARFARE COMING TO YOU STRAIGHT FROM SATAN AND THE DEMONIC, CUSTOM DESIGNED ESPECIALLY FOR YOU TO KILL, STEAL, AND TO DESTROY YOUR VERY EXISTANCE AND SEPERATE YOU FROM GOD. Just read the (1st chapter of the book of Job) to get an in-depth description of what I'm talking about.

For someone to make a statement about marriage problems, drug addictions and sickness like "Oh it's just life" or "Well, everybody is going through it, so I guess I will too," is to openly accept every attack Satan and the demonic have planned for you and your family. You will not have the spiritual maturity and discernment in the Word and the Holy Spirit to recognize the difference. This is exactly why I'm writing this book. I have found so many Christians who have been in churches for decades and who have never heard the term spiritual warfare, and I know many who also do not believe in Satan, or the demonic spirits, or believe that these demons have an actual spiritual kingdom.

This is because they have never been taught what the Word of God says. There are so many ministers, who either do not believe, or just do not want to believe, because they are too afraid they will have to face the demonic, so they will not teach it. I don't claim to be any smarter than anyone else, I don't know everything there is to know; I don't claim to be any kind of a leading authority, but I do claim to have "THE" authority that Jesus gave me in (Luke 10:19) And authority does not ask will you please, authority does not beg and plead; AUTHORITY COMMANDS. And when you have the authority, you are obeyed.

(SAMUEL 17:1) NOW THE PHILISTINES GATHERED THEIR ARMIES FOR BATTLE AND WERE ASSEMBLED AT SOCOH, WHICH BELONGS TO JUDAH, AND ENCAMPED BETWEEN SOCOH AND AZEKAH IN EPHES-DAMMIM.

The word "encamp" means to "set up." Have you felt like you've been set up by the devil? You get blindsided, you didn't see it coming, and you thought you had everything under control and, wham; it comes out of seemly nowhere. The unexpected financial blows, the unexpected sickness, yielding to the temptation, before you even realize it can knock you off your spiritual feet if you're not ready for it. Well, guess what? It was a setup, and it's called spiritual warfare. And you are the target.

This verse says the Philistine, who represents our demonic enemy, has gathered the army for battle. You are going to be attacked whether you're a Christian or not. Because (John 10:10) says Satan wants to steal, to kill, and to destroy you, your family, your finances, your faith, your health, and your total existence. And it is all because

God loves you.

Verse 2: SAUL AND THE MEN OF ISRAEL WERE ENCAMPED IN THE VALLEY OF ELAH AND DREW UP IN A BATTLE ARRAY AGAINST THE PHILISTINES.

The word "array" means getting the troops together in order and ready to fight. Part of this order is having and knowing how to use the intel that you know of the enemy. If people have never heard the term "spiritual warfare" then how can they get ready to fight? They won't, and they will be defeated and not even know it.

Verse 3: AND THE PHILISTINES STOOD ON A MOUNTAIN ON ONE SIDE AND ISRAEL STOOD ON A MOUNTAIN ON THE OTHER SIDE, WITH A VALLEY BETWEEN THEM.

Sometimes when you're IN a spiritual battle, everything is coming at you from every angle, and you can find yourself IN the valley with the enemy perched high above you like vultures, where he can see your every move. In the valley of depression, panic attacks, feelings of dread, you may just give up. You are defeated IF you stay there in the valley. This is a spiritual attack against you. Not only will this enslave you, but also your children, too.

Verse 4: AND A CHAMPION WENT OUT OF THE CAMP OF THE PHILISTINES NAMED GOLIATH OF GATH.

It is estimated that he was between 10 and 13 feet tall. He went out to the front lines twice a day for 40 days. That would be annoying, wouldn't it? "Annoying" means to hate and to irritate by repeated action. Constant battle and temptation will soon wear you down spiritually. Another similarity between Jesus and Satan and the story of David and Goliath is that Jesus fasted 40 days and Satan came to Him to tempt Him. The K.J. Bible says that Goliath defied the Israelites, meaning to resist, oppose, to dare and challenge them; so, daring someone can be a form of temptation. When Satan does it to us, it is spiritual warfare.

Verse 8: GOLIATH STOOD AND SHOUTED TO THE RANKS OF ISRAEL, WHY HAVE YOU COME OUT TO DRAW UP FOR BATTLE? AM I NOT A PHILISTINE? AND YOU NOT A SERVANT OF SAUL?

Has Satan ever had people in your life that put you down verbally? You're stupid, you're ugly, and you're worthless and no good. You don't have enough sense to do any better than that? You're as dumb as your father. Have they ever told you, you're a nobody? You're too stupid to ever amount to anything. You will never be able to quit the drugs, the alcohol, there's no use in even trying. You'll never be able to live a Christian life; you don't have what it takes. You'll never be able make it through the divorce, because you don't have what it takes, you're not strong enough. You're not good enough, and you never will be. A lot of us have heard all that before, haven't we? Well, they are lies from Satan. It is word curses that were placed on us by others, and we are sending them on down to our children, co-workers, and even church members. Spirit ties can sometimes be created through this. This kind of verbal word curses can create mental and spiritual strongholds that can control your life in defeat.

During the 40 days of Jesus' fast, Satan kept saying, "If you be the son of God." When you mess up, how many times has Satan said to you, "If you call yourself a Christian how can you do what you just did?" And he will beat you up over it. Confess your sin out loud so he can hear you, and then tell him, "I'm forgiven; now, shut up."

Verses 8 & 9: CHOOSE A MAN FOR YOURSELVES AND LET HIM COME DOWN TO ME. IF HE IS ABLE TO FIGHT WITH ME AND KILL ME, THEN WE WILL BE YOUR SERVANTS; BUT IF I PREVAIL AGAINST HIM AND KILL HIM THEN YOU SHALL BE OUR SERVANTS AND SERVE US.

One of the meanings of the word "servant" is to endure a term of

106

imprisonment. If David had lost the battle, it would have changed the entire course of history, as we know it today. Israel would have become slaves again, except this time to the Philistines. Israel was spiritually affected in Egypt as slaves by their constant exposure to all the demonic gods the Egyptians worshipped. They would have been enslaved spiritually even more by the demonic spirits the Philistines worshipped as idols, furthering them from God. The world as we know it today would have been different from what it is now. It would have tipped the world scale even more in Satan's direction. That is why it so important that our heritage is (and be) power, authority, and victory over Satan, because we will also change the course of history. It is the battles that we fight and win that will keep our descendants and everyone else free from demonic slavery and THIS is our heritage. Notice Goliath said that if you win then we will be your servants and slaves. He lied; Satan and the demonic also lie. All the Philistines fled in fear after Goliath's defeat. I want to refer to the last part of (Isaiah 54:17) that our righteousness is of God, through that righteousness we have authority and that will make Satan flee from us.

Verse 10: AND THE PHILISTINE SAID, I DEFY THE ARMIES OF ISRAEL; GIVE ME A MAN THAT WE MAY FIGHT TOGETHER.

The word "defy' means to resist – "resist" means to withstand, to fend off, to oppose; "oppose" means to contend; "contend" means to fight or to argue with. (Ephesians 6:10-18) tells us to put on the whole armor of God and to withstand to battle. The word "withstand" means to oppose, to resist, and to endure successfully.

Verse 11: WHEN SAUL AND ALL ISRAEL HEARD THOSE WORDS OF THE PHILISTINE THEY WERE DISMAYED AND GREATLY AFRAID.

"Dismayed" means to be startled and discouraged by someone making it difficult to resolve. Satan and the demonic will speak words of discouragement, doubt, fear and just total defeat into your spirit man. When you allow it to control you, then you are coming into agreement with them. The Israelites did not have their faith in God. They did not remember the promises to them in His Word. This is the only way that we can win in spiritual warfare.

Verse 16: AND THE PHILISTINE DREW NEAR MORNING AND EVENING AND PRESENTED HIMSELF 40 DAYS.

Twice a day, for 40 days, Goliath did this. This is just like Satan and the demonic. It's very annoying. Again, the word "annoy" means to hate and to irritate by repeated action. This constant, ongoing confirmation from the demonic can cause spiritual exhaustion.

Verse 21: FOR ISRAEL AND THE PHILISTINES HAD PUT THE BATTLE IN ARRAY ARMY AGAINST ARMY.

The battle we are in right now; God and us against Satan and the demonic.

Verse 23: BEHOLD THERE CAME UP THE CHAMPION, THE PHILISTINE OF GATH, GOLIATH BY NAME, OUT OF THE ARMIES OF THE PHILISTINES, AND SPAKE ACCORDING TO THE SAME WORDS, AND DAVID HEARD THEM.

Now before when Goliath spoke to the Israelites, they were afraid. David had no fear because he trusted God. In verses 33-36, God had already allowed him to experience fighting the lion and the bear; I believe to allow him to know that God could win the battle for him. I believe this is a word from God right now for you reading this book: God is saying, I have killed the lion for you, I have killed the bear for you, and because you have seen me do that, you can watch me destroy your other enemies.

Many of the battles that we fight, if we will allow, God and his angels will fight the battle, so we can see His victory and be ready next time to expect victory again and again. In a dream that God gave me a few years ago, while in battle, I saw a demonic spirit walking up to me. It was extremely angry, hate in its eyes, growling and snarling at me. In this dream I felt no fear; I also felt no great outpouring of a blessing and no outward filling of the anointing. Spiritually, I felt about as dry as a bowl full of dust. But that did not matter because I know the Word and my authority. I looked at it and said, "In the name of Jesus," and before I got the words out, "I rebuke you," it fell on its belly with a tremendous look of fear on its face. It began to back away and would not turn its back to me, as it disappeared into the darkness. God used this to teach me his authority at a time of a very long drawn out attack that I was experiencing almost every night for several months. This dream was instrumental in bringing me from fear to victory. Had I not learned, I might have been destroyed.

But these verses also show David's faithfulness to where and to what God had called him. And in verse 37 David told Goliath, "THE LORD THAT DELIVERED ME OUT OF THE PAW OF THE LION AND THE BEAR, HE WILL DELIVER ME OUT OF THE HAND OF THIS PHILISTINE.

Verse 40: AND HE TOOK HIS STAFF IN HIS HAND.

God gave me the Dream of the Staff (in a previous chapter), showing the staff as being a representation of his anointing on our lives.

Verse 43: AND THE PHILISTINE SAID UNTO DAVID, AM I A DOG THAT THOU COMEST TO ME WITH STAVES? AND THE PHILISTINE CURSED DAVID BY HIS GODS.

Demons want to enslave you by agreement with them, causing you to accept their bondage. Instead, Christians should proclaim: "Do you not know who I am, my strength, and who you are dealing with? You're a dirty, rotten lying thief, and all you ever want to do is give us grief. You may try to come in like a flood, but you can't conqueror us, Satan, because we're covered by Jesus' blood."

Goliath cursed David by his gods. These were demonic spirits that the Philistines worshipped as idols. And it also shows that Satan, and the ruling principalities under him, will send every demonic spirit to attack you. If someone accepts these curses by agreement it can open the door to their attack.

Verse 46a: THEN DAVID SAID TO THE PHILISTINE, THOU COMEST TO ME WITH A SWORD, AND WITH A SPEAR, AND WITH A SHIELD: BUT I COME TO YOU IN THE NAME OF THE LORD OF HOST, THE GOD OF THE ARMIES OF ISRAEL WHOM THOU HAST DEFIED. THIS DAY THE LORD DELIVER THEE INTO MINE HAND; AND I WILL SMITE THEE.

David said deliver, not delivered, meaning present tense, right now, not later, not someday, not maybe, not hopefully, but right now in the present, at this very moment. David said God has given me authority and victory over you and you are defeated.

Verse 46b: AND I WILL GIVE THE CARCASS OF THE HOST OF THE PHILISTINES, THIS DAY UNTO THE FOWLS OF THE AIR, AND TO THE WILD BEASTS OF THE EARTH; THAT ALL THE EARTH; MAY KNOW THAT THERE IS A GOD IN ISRAEL.

Sounds like David may have gotten a little angry with Goliath. When you get angry with Satan and the demonic then you can achieve results. "How dare you come against me and my family, in the name and authority of Jesus Christ get out!"

Verse 47: David said, "THE BATTLE IS THE LORDS AND HE WILL GIVE YOU INTO OUR HANDS."

We can give the addictions, the problems, the hurts, and the whatever to God to fight it for us. God has given us promises that he will deliver us, but first we must stop denying the problem exists. Then we must admit and confess to him what we've done. Very strong spiritual warfare exists in this area because, Satan does not want the bondage broken, and it can never be broken until we do this. The spirit of bondage is often working in this area.

Verse 49: AND DAVID PUT HIS HAND IN HIS BAG, AND TOOK THENCE A STONE, AND SLANG IT, (showing David took an action of faith) AND SMOTE THE PHILISTINE IN HIS FOREHEAD; THAT THE STONE SUNK INTO HIS FORHEAD; AND FELL UPON HIS FACE TO THE EARTH.

David took what he had, even though it seemed too small to do the job, he used his faith, and God took over from there, getting behind the stone, empowering it to do what normally would have been impossible, hitting one tiny vulnerable spot. Sometimes, we have to do that also. As a musician of many years in praise and worship, there has been many times that I would feel the anointing settle over me, and at those times I could play in ways that were so far above my normal ability. If I ever gave myself the credit for it, it would immediately leave, but so, long as I gave God the praise for it, and worshipped with it, it would continue throughout that service. Later, after the anointing was over, I would try to play the same thing again, only to realize that I couldn't.

We may not even realize the moment that we're stepping out on faith, but we are.

Several years ago, I was homeless for a period of time. One day I decided I was tired of living in the back of a van, and I was going to do something about it. I had a piece of land, so I put a tent on it and began living there. A storm came and destroyed my tent. I decided that I would not give up. I would buy whatever I could in lumber, even if it was only one board at a time. People, some I did not even know, began giving me bricks, concrete blocks, lumber, an AC unit,

111

plumbing, lighting, and many other things. I know it was all from God's blessings. One day I had an entire house built, debt free. But what I did not realize then, I stepped out in faith with a mission in mind, not accepting defeat as an option. And since that was faith God rewarded it.

Verse 50: SO, DAVID PREVAILED OVER THE PHILISTINE WITH A SLING AND WITH A STONE, AND SMOTE THE PHILISTINE, AND SLEW HIM; BUT THERE WAS NO SWORD IN DAVID'S HAND.

Do not look at yourself and think there is no way that you can stand up to this battle, or that you do not have the ability to do a certain thing. (Philippians 4:13) says that I (you) can do all things through God, Who gives you the strength. (Romans 8:37) says that you and I are more than conquerors. A conqueror has already overpowered and won, and yet we are to be MORE than a conqueror. It is not the size of your weapons; it's the size of your God and Father behind you, He has your back.

An example of this: As I said, I had always been a musician, something I could do almost asleep. When God called me into ministry, outside of music, it was to teach and preach the Word, and co-pastor a recovery ministry. I had never spoken in front of people before and really didn't want to do this, but the pastor of the ministry didn't give me a choice. I feared it because I listened to the enemy, telling me that I couldn't do it. In my childhood I had a speech handicap that the doctors could not cure. They said there was very little hope for me to ever speak normally to where I could be understood. Years later after God had healed me and being from Alabama I developed a southern accent, something that I always disliked about myself. Satan had tried to defeat me with this from my childhood. He had people placed throughout my life to make sure I was defeated by this. I wondered why God gave me this accent many times, but when I begin to work in this area of ministry, I realized the people I was working with related and bonded to me because of my accent. It made them feel like I was one of them. God knew what I needed to be equipped with, even though I thought it was a negative in my life, and by that He gave me the means to accomplish it. Today I teach and preach anywhere I get a chance to, just ask me.

In the beginning I would have to have everything I planned to say written down on a piece of paper. But over time, it began to get a little easier, to the point where it no longer frightens me, even if I need to teach at the last minute, with no time to prepare. God gives me the words at the exact moment. Many times, I would start a sentence with a word with no clue what the rest of the sentence would be, but God gave it to me word by word. People began to tell me how much they received from it, and how much they enjoyed listening to me. It was not me, not by my ability, because I do not have the ability, it is only through God. Many times, I have said, "God if you don't, I can't."

It was stepping out in faith, David trusting God, one step at a time, giving him what seemed so small and impossible on his part, but he took it and multiplied it, and used it. Even though what you do may seem very small, it is all these parts fitting together that makes up the entire work of God's plan. And it may be your work that brings down the giant.

Verse 51a: THEREFORE, DAVID RAN AND STOOD UPON THE PHILISTINE, AND TOOK HIS SWORD (GOLIATH'S SWORD) AND SLEW HIM AND CUT OFF HIS HEAD.

Psalms says that the enemy's sword intended for us will be turned and enter their own heart. (Isaiah 57:17) says that no weapon formed against us shall prosper against us. And this shall be our heritage. The heritage that we pass down to our children and others; we teach them by our actions and leadership.

PAY CLOSE ATTENTION TO WHAT Verse 51b SAYS: "AND

WHEN THE PHILISTINES SAW THEIR CHAMPION WAS DEAD, THEY FLED.

Verse 52: AND THE MEN OF ISRAEL SHOUTED AND PURSUED THE PHILISTINES.

"Pursue" means to chase, overtake and capture, and to continue to annoy. The table has been turned now, and it is God's people who are overtaking and annoying the demonic. When you allow God to take the battle, the struggle, or to use you, when He does then the victories that He gives you are pursuing the enemy, standing on top of them and destroying them with their own weapons. A soldier's purpose is to kill or to take captive, not to be defeated.

Verse 53: AND THE CHILDERN OF ISRAEL RETURNED FROM CHASING AFTER THE PHILISTINES, AND THEY SPOILED THEIR TENTS.

When we use the authority, Jesus gave us in (Luke 10:19), and we speak to the enemy, they have to obey that authority. The seventy disciples mentioned had this authority in Jesus' name. Today, they would probably be called the laymen in the church; this proves that anyone can have this authority, not just the pastor.

Let's look at this spiritually another way.

Goliath was the reigning champion over the entire Philistine army. We can say that Goliath "represented" the entire Philistine army. Verse 43, Goliath cursed David by "his" gods, the demonic spirits; this shows authority, a covenant, a contract, an agreement that he had with them. All the Philistines worked under the authority of Goliath in covenant and agreement with Goliath. Once Goliath was killed and defeated by David in the name of the Lord, all the Philistines under his authority, in covenant, in contract, in agreement with him, fled. Their champion was gone. David cut off Goliath's head to show the removal of headship from Goliath.

Spiritually, I believe Jewish tradition also says that Goliath represents the demonic strongman, the head principalities over every demonic spirit in (Colossians 1:16, 2:10; Ephesians 1:22, Ephesians 3:10, Ephesians 6:12 and 2 Peter 3:22). (Daniel 10) is a good example of this.

Daniel had prayed for 21 days. The angel appeared to Daniel with a message that God had heard and had sent an answer 21 days ago, but he (the angel) had been in spiritual warfare with the prince of Persia. The prince of Persia not only wanted to steal Daniel's answer, but he wanted to tear Daniel down mentally and get him spiritually exhausted.

After enough of this, you will become physically exhausted, and it will begin to affect your home life, your job, your attitude, and your relationships; leaving a path of destruction in its wake is its plan. This will get your mind on the problem and off God. At this point, a person will become useless to God's kingdom.

Finally, Michael, the archangel, was sent to fight the war. The angel tells Daniel that while Michael was fighting, he remained there with the kings. These were demonic kings. We see from this the demonic are in rank of a military type power and authority as in an earthly kingdom. Jesus said in (Matthew 12:26) that Satan has a kingdom.

Some of these demonic spirits work in collusion together. They are bound together by an agreement, a covenant, a contract, or an agreement to work together. This is what Goliath said in verses 8-9 when he admitted that if you can find a man that can fight against him and win, then me and my entire army will be totally under your power and submission and will be defeated and enslaved together. That is why the Philistines all fled when Goliath was killed. In other words don't waste your time fighting all the little demonic foot soldiers one by one, only to work yourself into spiritual exhaustion, but go to the head principality who is responsible for originating the plans of the attack against you, take that one out, and you will take out all the demons under his authority. They are bound by their own contract together, and they will all be defeated together at one time.

Chapter 9

The Satanic Kingdom

Let's look at how this is set up in the spirit realm. First, let's look at (Ephesians 6:12) where Paul said, "For we wrestle not against flesh and blood, but against principalities, against powers, against the rulers of darkness of this world, against spiritual wickedness in high places."

In (Ephesians 6:12) the Greek word "wrestle" is "pale" and means one on one; (Ephesians 6:17) tells us to take the sword of the spirit which is the word of God.

The word "principality" means a prince or a chief that rules over a territory. The Greek word for principalities is "archas" which refers to the top ranking demonic positions over geographic regions of the earth. (Ephesians 6:12) in the amplified Bible say "despotisms" which are basically the same, but explain it a little deeper. "Despotism" means, a system, or government, with a ruler having absolute authority over; a form of government system ruled by a tyrant, dictator, and a master of slaves.

(Ephesians 1:20-21) says that we are seated with Christ on heavenly places far above all principality and power.

The word "powers" means one with influence over other "nations," a person or thing having influence, force, or authority, legal authority and vigor, force and strength. Here it is referring to demonic spirits who are second in command below the principality. This is the territorial spirits who are over geographic regions of the earth, broken down into smaller areas, with others under their authority who carry out commands and strategies against the saints. The word "powers" in Greek is "exousia" and means delegated authority. The word "delegate" means a person authorized to act under the rule of another's representation, and to entrust power and authority to another of higher authority. They are given orders to be carried out for all kinds of evil.

"The rulers of the darkness of this world": "ruler" meaning one who governs smaller territories. It is taken from the Greek word "kosokrateros" and is made up of two other words: "kosmos" and "kratos." The word "kosmos" means "order" or "arrangement". "Kratos" means "raw power"; this means raw power that has been harnessed to be put into an order. The word was also used by the Greek military to describe certain aspects of the military.

Look at it this way; remember that what we see in the physical realm where we exist reflects what is going on in the spirit realm where the demonic kingdom exists. The Greek army had a lot of young strong soldiers who had a lot of natural fighting ability, strength and energy or raw power. For that raw power to be harnessed and effectively used in battle, it had to be harnessed, trained, and organized by top ranking officers, thus providing a strong military, instead of confusion and weakness.

We are on a battlefield also. The war that we're in does not have cease fires. Even if you're not directly under fire at this moment, you are still a target and are on the battlefield because you are a threat to the enemy. That's why we must stay constantly in prayer and in God's Word, learning how to use it. We are an army, and we need to join and fight as an army, instead of saying, "you're not of my denomination." Oops, I shouldn't have said that. But getting forgiveness is easier than getting permission.

"Spiritual wickedness in high places": The Greek word for wickedness is "ponerias," the meaning of which comes down to fornication and pornography. It also means vicious, impious and "malignant;" that which is evil, malicious, very intense and forceful, having an evil influence over, likely to cause death, cancerous, and having no reverence for God.

"…high places:" The Greek word here is "epouranois" which means heavenlies. Paul said in (Ephesians 2:2) that Satan is the prince and the power of the air. It also refers to references throughout the Old Testament where it repeatedly refers to idol temples being built on high mountains or in high places. Paul is telling us here that we are still fighting the same idolatry as thousands of years ago, proving that it has never died.

You will later see that I refer to Beliel as a strongman, here is why. He's just one of many that are in demonic authority under Satan. Jesus said in (Matthew 12:29) and in (Mark 3:27) that if we want to spoil and plunder the strongman's house we must bind the strongman. Paul said do not be ignorant of Satan's devices. We must know everything there is to know about our enemy, if we expect to win. Where he is, who he is, how he fights, his strengths, his weaknesses, what we do that brings on his attacks, and how "we" fight back. If we don't know these factors it's like sending a spiritual prayer missile off into the darkness, hoping that we hit something. Yes, we can get close; yes, we can hit something with the concussion of our missiles. But it takes a lot more work in prayer this way. If we know all these factors, and exactly who and where the enemy is, then we can send the missiles of our prayers, and of our words, and make a direct hit, taking out and binding the demonic strongman.

Satan our enemy:

Some of this is a review of what we have already covered before but we will also be dealing with the descriptions of Satan here.

The name Satan is mentioned in Scripture 53 times, and referred to over 200 times in other Scripture. The word devil is mentioned 60 times. He was created by God as an archangel, meaning he was a chief angel, very high in angelic rank, probably just below the Trinity, but limited in power. He was created as the original praise and worship leader of heaven, having pipes for music created in him.

119

After his fall from heaven, he masquerades as an angel of light and commands a hierarchy of demons. He thought he could be equal to, or above, God because of the pride of his own beauty (see Ezekiel 28:11-17). He tried to exalt himself above God. In (Isaiah 14:12-14) K.J. it says, "How thou art fallen from heaven, Lucifer, son of the morning! How art thou cut down to the ground, which didst weaken the nations! For thou hast said in thine heart, I will ascend into heaven, I will exalt my throne above the stars of God: I will sit also upon the mount of the congregation, in the sides of the north: I will ascend above the heights of the clouds; I will be like the most High. Yet thou shalt be brought down to hell, to side of the pit."

This was the first of three falls of Satan. During this first fall, the exact number is not known, but one-third of heaven's angels fell with him. The second fall will be in (Revelation 12:9) during the tribulation when he is cast down to hell and bound for 1000 years. The third will be when he is released at the end of the millennial reign of Christ and cast into the lake of fire forever (Revelation 20:10).

But first Lucifer, who is later to become Satan, was created by God, along with the rest of the angelic beings, who have a spirit body, soul, and a free will. (Ezekiel 38) tells us his free will led to his rebellion against God. In (Ezekiel 28:12-19) says that he was the anointed cherub, and that he was created as a beautiful creation. (Ezekiel 28:13) refers to musical instruments being created within him the day he was created, giving him the ability to create music within himself. This is why some people believe he was the first worship leader of the heavenly host before the fall. Even though Satan has fallen, he still holds a rank as a dignitary. In (Jude verse 9), the archangel Michael did not bring railing accusations or judgments against him, but said the Lord rebuke you.

(Genesis 1:10 says: "In the beginning God created the heaven and the earth." (John 1:3) says: "All things were made by him, and without him was not anything made that was made." The amplified

Bible says that "all things were made and came into existence through him, including the angels." (Colossians 1:16) says: "For by him were all things created that are in heaven, and that are in earth whether they be thrones or dominions, or principalities, or powers."

All things were created by him and for him. This means everything in the earthly and in the spiritual realms. Another reference to this is (Job 38:4-7): "Where wast thou when I laid the foundations of the earth? ...who laid the corner stone thereof, when the morning stars sang together, and all the "sons of God" shouted for joy?"

The heavens and its hosts were created first, or they could not have sung together at Earth's creation, and the phrase "sons of God" is mentioned 5 times in the Bible and in all 5 scriptures refers to angels, because human man could not do what is described that the sons of God do in presenting themselves in heaven before God.

(Genesis 1:31) says: "God saw everything that he had made, and behold it was good." So, I said all of that to prove by Scripture that God created Lucifer; and it sounds like (at first) he was still perfect, and the fall had not taken place yet. (Genesis 2:1): "The heavens and the earth were finished, and all the host of them." The Hebrew here is "tsaba" meaning the mass of persons or things, and means everything created was totally finished.

The name "Lucifer" in Hebrew is 'heylel" and means brightness, morning star, and to shine. Remember (Job 38:7) where the morning stars sang together. And it isn't just a coincidence that Paul said in (2 Corinthians 11:14) that Satan can be transformed into an angel of light, with his ministers performing great signs and wonders to deceive the weak-minded people as in (Matthew 24:24) and (2 Thessalonians 2:8-12). He will use this work through the antichrist, exhibiting the counterfeit gifts during the Tribulation to gain power over the masses of people that are left behind.

In (2 Corinthians 11:3) Satan is the deceiver that wants the believer to be blinded to God's Word, the truth, and he uses every possible means to do this such as establishing false religions that deny Jesus is God's son and the only sacrifice for our sin.

Other names given to him are: devil in (Revelation 12:9), Beelzebub in (Matthew 10:25 and 12:24), and adversary in (1 Peter 5:8-9). The word "adversary" means an opponent and foe. The word "opponent" means the one who is opposing or fighting us. The word "foe" means enemy, and the word "enemy" means one who hates and wishes to injure another. In (Revelation 9:11), he is called "abaddon" which is "apollyon" in the Greek, and means "destroyer."

He is also called a serpent in (2 Corinthians11:3) and (Revelation 12:9). We know that a serpent is a snake. One definition of "serpent" is "to creep." "Creep" means to move stealthily, to be ready to attack, to give the feeling of fear and disgust, and to be annoying. The word "annoys" means to hate, and to irritate as by repeated action. Doesn't that sound like the temptation that we encounter? And the word "encounter" means to meet, as in battle.
(2 Corinthians 4:4) refers to him as the god of this world, where he rules by the operation of his demonic hierarchy. (John 12:31) says he is the prince of this world; (Ephesians 2:1-3) says he is the prince of the power of the air.

In (Revelation 12:10), he is the accuser of the brethren both day and night. We also see proof of this in (Job 1:6), where Satan went to God accusing Job. We can say from these two verses that Satan still has access to come before God's throne. He is accusing God's people, which are one of the acts of the sons of Beliel in the Old Testament in (Psalms 37:32). Satan accuses believers before God of their sins which are seen by the demons who report back to Satan, using this as ammunition against you. Satan will always lie to you when it comes to talking to you about God, but he wants to tell the truth when he's accusing you to God. Satan wants to keep you in condemnation over the things that you've done in the past, to make you feel unworthy to come to God and receive His love, mercy and forgiveness. He wants you to feel excessive guilt but not repentance. This excessive guilt and condemnation can lead us to seeing God, not as a loving Father, but as a mean, vindictive God, who is ready to crush us at everything we do wrong. This can cause depression and despair, and will keep us in defeat.

(Matthew 13:39) says he is the tempter and the enemy and the sower of discord. (Matthew 13:19, 38) call him the wicked one. In (2 Corinthians 11:30, he's the deceiver; in (Revelation 12:3), the great red dragon; in (John 8:44), he's the father of lies and murder. In (Ephesians 2:2), he's the spirit that works in the children of disobedience. In (Matthew 12:29), he's the strongman. In (John 10:10), he's the thief. In (James 4:70, he is a coward that will flee from us. Satan does not possess mercy or goodness; he cannot be loving, kind, gentle, pitiful or patient.

Some people don't believe in Satan because they do not believe that we encounter him. "Encounter" means a direct meeting, as in battle, or meeting in conflict with difficulties. With Satan being a spirit being, who directly meets us in conflicts as in a battle, we call it spiritual warfare.

The word "war" means armed conflict, and to contend, to strive in a state of active armed conflict. The word "conflict" means to fight, to war, a sharp disagreement, (which we have because of agreeing with God and not agreeing with Satan). It also means an emotional disturbance, commotion, and disorder. It doesn't matter how you look at this, it describes spiritual warfare which means to steal, kill, and destroy you physically, mentally, emotionally, and spiritually.

Start standing your ground, using your authority in Jesus' name, taking dominion over Satan and the demonic principalities, and you will begin to see and understand the difference between what is spiritual warfare and what is "just life." A lot of Christians wouldn't know spiritual warfare even if it announced itself and set an appointment time when it was going to arrive, or what the attack would consist of.

Eve encountered Satan in (Genesis 3:1-13). Satan first seemed to be her friend, then he lied to her, then he deceived her to commit sin, then he used her to drag someone else into the same sin. King David encountered Satan in (1 Chronicles 21:1). Satan opposed Joshua in (Zechariah 3:12). Jesus encountered Satan, and overcame his temptations in (Matthew 4:1-11). In (Matthew 16:23), Satan desired to sift Peter as wheat. The Israelite woman was bound by Satan with her health problems for 18 years in (Luke 13:16). Judas was controlled by Satan in (John13:27). Paul was harassed by Satan in (2 Corinthians 12:7) when he sent a messenger to buffet him. The word "buffet" means to punch, hit, to thrust about, to give a striking blow. And (1 Thessalonians 2:18) says he was hindered by Satan.

In (1 Timothy 1:19-20), Hymenaeus and Alexander were delivered to Satan because they had shipwrecked their faith. In (Acts 5:3), Ananias and his wife Sapphira were tempted to lie to the Holy Spirit by Satan and it cost them their lives.

In (Luke 13:16) and in (Acts 10:38), we see that he is the cause of sickness and disease. He had the power of death until Jesus defeated him according to (Hebrews 2:14). In (2 Corinthians 11:13), and in (Matthew 24:5), he deceives many with his false prophets. In (James 1:5-9), he causes unstable minds. He and his workers hinder prayers in (Daniel 10). He hinders and perverts the gospel in (Acts 13:10). In (2 Corinthians 4:4), he blinds people from God's truth. In (Luke 22:3) and (John 13:2), we find proof that people can come into union or agreement with Satan. In (2 Corinthians 12:7), he sends his messengers or demonic spirits to fight us. The Greek word for messengers in this verse is "aggelos" and means angel of Satan. In (2 Peter 1:9), he can cause spiritual blindness. In (Ephesians 6:10-18), he causes war on the saints. In (Matthew 13:19) and (Luke 8:12), he steals God's Word after it is sown into hearts. In (1 Timothy 3:7), he sets snares of temptation to trap us. And in (2 Timothy 2:25-26), he tries to keep men in bondage, not wanting them to repent. Are you beginning to understand the character of Satan? And that he is a real enemy?

I said in the above paragraph that Satan is a real spirit being, so let's look for proof of this. The Bible tells us things that he did, as in (Job 1:6) when he goes before God's throne. In (1 Peter 5:8-9), he's a roaring lion. Jesus dealt with him on a personal level in (Matthew 4:1-11). In (Luke 10:18-19), Jesus taught that Satan was a real being and gave us power over him. You can't have power over something that doesn't exist. The apostles fought with him; personal pronouns are used of him (see Ephesians 4:27; Matthew 12: 26). Statements are made to him (see Matthew 4:1-10; Job 2:1-7, 1:6-12; Isaiah 14:12-14). Descriptions are given of him in (Isaiah 14:12-14) and in (Jeremiah 28:11-17).

According to (Job 2:1-3), he goes from place to place, throughout the earth. He has a kingdom divided into a military type authority. (See also: Matthew 12:26; Mark 3:22-26; Ephesians 1:21, 6:12, 3:10; Colossians 3:14). He rules over the demonic spirits in (Matthew 25:41).

Satan and Job:

Some of the works of the devil are sickness, sin, controlling, fear, death, temptation, depression, lust, deception and more. (1 John 3:8) says, "For this purpose the son of God was manifested that he might destroy the works of the devil."

God would never use the devil's works to punish his children. God would not have sent Jesus to destroy Satan and his works, he would not have sent Jesus to give His life to redeem us, if he was going to use those works against us or not give us the power over Satan's works. Many people have unfairly blamed God for Satan's works. If Satan can keep people in this deception, then people who believe it is from God will blame God.

In (Ephesians 4:27), Paul said "neither give place to the devil." I like what the amplified Bible says, "leave no room or foothold for the devil, and give him no opportunity." When we believe the deceptions, we hold a door wide open for Satan to have a free, open door of legal access to attack us physically, mentally, emotionally, and spiritually.

Let's look at the story of Job that is found in the (1ˢᵗ and 2ⁿᵈ chapters of Job). We find that Satan is a being; that he has access to heaven and to God, and God addressed him by name. We find that he is the father of all lies in (John 8:44) and he falsely accuses Job. This shows that he plans personal attacks against people and not God. Sometimes people, by their sinful actions, open doors for him to bring the attack upon them. Satan envied Job's blessings and desired to steal them from him. God gave Satan limited permission to touch Job, but he could not kill him. Satan stole his home, wealth, and his children. He thought he could cause Job to curse and deny God.

In (Job 1:15-17), Satan has those under his power attack Job physically. Then in verses 16-18 he controls the elements, the earth, wind, and fire; and to bring a storm upon Job that destroyed his house. This could have been a powerful thunderstorm, with lightning and tornados. Remember (Ephesians 2:1-3) says that Satan is the prince of the power of the air. The word "prince" means the head of a principality. "Air" means the invisible area of gases surrounding the earth between the surface and outside of the atmosphere. Satan controls this area, causing destructive storms around the earth. We see this from Jesus rebuking the storm in the book of Matthew. Sometimes this attack is spiritual.

I shared part of this dream before, but I and many other people were in ships on a large body of water that I assume was the ocean. Around us was a huge storm, like a hurricane, very large waves and hurricane force winds. But although we were in the same body of water, and the storm waves were only about 25 feet away from us, the water around us was perfectly calm and smooth as glass, with no wind hitting us. The ships did not even create a wake as ships normally would.

As we sailed on, I realized what I was seeing; that this chaos was symbolizing what was going on around the world. The wars, the natural disasters, the world economy, and things all the way down to the spiritual battles going on in people's personal lives. I was reminded of (Matthew 24:5-8): "For many shall come in my name saying I am Christ and shall deceive many. And you shall hear of wars and rumors of wars, see that you be not troubled, for all these things must come to pass, but the end is not yet. For nation shall rise against nation, and kingdom against nation, pestilences, famines and earthquakes in diverse places."

All these are the beginning of sorrows. After that, I began to think about the rapture and the tribulation. I heard the Holy Spirit say, "That time is not very far away." I watched the storm a little longer. Then I realized that all the chaos I was seeing was the result of the disturbances caused by extensive spiritual warfare, caused by the massive amount of demonic activity that was going on, encircling the entire planet Earth. What was going on in the spiritual realm was affecting the physical realm around the world.

I was reminded of (Romans 8:22), "For we know that the whole creation groaneth and travaileth in pain together until now." The planet Earth was shaking, quaking and was not able to withstand the demonic effect on it, creation was wanting to return to the perfect state it was first created in, and it could not do it. I bent over the side of the ship to look straight down at the water. It was still perfectly smooth and calm, not the slightest ripple, although the storm was raging and intensifying with strength only 10 feet away from us. We were untouched and totally safe. I was then reminded of the entire (91st Psalm).

But in (Job 2:7), Satan also afflicted Job with a physical disease, proving that it is Satan, and not God, that sends sickness. Sometimes people open the door themselves by sin and that allows Satan free legal access to inflict sickness and disease on them.

Well, if that is still not enough to convince you, here's more proof.

It was Satan, not God, who smote Job with boils in (Job 2:7). And it was "God" who turned or delivered Job's captivity from Satan's attack in (Job 42:10). In (Matthew 12:22) there was a man possessed with a blind and dumb spirit. In (Matthew 9), and (Mark 5), a man was possessed with a devil. In (Matthew 17:18) Jesus rebukes the devil, not God. In (Luke 9:42), it was the devil that threw the boy down on the ground, causing him to foam at the mouth and bruising him. Not God. In (Luke 4:19), God anointed Jesus with the Holy Ghost and with the power to heal all that were oppressed of the devil. In (Mark 6:7-13), they cast out many devils, and many who were sick were healed. (Luke 13:16) Jesus healed the woman that he said had been bound by Satan in sickness for 18 years. So, by now, you either believe it or you don't.

Chapter 10

How Satan Works

Satan uses everything that he can to keep the human race in bondage to him. Generational curses are an example. He tries to keep people in ignorance of how to be set free. He will try to ruin a believer's testimony and the influence that they may have on an unbeliever. He tries to get believers into a lukewarm state as in (2 Timothy 3:1-9). At first, he causes a false condition of peace, which is pleasing; he makes the lake look so good on Sunday, and, after all, you have worked hard all week. You deserve it, don't you? And what's wrong with just one beer every now and then, huh? And what's wrong with looking at pictures of a few beautiful women? After all, God did create them, didn't he? You say, "I'm just admiring his handy work, right?" You see, Satan can make it seem so good. Even innocent, so simple, that we can be deceived very easily.

Satan will create situations for you. One example and I will try to be tactful.

In the office where I worked, my coworker and I are out of the office on the road a lot. The package delivery service leaves our packages at the office next door when we are gone. In that office, there are two nice looking women who work there, and they both make it a point to bring our packages to us together. Their message is very clear, what they are trying to do. In our front office, we have a weight scale next to a large glass window, and one day both women decided to weigh themselves. The comment was made, by them, that they could not get an accurate weight with their clothes on, and if we would cover up the window, they would take all their clothes off, so they could get an accurate weight. They wouldn't mind at all. The ball was in our court.

Both of us being Christians, involved in ministry, happily married, and wanting to stay that way, loving God and our children, our testimonies and our places in ministry at our local churches, we left the ball right where it landed and did not return it. We did not cover the window up.

You don't think Satan tried to plant thoughts and desires? He said, "No one would know; you know a chance like this doesn't come around very often; you know it would be fun."

Yeah, it would be fun, all the way to divorce court, but even worse, God would be displeased. Satan and the demonic spirits involved would know, and generational curses would be accepted into our lives. We would be opening doors for the demonic to have power and legal access over us. No thanks. In doing this, he can cause a person to give away their salvation and maybe even lead to a wrecked life, even driving them to suicide. He causes unholy passions in men and women that cause them to totally lose their restraint from sin.

Satan dares us to do things we would not normally do. He makes people feel like they are missing a great chance if they don't do it. When he stirs up these unholy passions, causing people to lose their values, it makes them think there is more joy in pleasure than there is in serving God.

Chapter 11

Why Does God Allow Satan to Continue?

I've heard many people blame God for bad things happening to them. "Why did God let this happen to me?" Well, let's see, first you listened to the temptation and came into agreement and covenant with the demonic spirit, who brought the temptation and then you obeyed and did it. At that moment, whether you realized it or not, you accepted the terms and consequences of your actions, which resulted in something bad happening to you.

Hopefully, by now you see that it is Satan and not God who steals, kills, and destroys, and Jesus that gives life (John 10:10) and God who gives good gifts to his children (Matthew 7:11). And in (James 1:17), every good and perfect gift comes from God. But Satan wants us to stay ignorant to this truth. This is why Paul said in (2 Corinthians 4:3) that if the gospel is "hid" it is hid to them that are lost. This means to keep out of sight, to be concealed, to keep it as a secret. In (Isaiah 5:13) God said, "My people have gone into captivity because they have no knowledge." This means they have no range of information. Satan uses this ignorance to keep people bound down.

Let's look at some Scripture to find a purpose for Satan being around. (James 1:12): "Blessed is the man that endureth temptation; for when he is tried, he shall receive the crown of life, which the lord hath promised to them that love him." In this verse, the Greek word "blessed" is "makarios" which translated means "happy" in six different Scriptures and translated "blessed," meaning holy, blissful, to bring comfort and joy, and to glorify in at least 43 different Scriptures. The beatitudes in (Matthew 5:3-11) being a good example. "Crown" in the Greek is "korone," refers to a wreath of victory, honor and reward worn on the head of a conqueror. Wow, think about this, by Satan's constant tempting, he helps us to gain crowns in heaven when we overcome him.

(1 Peter 1:7) says: "The trial of your faith is much more precious than of gold that perisheth, though it be tried with fire, and might be found unto praise and honor and glory at the appearing of Jesus Christ."

The "trials" mean hardships, sufferings, a test, and a source of annoyance that can work to make us stronger. Remember the word "annoyance" means to hate and to irritate by repeated action. This means a constant bombardment from Satan in temptations and attacks. The amplified Bible says the "genuineness" of your faith, meaning no counterfeit, no artificial, to be true and sincere; that it be purified by fire. When gold is melted down, it purifies the gold. All foreign particles and impurities are separated and removed from the gold. In this process, the gold is not diminished in any way whatsoever. It does not lose color or weight; if anything, it increases the value because it is now purer than before. Once gold is purified it can remain in that purified state forever. Then he says that our faith might be found as praise, honor, and "glory." This means being found of great worth, to express approval, to glorify, to have high respect, to exalt to honor, and to make better and greater than before. Wow, by Satan fighting us, we have the chance to become purer, of more worth, and our end being greater than our beginning.

In the ministry where I work, I was talking with a couple who had recently been saved. They shared with me how a year ago both were involved with drugs; they were separated, and had been living in a house that was falling in around them. Their lives were wrecked, and that's where Satan wanted them. They began coming to our Friday night meetings and turned their lives, their wills, and their control over to the will and control of God. They very quickly began coming to church on Sunday morning, so they could grow spiritually. Now, a year later, they both are off drugs, their marriage is restored, they are raising their children in church, they both have jobs, a smile on their faces all the time, and even have a better house to live in. You see Satan pushed them until they turned to God for help, and now their present is better than before.

In (2 Corinthians 2:11-12), we learn forgiveness, so Satan cannot control us. In (1 Corinthians 5:5), "To deliver such a one unto Satan for the destruction of the flesh that the spirit may be saved in the day of the lord Jesus." Satan's attacks can help bring someone to repentance. In the early church, when someone was bent against God, and prayers were no longer offered for the person, they were open to Satan's full attacks by their own sin rebellion which opened the door for free legal attacks by the demonic. It was not the attack that saved him, but it caused him to realize that God could help him and would cause him to return to God in repentance. The word "deliver" means to set free or rescue.

Chapter12

Us and Satan in Warfare

When we are born again, we are on a supernatural battle ground of warfare against Satan. Although this battle takes place in the spirit realm, it also affects our physical realm where we live and work. This affects us through our relations, where he causes strife to be in control, causing financial problems, where we run out of money and can't pay our tithes, causing sickness; keeping us so busy that we run out of time to spend with God in prayer and Bible study, causing fear of the situations that seem to be out of control, keeping us from trusting God to provide as in (Philippians 4:19), that says God will meet all of our needs.

The amplified Bible says God will liberally supply, fill to the full, all our needs. (Ephesians 6:10-18) says, "Finally my brethren, be strong in the lord and in the power of his might. Put on the whole armor of God that ye may be able to stand against the wiles of the devil." When we do this, we have our spiritual bodies covered, which, in effect, will cover and protect our physical bodies.

Know Satan's Tactics and Strategies:

Paul said in (2 Corinthians 2:11): "Lest Satan should get an advantage of us, for we are not ignorant of his devices." To keep him from gaining ground on us, we need to know his every tactic. The Greek word for "devices" is "noema" and it means thoughts, purposes, designs, plan, schemes, and tricks. This is the reason that I dedicated most of my study to spiritual warfare. This has lead me deep into studying how Satan works through witchcraft, the occult, Satanism, and the functions of different demonic spirits. How Christians can be deceived in these areas and have no knowledge of it. We need to know every method of attack that Satan has, so that it can strengthen us.

If a country is going into battle against another country, they need to know all the strengths, weaknesses, what kind to artillery and weapons the other country has. We need to know how they fight, where the attack comes from, and what brings on the attack. It's the same way in the spiritual battle that we are in. Begin to keep notes on the ways Satan battles you. Write down the time and date and the temptations that you face. Write down your weakness and make a strategy of how to guard yourself. Make a mental search into your past, asking God at the same time, to reveal what is in you, and in your past, that has happened to open a door that Satan can use to keep you torn down emotionally and spiritually.

If you read the chapter on generational curses you will find our ancestor's sins will give Satan and the demonic a legal doorway to attack with temptation. Also read the chapter on soul wounds. This is another area that can allow a legal doorway for Satan and the demonic to attack with temptations. This will keep you from fulfilling your purpose. And those things need to be destroyed. To do this, you can renounce the sins of your ancestors. Someone said, "That's crazy; the Bible doesn't say that." Yes, it does. (Leviticus 26:40) tells us to not only confess our sins, but also to confess the sins of our fathers or ancestors. This breaks those ties and closes those doors.

Chapter 13

Our Past Can Be a Strategy of Bondage

The events of our past, both good and bad, have affected us and those we love. You are a product of everything that you have been through during your entire lifetime. Only you can determine if it is going to ruin your life, or if it will be strength to your life. Our hurts, choices, resentments and our fears are often traced back to our childhood memories, and the pain that we may have experienced. It takes courage to dig into our past to discover the source of our hurts and emotional pains, but we have to destroy this strategy that Satan uses to defeat Christians. Sometimes our past can cause generational curses that can be passed on to our children, and to their children. Facing it, we can put a stop to it. (Lamentations 3:40) says, "Examine our ways and test them, and let us return to the Lord." We need to make an inventory of our lives, writing down everything we have been through, to see what actions we need to take.

By doing this inventory of your past, you will learn how to maximize your growth process and minimize the pains of your hurts and failures from the past. Our past, no matter what it may be, abuse, molestation, a bad childhood, addictions, what people have done to us, can bring us into bondage. And as I've said, before breaking generational curses that have been passed down to us, is a great way to begin this deliverance process.

Unfortunately, we can't always ignore the hurts. And time does not always heal the hurts. WE must face it head on, acknowledging what God shows us. If we don't, and we leave it unresolved, it will fester and cause a spiritual cancer in our lives. This can cause denial. "Oh, it wasn't all that bad. I'm alright. I deserved getting hit. Nothing ever works out for me. You don't need to trust anybody, they will all do you wrong." This is the hurt talking.

This kind of thinking causes people to justify their past, and causes them to have a bad outlook on the present, where they are never satisfied with anything, causing divorces, where the other person can never make them happy, broken relationships, where they will end it before the other person does anything to them, bad spending habits, trying to find happiness in new things and so forth. But it doesn't work. It causes debt, and fears of the future. Satan will keep using those things to keep us in bondage, frozen, unable to move forward with any of our relationships with God and others. When we get them out into the open, before God and someone we trust, Satan no longer has anywhere to hide and torment us with our past faults, failures, and things that have hurt us.

(Psalms 107:13-14): "They cried to the Lord IN their troubles, and he rescued them….and snapped their chains." God didn't wait until they had their lives straightened out before He healed them; He healed them as they were when they came to Him. "Chains" means shackles, captivity, bonds, and to restrain. These chains can cause low self-esteem, and spiritual strongholds that cause incorrect thinking. This can distort our seeing the truth of what God's Word says about us and not seeing God as our loving Father. We see ourselves as a failure, instead of as victors in God.

You need to make a list of the good and bad things that have happened in your life and how they affected your past, how they are affecting your present, and how it will affect your future if you don't get it resolved and healed. And be honest about it. Seeing our past in print helps us to come face to face with our character defects and see who we truly are down deep. This can also be referred to as "peeling off the layers of the onion." Peeling away layers that can get down to the core of our problems can cause you some emotional pain, and it can also make you very uncomfortable. But as you peel away those layers, God is getting you to the point where He can start rebuilding you to what he wants you to be. He gets rid of the garbage that you have collected and has been placed on you by others throughout your life. As I did this in my own life, God began to show me hurts that I had, that I didn't know I had, and why I am as I am today. Getting all that healed gave me a whole new outlook on my spiritual life. And when you cook that onion in a stew, or grill it with some olive oil, after peeling off the undeserved skin, it is a good thing.

But let me say that while we look back and recognize our past actions, we do not dwell there; we move forward to get past the past, focusing on the future for freedom and permanent victory where Satan can no longer use this strategy against us.

While making this list, we must admit and recognize that we've had past hurts and uncontrollable bondages to sins that were out of our control. It could be that someone else has had dominance and control over us, or that we've let something keep occurring, but that we also want to eliminate the dependence that is controlling our lives.

Set aside a day to be alone with God, so you can pray. And take time to let God speak to you, to bring things back to your memory that you have pushed so far back that it's repressed you, and you really don't realize or remember it anymore. Repression is a form of denial and is also a defense mechanism. Make it a time when you can clear your mind, and in a place free from distractions if possible.

(Job 33:33) says: "Listen to me and I will teach you wisdom."

Open your heart and mind to allow yourself to feel and deal with the pain the past has caused. Wake up your feelings by thinking back on the past, by putting a stop to denying the past, as God reveals to you those hidden things. Some people never deal with this, they push it back, yield to it, and get used to it. At that point, it's controlling them, and Satan's strategy is working.

Chapter 14

Satan's Strategy Against Confession

Satan does not want us to use the power of confession, be it to God or anyone else. God tells us in his Word to confess our faults one to another that we may be healed from not just physical healing but also for soul healing. There is freedom in confession. It is simply admitting and acknowledging a fault.

After going into ministry, I knew that I would have to tell my testimony at some point. My wife did not know what I was in those years before we met and married. Satan was holding me in fear-bondage because I did not know what her reaction would be when she finally knew. I wrote it all down, and gave it to her to read. She never asked me any questions; she just accepted it, with no problems.

Then there were the people who I am in ministry with, what would they think? How different would they treat me after knowing? Would they still want me in ministry with them? Satan tormented me with this. It affected me mentally, emotionally, and spiritually.

One night I was teaching a lesson on "denial." I prepared a lesson, but God said that was not what He wanted. He wanted me to speak from my heart. I knew what He wanted me to say. He wanted me to talk about my past because I was still denying it. So, I prepared another lesson, and again God said the same thing. Five times I did this, until finally I said, "Ok God, I'll do it."

That night I confessed to my ministry team what I used to be, and the life I had lived. When I released my past to them, they loved me that much more. Two weeks later, people were still telling how much they needed to hear that, and how much it helped them to be set free. My pain was blocking the feeling that I was trying to get out in the open. I was never able to move forward, nor was I able to fully recover, until I confessed. I broke Satan's fear-bondage with confession.

When you find yourself giving in to a sin, Satan will try to keep you in condemnation over it, trying to keep you wallowing in it, beating yourself up over it. Not forgiving yourself is a strategy to keep you defeated. So, OK, you sinned, that's bad. What should you do? OUTLOUD, confess the sin to God according to (1 John 1:9), asking God OUTLOUD to forgive you, so Satan and all the demons can hear you. When you do this, Satan cannot stand against you or harass you. This is a God-given strategy that we have, and it works.

(Job 7:11) says "Let me express my anguish. Let me be free to speak out of the bitterness of my soul."

I used to feel so guilty when I was back in sin that I'd cry myself to sleep at night, promising God I'd never do it again, but I would sin over and over, usually the next day. I had not dealt with the root cause, thus causing the anger, the revenge, the pain I caused others. I found Scriptures telling me what God said about forgiveness. I wrote those down and used them in prayer and praise and thanksgiving over my life.

(Romans 8:1) says: "There is no more condemnation for those who are in Christ Jesus." When we accept Jesus, and the work of His shed blood, we are forgiven of our sins and we're not under condemnation any longer.

(Romans 5:1) says we are justified by His grace, just as if we had never sinned. Psalms says God said that he will cast our sins as far as the east is from the west, never to remember them anymore. As a hint, if you do sin, pray out loud to God for forgiveness, so Satan can hear you, so he will not have any ground to stand on to continue to condemn you.

But remember, when God forgives us, we have to forgive ourselves and not beat ourselves up as I used to do. This is a trick of Satan to keep you in bondage, causing you to feel unworthy, not good enough, that God couldn't possibly love you. This keeps you from being what God wants you to be. WE have to accept His forgiveness, and know He has forgotten it, never to remember it anymore. Not forgiving ourselves is a trick and a scheme of Satan to keep us in bondage. That's a form of condemnation but it is not from God.

(Romans 10:9-10) tells us to make confession unto salvation. In (Matthew 1:21) the angel said his name shall be called Jesus because he shall save his people from their sin. The name Jesus means savior. From that we get the word salvation. Many people assume the word salvation only means being forgiven from their sins. But it means so much more. The word "salvation" is translated throughout the bible as heal, health, healing, deliverance, deliver, safety, protection, welfare, rescue, avenge, forgiveness, and many more. So biblically we can confess, "I am healed in Jesus name." "I am protected by God in Jesus name," and so on. Tell Satan, "Oh no you don't, I AM HEALED, I AM DELIVERD, GOD SAID I AM AND I AM." Stand your ground on the scripture and don't back down.

I drove a truck over the road for a time. Every day before I would pull out on the road I would pray this prayer. "God in the name of Jesus I ask you to keep your hand of protection over me, this truck and the other drivers around me. Give your angels charge over me to rescue me if it's needed, stop or move this truck, to keep drivers from causing an accident, and make me aware of a hazard. And Satan, in the name of Jesus I rebuke you from any hindrance or accident on this trip. It worked.

Resentments: Satan's Strategy for Bondage

I had to also ask myself about all the resentments that I once had against people. "I hate so-and-so for what they did to me. The abuse from others ruined my life; I deserved that promotion, not them." I

141

resented others for things in my life that caused my life to turn out wrong. I wrote these resentments down and then found Scriptures dealing with these issues and used them in prayer and praise over my life.

The things that used to cause me anger also led me to acts of revenge against people. I was very inventive at being able to get revenge. There are still people I hurt in the past who knew that someone did something to them, but they don't know who, because I never got caught.

When I begin getting serious with God I knew I had end the revenge. God said vengeance is mine, I will repay. Someone owed me $700 and they told me that I would never get the money. Thoughts of revenge begin to run through my mind. The Holy Spirit spoke to me and said, "let me handle it." I finally said, "Ok, handle it." Within about 2 weeks I received the money.

Another time at the company I had worked at for 30 years I was attacked by a coworker of higher rank. He would fabricate every lie against me that he could. He would put other's mistakes on me. He, being of higher rank had the owner's ear and the owner believed whatever he said about me even though I had the paper work to prove my innocence. It didn't matter. I had a service manager who would not stand up and say, "You're wrong for treating Nathan this way." It finally cost me my job of 30 years.

I had to really pray hard to not have resentment and unforgiveness against them for the attack that I did not deserve. I always did everything I was asked, I worked all the overtime required, and never complained. I made a lot of money for that company and was thrown out like I was worthless. I had the thoughts of revenge come into my mind. Instead I prayed for them to be saved and forgiven. I purposed to forgive.

When dealing with resentments write it all down. The anger and the resentments are a result of burying your hurts, not getting them out in the open, and dealing with them. By not going to the person that wronged you, it causes anger that leads to frustration and oppression and depression. This can even lead to health problems like depression, which will hinder your walk with God as it keeps you from seeing God as the loving Father. It will hinder your faith level. It can break up relationships, cause loneliness, missed opportunities, dread, and panic. And the list goes on and on.

The anger, grudges, and unforgiveness will keep us out of heaven. It stops God's blessings on our lives and keeps Him from hearing our prayers, until it is dealt with, and we ask His forgiveness. The strategy of warfare on resentments is to pray for the person to be saved, healed and blessed. Purpose that you want to see them in heaven, not that they go to hell. Pray for no ill will to come to them. If they stole from you, say, "God in the name of Jesus I GIVE it to them, so they won't be responsible for stealing it." If they have slandered you, do not curse them, do not slander them back, pray for them. Be kind and at peace with them. Do this even if you don't feel it at first. Ask God to get you to the place where you can honestly do this and mean it. If you will, He will. This will bring power and freedom in your life.

Chapter 15

Satan's Strategy of Fear

The Spirit of fear will keep us from being open and honest with ourselves and with God, by keeping and hiding secrets we don't want anyone to know about. Being truthful with another person will tear away our denial and our fear. Fear is False Expectations Appearing Real. Fear is a paralyzing force that stops God from working in our lives because fear gives Satan access to work in our life. Fear also contaminates our faith. (John 4:18) says: "Fear has torment." The word torment means a great physical pain or mental anguish and anxiety. Fear is a spiritual force that WILL bring about negative spiritual manifestations in your life, just as faith will bring a positive spiritual effect in our life.

Where there is no fear Satan has no access to your life. Fear comes believing that God will not do what He has promised in His Word that He would do for us. Remember that for everything that God created, Satan has a counterfeit, and that God did not create fear; Satan did as a counterfeit to faith. Fear is not the nature of God, so it shouldn't be ours. Fear expects bad things to happen because fear believes the word of Satan instead of believing the Word of God. We can attack fear with God's Word, with prayer, with praise, and with thanksgiving.

In (2 Timothy 1:7), we read: "For God has not given us the spirit of fear; but of power, and of love, and of a sound mind." The word power in this verse is "dunamis." In the Greek and means inherent power, able to reproduce itself. The word "power" also means the ability to get results, the legal authority, force, strength to supply with source of power given to do great things. (Daniel 11:32) says: "The people who do know their God will be strong and will do exploits."

(Joshua 1:9): "Do not be afraid or discouraged for I the Lord your God am with you wherever you go." (Isaiah 41:10): says "Fear not for I am with you, be not dismayed for I am your God, I will strengthen you, I will help you, I will uphold you with the right hand of my righteousness." The word "uphold" means to hold up, to keep from falling, to come up under and support, to sustain. That's what God does for us, if we let Him by turning our will over to HIS control instead of Satan's strategy.

We must learn to rely on God for our help. (Isaiah 40:29) tells us that God gives strength to the weary and increases the power of the weak. Relying on God is a form of faith. Faith is having confidence in God. Trust is being committed to God That No Matter What happens, if things don't work out like we want them to that we will still trust Him. That reminds me of the old song, "I shall not be moved; just like a tree planted by the water, I shall not be moved." (Psalms 31:23-24) says: "Love the lord, all of you who are his people, for the lord protects those who are loyal to him." So, cheer up, take courage if you are depending on the Lord.

Another strategy of Satan when talking about fear is to cause you to give up and lose sight of the answer that is on its way. (Isaiah 40:29-31) says: "He gives power to the faint, and to them that have no might he increases strength. Even the youth shall faint and be weary, and the young men shall utterly fall, But THEY THAT WAIT UPON THE LORD SHALL RENEW THEIR STRENGTH, THEY SHALL MOUNT UP WITH WINGS AS EAGLES, THEY SHALL RUN, AND NOT BE WEARY AND THEY WALK AND NOT FAINT." I like what the amplified Bible says: He causes our strength to multiply and making it to "abound," meaning to be plentiful and rich. And they, who expect, look for, and hope in God shall change and renew their strength and power.

You see, Satan will cause us to begin to look at the situation we are facing, and just as Peter looked around at the waves when he was walking on the water and began to sink because of fear, the same

145

thing happens to us. Sometimes we pray and do not see the results, and we began to doubt, playing into Satan's strategy. Let me give you two examples of this.

Satan is a master "illusionist," which means a false ideal or conception, to create an unreal or misleading appearance or image; it also means to mock, which is a sham, an imitation, false, fraud and a fake. Here is what happens:

You are praying about something. The more that you pray the worse the situation seems to get. But it's just an illusion. If Satan can get you to give up faith and hope, then you have lost. So many people quit when they are only a step away from the answer coming through, and then they have lost. All because Satan gives the illusion that everything is getting worse instead of better. But the entire time God is working. You must understand that God is our Jehovah Jireh, God is our supplier. He is the source of our supply.

Now, let's go to (Daniel 10). Daniel was on a three-week fast. In (Daniel 10:12), the angel of God appeared to Daniel and said from the first time you prayed, on the first day that you prayed, God sent me with the answer, but the high ranking demonic spirit who ruled over that geographical region of the earth called the prince of the kingdom of Persia withstood him in spiritual battle for 21 days to keep the answer from getting through until God sent Michael who verse 13 says was one of the chief princes.

Verse 13 proves that the prince of Persia is a demonic spirit, if the chief prince Michael who was an angel of God had to be sent to defeat him. And in verse 13 the angel tells Daniel that while Michael was fighting with the prince of Persia that he (the angel) remained there with the kings. This was in the same spirit realm where the war was being fought, farther proving the military rankings of the demonic and angelic forces. And the very same prince of Persia, as well as the same kings, is still in power today hindering prayers from getting through.

Well, you may not live in Persia, but the same thing happens where you live. There are demonic spirits of high rank over your geographical area where you live, who are hindering your prayers from getting through. But God will also send His angels to help if you will hold on and not give up.

Another example of this: I was working all over the north Alabama area. On my way home out of south Huntsville, I would pass a place of ill repute. It was a spa, where anything sexual that you wanted was there if you had the money to pay for it. Well, every day as I would drive by on my way home I would say, "You are cursed by your own sin, and in the name and the authority of Jesus Christ you are closed down and you are out of business. God, send your angels and set into force what it takes to accomplish it." I prayed that with no visible evidence of anything happening at first. Then one day it burned to the ground. Well, shortly after they rebuilt it. But don't ever give up praying and believing. About a year passed, and it was raided by the sheriff's department and permanently closed. A prostitution ring was working out of it that reached from Huntsville to Birmingham, and the owners were put in jail. Don't look at the situation; don't look at the visible manifestations until Michael has arrived with your answer. Faith creates freedom, (John 8:34), "Who the son sets free is free indeed." GIVE SATAN NO GROUND.

(EPHESIANS 4:27) SAYS: "NEITHER GIVE PLACE TO THE DEVIL."

Chapter 16

Demonic Spirits

The word demon does not appear in the King James Bible. But the word devil appears 60 times and devils appear 55 times. Another name for demon is evil spirit. The Greek word for devil is "diabolos," which means adversary, false accuser, and slander. This also describes the way they attack us.

There are some different ideas concerning where demons are believed to have come from, and the Bible does not say exactly which one is true. But we know they are of Satan and are the workers in his kingdom who carry out the plans of attack against us, and we, as believers, have authority over them, which we will get into later.

Some believe that demons are the one-third of the angels who fell with Satan when he was cast out of heaven. They believe that since God's angels are carrying out His commands, helping the human race, that the fallen angels, as demons, are doing the same job but now doing it for evil, carrying out Satan's commands.

The apostles (and Jewish) belief is that the ruling principalities are the fallen angels, and the demonic spirits are the result of the union between the sons of God and the daughters of men (Genesis 6:4). They believe this union between angel and human created half-flesh and half-spirit beings which were giants called the Nephilim. After they died their departed spirits became the demonic spirits who now roam the earth, attacking the human race. The belief is since they had a physical body, and they knew the human appetites of lust, sex, perversion, and murder, they now push that on the human race.

The book of Enoch, which claims to have been written by Enoch himself, is not part of the King James Bible. I do not use it as scriptural proof, although the book of Jude which is in the Bible quotes Enoch in verses 14 &15. This would prove that the apostles used it as scripture. But I do love history and many historical documents are true and accurate.

Some people believe the demonic spirits, which possess human beings, are the fallen angels which fell with Lucifer, with at least some being in Hell, in chains, and are different from "evil spirits." Because of Jewish tradition, and the book of Enoch, others believe that the evil spirits or demons are the departed spirits of the dead giants from the spirit angel fathers in (Genesis 6). Now, as I have said many times, I do not teach the lost book of the Bible as Scripture, but I do love history, and as an ancient historical document, I believe it has some value. In Enoch 15:8-11, we read: "And now the giants who are produced from the spirits and flesh, shall be called evil spirits upon the earth, and on the earth, shall be their dwelling. Evil spirits have proceeded from their bodies because they are born from men and from the holy Watchers. As for the spirits of heaven, in heaven shall be their dwelling, but as for the spirits of the earth, which were born upon the earth, on earth shall be their dwelling. And the spirits of the giants afflict, oppress, destroy, attack, do battle, and work destruction on the earth, and cause trouble: they take no food, but nevertheless they hunger, and thirst, and cause offences. And these spirits shall rise against the children of men and against the women, because they have proceeded from them."

These were half-human and half-spirit beings, so when they died, the human part was gone, but the spirit was then loosed and freed from the body and became the evil spirits to attack the human race. And it also states that having lived in a body knowing and understanding the appetites of human lust, and longing to be in a human body.

This describes exactly what we see evil spirits doing today. Satan does not have the power to create but both factors were already there: the daughters of man, to whom God had given the law of reproduction, and the sons of God, who in the human form, are believed to have the same capability. Satan will use and pervert what is there at his disposal.

Enoch makes it very clear where he believed demons came from, and that he believes they did not leave earth, they stayed to cause torment, pain and to inhabit bodies. Many believe the giants, the Nephilim, are the gods of Greek Mythology. The word "daimon" is translated as "demon" in the New Testament which also is referred to by pagan Greeks to describe their mythological gods. The similarities are there. Zeus married an earthly woman, and had a half human, half god child with super human strength. In (Acts 14:12), the people of Lystra thought Paul and Barnabas were two of these gods. The Greeks believed their gods to be beings of super human strength and abilities that were born when the gods came down to earth and intermingled with human women. In the ancient world many myths were rooted from factual information. Could this be one of those times? We may never know. I believe it is possible.

The word nephilim not only means tyrant and bully but also tormentors. Jesus used the word tormentors in (Matthew 18:35) in referring to demonic bondage that is due to unforgiveness that creates spirit and soul ties linking the human race. The fact is demons work under Satan; they carry out plans of attack against us.

I suppose it really doesn't matter where they come from, we know that they work for Satan, they are our enemies, and we have been given authority over them. Everyone has their own opinion, but my personal belief from my study is that fallen angels are still holding the same power and rank that they had as angels of God in heaven, only now they have changed sides, working for Satan. They have lost no power or ability from what they had before the fall as spirit beings. Angels of God cannot possess a human being, so why would a fallen angel, now working for Satan, suddenly be able to possess a human being when they couldn't before? Yet we know from Scripture and from ministry that people do get possessed. This is where I believe the book of Enoch had it right; that it is the evil spirits departed from the giants that are bound to the earth who are able to possess and inhabit human bodies. Also, angels, both fallen and unfallen, have their celestial spirit bodies and do not have any need for a human body, but these evil spirits desire one. You and I may not totally agree on this theology, but so, long as we agree that they are from Satan, we fight them, at least some can possess, and that Jesus through His shed blood on the cross gave us authority over them, then we together can win the battle.

Another difference is angels can transport or "fly" from place to place, and Jesus said in (Matthew 12:43) that an "unclean spirit" or demon, after it has gone out of a man, "walks" through dry places, seeking a place to rest. Being basically disembodied spirits, who once had a body; this causes them to desire another body.

According to what Paul said in the (6th chapter of Ephesians), they are highly organized. We can find them in Scripture from before time until the time they are cast into Hell at the end of this age. We find in many Scriptures that Jesus had power over them and cast them out everywhere he went. Matthew, Mark, Luke, and John all record at least 26 different times that Jesus encountered them with victory. We also find that He gave us the same power in (Luke 10:17-19) and (John 14:12).

(Luke 8:27-30) tells of a man possessed by many demons and their name was Legion. Roman legions were 6000 soldiers. They are referred to by the personal pronoun of "he," showing a personality. He recognized and obeyed the authority of Jesus. Legion knew and feared the judgment that was awaiting them and begged Jesus to not send them into the "deep" which referred to the bottomless pit. This showed they are individuals who are not human and not angelic. It also shows they have knowledge, emotions, desires and wills. This also proves that they have power over unbelievers who are not covered by the blood of Jesus.

The name Legion is just one of many names of demons given in Scripture; most are mentioned in the Old Testament, and were worshipped as idol gods. In (Matthew 10:1), they are "unclean spirits." In (Luke 7:21), they are "evil spirits." In (Matthew 12:45), some are more wicked than others. In (1Timothy 4:1), they have a doctrine and are evil teachers of false cults and religions. (James 2:19) says that they believe and tremble, meaning they shake and shiver from fear because of the anxiety of knowing the punishment that awaits them and the authority of Jesus Christ who is over them.

Chapter 17

Territorial Level Demonic Spiritual Warfare

Throughout history, since the beginning of time, there has been as Jesus described in (Matthew 5:8) a history of wars and rumors of wars. That is in the natural world, but there also is a war going on in the spiritual world. In the spirit world, which is just as real as the one that we live in, there are two kingdoms: the kingdom of God, and the kingdom of Satan. People have no problem believing that God has a kingdom, but many people do not believe that Satan has a kingdom, although Jesus told us this in (Matthew 12:26). Both these kingdoms operate with a delegated system of power, rank and authority just as earthly military kingdoms do. Paul tells us this in the (1st, 3rd and 6th chapters of Ephesians).

Spiritual warfare is the participation in the actual battle that is taking place between God, his angels, God's believers, and Satan, demonic spirits, and Satan's believers. In this battle, we must know our enemy; we must know the tactics and strategies they use so we can defeat them.

Demonic spirits affect the human race in different ways. In (Luke 13:11-16), we find a woman who Jesus said had been bound physically by a demonic spirit for 18 years. This bondage was to the point that her physical body was bent over. In (Job 1), we find that Satan was the reason for every bad thing that Job suffered. This proves where physical suffering comes from. In (Mark 5), we find the story of the man possessed by Legion. This man was affected physically, mentally, emotionally, and spiritually. He was under such extreme torment that he had no peace. The story of King Saul in (1 Samuel 16:14) also shows how Saul was tormented mentally by demonic spirits that caused him to have the outward evidence of mental illness. Spiritual oppression always shows up whenever mental illness is caused by demonic spirits. The open door to this is

153

always sin, rebellion, and disobedience in some way, either by the person themselves or from a generational curse that has been passed down through the family blood line. In (Luke 8:27-35) we find the story of the boy that was called a lunatic and that he was vexed, being thrown into the fire and water. Jesus cast a demon out of the boy and he was restored to a sound mind. These stories prove how Satan can affect people physically, mentally, emotionally, and spiritually.

Being involved with the occult, witchcraft, and Satanism will always bring demonic activity, oppression, and possession. In (Acts 16) we find the story of Paul who encountered the girl who was involved in divination, or fortune telling. This is performed through the help of a familiar spirit. Paul prayed for her and commanded the demonic spirits depart from her and they did. In the Greek this was the spirit of python which all divination works through. A person can open the door to this spirit by becoming involved in the occult, witchcraft, or going to fortune tellers. This proves the demonic are at work behind certain books, movies and video games about demons, witchcraft, casting spells, fortune telling, communicating with the dead, and so on.

As believers, we always have authority over demonic spirits according to (Mark 16) and (Luke 10:19). But according to (Matthew 17:14-21), some demonic spirits require more work than others to be cast out. In this story the disciples had prayed and rebuked all they felt like they could and still the demonic spirit had not been cast out.

After explaining this to Jesus and asking, "Why could we not cast him out?" they found out the reason. Jesus said, "because of your unbelief." Jesus also told them that this comes only by prayer and fasting.

In (Matthew 12:45) we find that some demonic spirits are eviler than others. Jesus said that when a demonic spirit is cast out, after wondering for a time, it will return to its former house and if it is full of God and His word, it will return with seven more who are more wicked than itself. At this point Jesus said the latter state of that person would be worse than the beginning. (2 Peter 2:20) also tells us that if a person becomes entangled in sin again after the knowledge of salvation, the latter end is worse for them than the beginning. This is why we see so many people who seem to get delivered and in a short time are back in even deeper sin than they were in before. This story, and the story of Legion, proves that demonic spirits can and will work together to achieve their goal. One interesting fact here is that they were working together to the point that there was no confusion between them, they all agreed on being cast into the pigs. One of the demons took the role of spokesman and spoke intelligently to Jesus, answering all His questions.

Many times, certain manifestations accompany demonic spirits. In (Mark 1:26), the demon caused convulsions and screamed with a loud voice as it was being cast out. Again, in (Mark 9:20) the demon caused convulsions, wallowing on the ground, and foaming at the mouth and screaming loudly. A few times, I have been praying for deliverance of people and have witnessed this happening. I've also witnessed some of these people speaking in voices that were not their own, having to be held down by several people because of their excessive strength. But always remember (Mark 16), Jesus said the signs of casting them out would follow those that believe. He gave us this authority through His name to cast out demons.

Territorial Demonic Principalities

In the spirit realm there are also territorial demonic spirits called principalities, or those of high enough rank to be called demonic princes who are ruling these kingdoms. I realize I've already stated this before in my study of ancient worship of gods, goddesses, and idols. I have found that some of these ancient cultures believed that there were gods who ruled over towns and geographic areas. This is Strategic level warfare.

At the strategic level, the ruling demonic princes plan and direct the attacks being handed down, to be carried out by the mid and lower rank spirits against God's people. This is to prevent them from ever reaching what God has for them. Israel is an example of this. In (Deuteronomy 7:1) God told Israel to go in and possess the promise land. The word "possess" means to take, gain and maintain control of something, and means to have as belonging to someone. God told the Israelites that he would deliver the Hittites, Girgashites, Amorites, Perizzites, Canaanites, Hivites, and the Jebusites to them and they were to destroy them. That meant they were to absolutely and unconditionally destroy them, keeping no captives alive. God said do not show them any mercy. Do not make any covenants with them. Do not marry any of them. In other words, do not come into agreement and covenant with the demonic spirits operating through them by obeying their temptations. This increases the strength of the spirits who are in control of that geographical area.

A good example of this are places like Las Vegas where there is a very strong demonic presence working in gambling, sexual immorality, and even death. The more people who come into agreement and covenant with them through obedience, the more generational curses, spirit ties, and soul ties are created. This can end up linking millions of people together all over the world in spiritual bondage. For this reason, people need to destroy the sexual, mental, spiritual, and emotional strongholds of bondage in their lives. If they don't, Satan will keep them from advancing into God's word and victory, not only ourselves but to others. By allowing strongholds to control us, we struggle trying to maintain instead of conquering.

From (Daniel 10:10-21), we see there are territorial spirits such as the prince of Persia, and the prince of Greece, who interferes with and hinders our prayers and earthly events. Both are fallen angels, who before they fell were high ranking angels of great responsibility in God's kingdom. They were no doubt over many other angels in carrying out God's plans and ruled over territories. Now they are doing much the same, except in reverse and under the direction of Satan, who according to (2 Corinthians 4:4) is the god of this world. Where God's angels deliver answers to our prayers, these demonic princes cause warfare with these angels to destroy our answers to the prayers that we pray. So, next time you don't receive the answer when you think you should, just remember maybe your answer is caught up in warfare and keep on fasting and praying.

The chief archangel Michael was sent to personally fight and subdue the prince of Persia who was withstanding the unnamed angel who was sent with Daniel's answer. One interesting fact in this scripture is the angel tells Daniel that while Michael was fighting the prince, he remained there with the kings. Where? Remember the angel was still in the spirit realm while Michael was fighting, so they had to be demonic kings.

In (Daniel 10:21) he uses a personal pronoun and calls Michael "your" prince. This is not saying that Michael was Daniel's personal angel, but that he was chief angelic prince of Israel where Daniel was, or God's territorial archangel over Israel and God's children. (Daniel 12:1) says Michael is the great prince which protects the children of God. God has placed his most powerful archangel over His people. One rule of the spirit realm is what you have on one side of the spirit realm you have on the other side. In (Revelation chapters 2 and 3) we find 7 more proofs of God's territorial angels. They are the angels of the 7 churches. These were 7 churches in actual cities and these angels were over that geographic area.

Now from what I said above on the power that is given to the territorial demonic rulers when the people of that geographic area come together into agreement and covenant of obedience with them, could you imagine if we could get all of God's people to come together as one? Instead of arguing over denominational issues, instead of criticizing one another over race, sex, or length of hair (for example), whether they were a spirit filled church or not, what if all of God's people came together, as one? Can you imagine the holy power that assemblage would create?

Daniel had to face the prince of Greece, who was another powerful territorial demon who directed the country of Greece. These demons are so powerful in the spiritual realm that they direct the affairs of the ruling earthly governments. They direct the strategies that bring the earth under their bondage. The chaos around the world that we hear on the news is not just the actions of mortal men, but it reflects the spiritual warfare that is going on in the spiritual realm influencing their thoughts and beliefs. These ungodly earthly leaders, and their people, are being influenced by these demonic princes to pass laws that are against Christian beliefs and to also bring about false religions to deceive people. That is why we see society going down as we do. We must fight this with prayer and fasting at the territorial level to win.

These territorial spirits can affect an entire area with many different symptoms. Sometimes after a survey is done, you find a mass of people having been hit by the same problems such as fear, depression, an uncommon amount of cancer, accidents, the same type deaths and suicides of a certain age group, similar types of sickness and diseases. Recently, in the area where I live, there have been about 7 or 8 youths die in what looked like questionable suicides. In these circumstances, people will say "this is weird, I just can't believe this many cases of the same thing are happening." This is the work of the territorial demonic spirits.

Sometimes past generations of occult activity, Satan worship and witchcraft can be the source of the spirit having its demonic hold on an area. This activity could go back before recorded history, or to a time when the first settlers moved into that area. Other times, it may be that there has always been a strong rebellious spirit at work in that area. The territorial spirits know that we, the Christians, are here and they do not like us invading their territory and taking away their control in the name of Jesus. They will try to attack the ministers and the churches with fear to diminish our advancement. But if we are doing our jobs these spirits will be afraid of losing their power. Remember in (Mark 5) the spirits "begged" Jesus again and again to not punish them before their time. Jesus used this example in (Mark 5) to show us that He gave US this same authority over demons that He has and has given it to us to cast them out.

Some of these territorial spirits are very powerful, and people have to come together in unity to pray against them.

(Isaiah 14) and (Ezekiel 28) both tell us that Lucifer, who is Satan, is the power behind both the earthly kingdoms of Babylon and Tyre. Satan, and his principalities, controlled the governmental and moral decisions that were made there. That is why in (Matthew 4) Satan offered Jesus the kingdoms not only of the earthly realm but also of the spiritual realm if He would only obey and worship him. We can say for sure that the 7 civilizations of people possessing the promise land, who were enemies of God, were controlled by the territorial demonic spirits because they were so deep into idol or demon worship. Satan had placed these 7 groups of giants there in the Promised Land ahead of time as a set up for defeat, just as he sets us up sometimes. God commanded the Israelites to destroy all the 60 cities and towns of the giants and their idols, images, demonic temples, and altars with fire. In other words, they were to have a spiritual house cleaning.

(Leviticus 18:27) tells us that the land became defiled because of idolatry and sexual immorality. Today, it would be cleaning our own houses of demonic books, games, movies, occult and witchcraft items, good luck charms, amulets, pornography and such items. In the book of Acts the people brought all these kinds of items to Paul to burn and destroy.

Now, we know we cannot go out into the community and begin burning everything ungodly, because we would be arsonists and would end up in prison. But what we can do is take authority in our own homes and areas where we live. Later, we will go into more detail on how to do this.

Sometimes we, as Christians, may come together in prayer against territorial spirits. When we do, we must bind any other spirits they may call in to help resist our prayers. If we continue, we will see results. But if we are not careful, we can begin to slack off and get lazy. When this happens, we will allow the territorial spirits to regain the power that we have taken from them, and they can gain a stronger hold than before.

Territorially, according to Ephesians, Satan is the god of this world. He has all his principalities working on many levels of rank, power, and authority. He controls his top generals all the way down to the foot soldiers who carry out orders to steal, kill, and to destroy, thus keeping the entire world in bondage and oppression. We must always remember this!

Chapter 18

Offensive and Defensive Warfare

When Rome was at the peak of its power, conquering the surrounding kingdoms, they had to set up military strongholds or fortresses to maintain their position of power. It took a well-trained army to accomplish this. In the same way, we as God's army with His authority can advance in an offensive attack against Satan's kingdom claiming territory he controls, taking away his domain. We must maintain that control and use fasting, prayer, and God's Word as our fortresses and stronghold. At this point, God's angels can take control and work more powerfully for God's army.

The earthly militaries have both basic and advanced training in the science of planning and directing the battle which is the strategy and tactics of warfare. The soldiers must learn not only their weapons, maneuvers, tactics, hand to hand combat, and their own strategies, but also their enemy's so they can fight an effective war. They must learn their enemy's strengths and weaknesses, where they are, where they attack, how they attack, and what brings on the attack. This is to make each attack count when they are mobilized for the invasion. Without all this an army is useless.

Basic training is useless without training on how to use the weapons. Without this spiritual foundation, we can never be successful. When a new Roman soldier joined the Roman army, he had to go through a very rigorous training that lasted for 6 months, day and night. It is the same with a Christian; we must be willing and patient to take time learning Scripture, praying, and learning to listen to the Holy Spirit. The Roman armies, like our own military, had soldiers specialized in different areas of warfare, using different kinds of weapons, hand to hand combat, vehicles, and armor. It is the same way in God's army.

Paul said in (Ephesians 4:11-12), "And he gave some apostles, and some prophets, and some evangelists, and some pastors, and some teachers. For the perfecting of the saints, for the work of the ministry, for the edifying of the body of Christ."

Some that he didn't list are the many people with the servants' heart like missionaries who risk their lives in the jungles to carry the gospel to an unreached group of people. The ones who make the Sunday service possible, the people who minister at the grocery store to someone in need, or the co-worker on the job. There is much ministry that takes place outside the four walls of the church building that the pastor by himself could never accomplish. All of this is defensive (and sometimes offensive) spiritual warfare on the enemy's territory.

Jesus said in (Luke 14:31): "Or what king, going out to engage in conflict with another king, will not first sit down and consider and take counsel whether he is able with ten thousand [men] to meet him who comes against him with twenty thousand?" This is where our training pays off in the spiritual war that we are fighting. The information in this book, along with the wisdom that we gain from God with each experience in the spiritual battles that we face, is a growing step-by-step process. No one, regardless of what kind of spiritual strength they may have in God today, started out that way in the beginning.

Satan has declared an offensive war on you. Offensive spiritual warfare is going onto the enemies' territory. So, you declare a defensive war back on him, going onto his territory. Often this spiritual attack is originated by the territorial spirits. These attack plans are made by Satan and the demonic and are given to the demonic spirits of mid- and lower ranks to be carried out against you and others. Sometimes it is personal; this is the "Ground Level" warfare. These can be attacks of fear, depression, discouragement, hopelessness, despair, rejection, word curses over your life, attacks of failure, and sickness. Sometimes "occult level" warfare comes through Satanism and witchcraft. This can create an attack on our children through books that teach witchcraft. This level can very easily lead to demonic possession. Sometimes this is on a governmental level to create spiritual oppression and bondage. One example was in 1951 when it became legal to be a witch. I believe in the not so far future we will see one of these territorial attacks against the church. But if Satan and the demonic can declare a Strategic level war on us then we can declare a strategic level offensive war on him through God, His authority, His word, prayer and fasting.

In (John 15:18-21), Jesus tells us that one phase of warfare that we are going to fight are the battles in our everyday social lives, at work, at church, our finances, and in our own families. In the 20th verse Jesus said that we would be "persecuted." In the Greek, this means to pursue with malignant intent, meaning having an evil influence, to wish evil, to be very harmful, to cause death, and also means cancerous. Cancerous in the sense that spiritual oppression and bondage can grow at an alarming rate if it is not dealt with spiritually.

In (Galatians 5:16-26), Paul tells us that one phase of our warfare is between ourselves, or the desires of our flesh, and the desires of the Holy Spirit for us. Another phase of our warfare Paul describes in (Ephesians 6:10-18) is one-on-one combat with the demonic.

Each one of these phases is where training in the tactical maneuvers of warfare is applied. In an earthly military the soldiers learn how to apply the training they have been taught in actual combat training situations. The only way that we will really learn is fighting through battles.

Chapter 19

Functions of Different Demonic Strongmen

We have already established that there are many demonic spirits with each one having their job to do. Jesus referred to these demons or evil spirits as the strongmen in (Matthew 12:29), and there are many demonic strongmen. Many of these spirits work together in collusion under the leadership of the spirit of antichrist. This means they work together under a secret agreement for a fraudulent or illegal purpose to trick or deceive someone out of their own legal rights. The jobs of these spirits are to oppress, influence, and possess. Oppression can weaken and paralyze a Christian. Possession totally controls someone who is not a Christian from the inside out. Being influenced is being attacked from the outside as in being influenced mentally/spiritually to do certain things.

In (Matthew 9:32-33) and (Mark 9:25) they cause dumbness and deafness. In (Matthew 4:23-24) they cause torment, sickness, paralysis, insanity, and disease. In (Matthew 12:22) they cause blindness. In (Matthew 15:22) a woman was "grievously vexed," meaning miserably possessed. In (Luke 4:35) they cause convulsions. In (Mark 5) they cause attempted suicide and pain. In (John 8:44) they cause lies and lust. In (2 Chronicles 33:6) they are used in witchcraft and the occult. In (Romans 8:15) they are the spirit of bondage and slavery. In (Acts 10:38) they cause oppression. In (John 13:2) they cause betrayal. In (Luke 8:27-30) they can speak out loud.

They are individuals, who are not human and not angelic. They have knowledge, emotions, desires, and wills. They have the knowledge and desire to gain power over unbelievers and believers alike to destroy lives. For these reasons, we must be covered by the blood of Jesus Christ, which gives us power and authority over them. In (Matthew 8:28) they caused two men to become physically stronger and more fierce than ordinary men. In (Exodus 20:5) they can enslave the human race in a global world-wide web of generational curses. But the blood of Jesus can destroy every one of these curses, all the way back to the root cause.

Satan's hierarchy works together for one common purpose, to carry us to hell. And as a Christian you WILL experience them and here are some of those ways.

Seducing Spirits

To "seduce" is to tempt into doing wrong, and to entice into illicit sexual intercourse. This leads to an emotional and spiritual bondage. Satan and the demonic can seduce us into unforgiveness causing confusion, division, church splits, anger, strife, slander, gossiping, and divorce. They cause people to make wrong decisions to wreck lives. All these work, together with the spirit of unforgiveness and strife to bring division.

The seducing spirit is a spirit of deception. The Greek word for seduce is "wonder" because it causes the mind to doubt or question God's Word. This can cause confusion making it easy for Satan to make someone question their salvation, question if God exists, question whether there really is a hell or not; and whether they really need a savior or not.

Satan has his false evangelists, preachers, and apostles. (2 Corinthians 11:13-15): "For such are false apostles, deceitful workers, transforming themselves into the apostle of Christ. And no marvel; for Satan himself is transformed into an angel of light. Therefore, it is no great thing if his ministers also be transformed as the ministers of unrighteousness; whose end shall be according to their works."

Jesus said: "Many shall come in my name saying I am Christ (or the messiah) and shall deceive many." Paul said in (Galatians 1:6-9), "I

165

marvel that you are so soon removed from him that called you into the grace of Christ unto another gospel; which is not another; but there are some that would pervert the gospel of Christ. But though we, or an angel from heaven preach any other gospel unto you than that which we have preached unto you let him be accursed."

What other gospel would this be that can cause a born-again child of God to be deceived to the point of believing something totally contrary to what they had first believed? (1 Timothy 4:14) says, "Now the spirit speaks expressly that in the latter times some shall depart from the faith, giving heed to seducing spirits, and doctrines of devils; speaking lies in hypocrisy, having their conscience seared with a hot iron." The bible says that there is a way that seems right to a man, but the end is death. We see so many religions that while some are so far from the truth, yet many are so close but leave out that Jesus is the only way of salvation. (Acts 4:12) tells us there is no other name given except the name of Jesus that we can be saved by. My son asked me once if someone spent their entire life ministering to people but never accepted Jesus as their savior would they miss Heaven when they died. I answered according to God's word the answer is yes. But the seducing spirit would make them believe a lie.

The Greek word for "depart" is aposteeontai meaning to slide back from; "giving heed to seducing, deceiving, and wandering spirits" in the Greek (I won't bore you with the word), but it means the teaching of demons. It also means the person has gone into apostasy. An apostate is someone who departs from the faith that they believe, that they know, that they have experienced and have understood, and the faith they have professed as a believer, and now comes to believe that the blood of Jesus Christ is not needed in their life for redemption. I have found this in so many of the cults and false religions I've studied. This is why we are seeing so many gay churches today; churches that rely on man's ability to save himself, leaving God out.

Paul said they have their conscience seared with a hot iron meaning that their hearts are hardened against God, where they cannot hear His conviction of sin speaking to them. Our conscience gives us the ability to determine right from wrong. After a person overrides his conscience long enough, he will no longer feel it is wrong. At this point, the seducing spirit has accomplished its job.

The seducing spirit can also work through sex and pornography. The constant temptation to give into premarital sex, prostitution, homosexuality, and the bondage of looking at porn will cause a bondage that can be impossible to break without God and a tremendous amount of work and prayer. This can destroy families, causing divorce, distrust, emotional hurts, molestation, and passing on generational curses.

Hindering Spirits

Some of the manifestations are hindering prayers, hindering God's work in His people, hindering people from reaching God's will and purpose, causing problems between Christians, and causing problems to not be resolved.

When I think of hindering spirits, I think back to when I was a very mischievous, sometimes cruel, young country boy growing up on a farm in Hayden, Alabama. I thought it was fun to shoot the cattle and hogs that we raised with a high-powered BB gun. I thought it was funny when they would jump and squeal. I would follow them around, shooting them daily, causing them misery because they couldn't get away from me. I was in control. I had superior intelligence over them (although you may be questioning that at this moment) and I had the means to outsmart them. Then I got caught by my dad, who had the authority to make me stop. He had the power to take the weapon out of my hands. You have to realize it was the 1960's and 70's, I was 12 years old and there wasn't much to do for entertainment back then in the country.

Hindering spirits can often work in the same way, constantly hitting us over and over. Many times, we wonder where the attacks came from, and how they came upon us. Hindering spirits are demonic spirits who are sent by the high-ranking principalities. Paul talked about them in (Ephesians 6:12). They are sent to stop us from getting to the purpose God has called us to. They often work through other people in word and generational curses of discouragement to cause inferiority and low self-esteem, for example. Sometimes they operate through distractions to keep you from having time to read your Bible and pray. They may cause financial troubles that keep you from paying your tithes and offerings to God, so they have an open door of attack on your life. They may operate through trials. (1 Peter 4:12) tells us: "Think it not strange concerning the fiery trial which is to try you." The amplified Bible says: "Do be amazed and bewildered at the fiery ordeal which is taking place to test you as something strange, unusual and alien were befalling you."

If the light switch on your wall breaks, then ok it's a man-made switch, things are going to break from time to time. Your car is going to break down also. But if you had a week like I once had when we had 22 flat tires, the microwave, stove and washing machine died, the engine in the car blew up, the roof began leaking, the water heater started leaking, and there were other things that also happened, then you may need to realize you could be under an attack of distractions, getting your faith level down, stealing your money from tithes and offerings.

WE, especially those of us who are close to middle age, having witnessed these spirits at work in the United States over the last several years by humanist, New Age beliefs, the occult and the morals of the overall society, know this firsthand. When once God was the forefront of the American belief system as a Christian nation, we now have many other religions that are against God, with some of these being held in high regard.

Here is another example of hindering spirits working through distractions. Let's say you are praying for a battle that you're fighting your way through. You don't see any evidence that God has even heard your prayer, or that any relief is on the way. You know that Jesus said for us to give Him our burden and He would carry it. We know that (1 Peter 5:7) tells us to cast all our cares on Him because God cares for us. But still it seems as if nothing is happening. Here is what is happening in the spirit realm.

Satan is a master illusionist. He, and the spirits working together under his command, will throw everything they have at you in warfare. At that point, your angel with your answer is in warfare with the demonic spirit who is keeping it from you. They will make it look as if God is not going to answer you, but God heard you the very first time that you prayed. He sent the answer, but it is being held up from getting to you, the same way that Daniel's answer was held up, giving you the illusion that you have lost the battle. If you will hang on, God will send more angels to do battle. But many people give up the fight during this process, when many times they are only one step away from receiving the answer. But they give up and quit, allowing Satan to win.

Many people do not believe that God will do this work for "ME," but he will. Why? Because "we" are the ones carrying on His work and His word for future generations to know Him. "We" are the ones that Jesus said would do even greater works than He did in (John 14:12). "We" are the ones who Jesus said would have the signs following us, (Mark 16:17-18). And because "we" are the ones who are heirs of God, and joint heirs with Jesus Christ in (Romans 8:17), "we" are the ones that Jesus gave all the power over the enemy to in (Luke 10:19). (1 John 3:8) says that Jesus was manifested, meaning to be revealed, to destroy the works of Satan, then that means it is our job also to destroy, expose, and reveal Satan's work.

A battle always comes before a breakthrough. I believe that somehow in the spirit realm the demonic can detect a blessing is coming for someone, or so it would seem, because they always

169

know when and where to attack beforehand. How we handle the battle determines the outcome. Always remember you fight Satan and the demonic from the highest rank down with God's Word, prayer, praise, and fasting. The stronger you are in the Word, prayer, and praise the more the angels of God are empowered to work on your behalf.

Also watch for the counter-attack! Most battles may be won on the first attack when you know and realize that you're in battle. When you are in the first of a battle your guard is up. But then, after you think it's over and you begin to relax, watch out for an unexpected and sudden counter-attack. This is when the enemy thinks, or knows, that your guard is down, or that you are spiritually exhausted from fighting, because after warfare you need time to recharge. Even after ministering, where you have brought the Word and have prayed for people, you can give out so much that you feel drained spiritually.

The warfare strategy here is to have a spiritual recharge. The only way to recharge is with God's Word, prayer, praise, worship and fasting. If you do not recharge, you can become so overwhelmed by the sudden counter-attack that you will be overcome.

The Spirit of Jealousy

The spirit of jealously does not want to share with others. It is a coveting spirit because it envies what someone else has. It gets its power from insecurity. The spirit of jealously creates a strong sense of ownership and obsession. It can cause anger, depression, anxiety, sadness, broken churches and relationships, and even death. Some other manifestations of this spirit are murder, strife, contention, lies, revenge, divisions, envy, spite, anger, accusations, backstabbing, belittling, bickering, bitterness, causing divisions, extreme competition, contention, criticism, discontent, dissatisfaction, distrust, fault finding and hatred.

I have seen husbands and wives who are so jealous of their spouses that they end up destroying the marriage. I have witnessed Satan cause situations and circumstances that did not exist in reality for no other reason than to cause jealousy to destroy a marriage. I have even worked in ministry with people who were jealous and envious of someone else's position, even to the point of tearing the ministry apart. Jealousies led Cain to kill Abel. Jealousy is a demonic strongman who influences the condition of someone's thinking, who is listening to, and operating off, what this demonic spirit is speaking into their spirit.

First, Satan became jealous of God in (Isaiah 14:12-14) and (Ezekiel 28:12-19). Jealousy is Satanic and demonic because of the bondage it carries with it. (Numbers 5:14): "And the spirit of jealousy comes upon him, and he be jealous of his wife..." The word "jealousy" means being resentfully suspicious or envious of a rival or a loved one. This can open doors to many other spirits.

Revenge is a door that is opened with the works of jealousy. (Proverbs 6:34) says, "For jealousy is the rage of a man: therefore, he will not spare in the day of vengeance." The word "rage" means a furious, uncontrolled and unchecked anger, with great force and violence. When a person yields to the rage, it can open doors to many things. Murder and competitiveness are two of these things. (Genesis 4:1-8) tells the story of Cain and Abel. Verse 5 says that Cain became competitive and was "wroth" or filled with "wrath" against Abel, meaning intense anger, rage and fury. Because of jealousy, murder was committed. According to (Proverbs 14:29) wrath can cause a "hasty spirit," using a lack of sense causing incorrect quick decisions, without praying or thinking it through, that can lead to wrong decisions. (Proverbs 22:24-25) tells us not to have ties to an angry person because learning their ways would become a "snare" or a dangerous trap to us, opening more demonic doors. (Proverbs 10:12) says "strife" and hatred are two more of the open doors linked to jealousy, anger, wrath, rage and being hasty.

(Proverbs 27:4) tells us it opens even more doors: "Wrath is cruel, and anger is outrageous; but who is able to stand before envy." The word "envy" means a desire, discontent and ill will for possessions of another. (Proverbs 14:30): "A sound heart is the life of the flesh: but envy the rottenness of the bones."

Envy, jealousy and hatred bring corruption to not only the spirit man but also to the human body. In (Galatians 5:19-21) jealousy, envy, strife, wrath, murders, and hatred are six of the seventeen things that will not inherit heaven. But these six will open a door to the other eleven to operate. Satan will bring people across your path to give you the opportunity to cause these things to rise in you, giving them the open door they need.

Sometimes it's people in our church, co-workers, and even our families that can cause the open doors in our lives. The main thing to remember here is do not have resentment, hard feelings, grudges or unforgiveness toward them, even though you may want to choke their eye balls out. You may want to curse them to have the fleas of a thousand camels in their bed. But don't, it's not totally them; they are being demonically influenced by this demonic strongman to cause the trouble because their spirit man is not operating off God's Word, and because they are not being led by the Holy Spirit, even if they do claim to be Christians.

As a strategy of warfare to counter-balance and destroy this in your life, Paul tells us in (Ephesians 5:2) to: "walk in love." And (Galatians 5:25) tells us to live and walk our daily lives in the Spirit. (Romans 12), (Ephesians 4:24-32), and (1Corinthians 13) tells us how to do this. Read it, learn it, and began to operate off it as a warfare strategy. Recognize the signs and begin to ask God to remove them from your life.

A Lying Spirit

I have known people who are habitual liars, who you could not believe anything that they said because they would lie about anything, sometimes so extravagantly that it was clearly a lie. I have worked with someone who would lie to me knowing that I knew the truth. Someone said, "They're crazy!" No, they are just listening to, and under the influence of, this demonic strongman, the lying spirit.

We find in Scripture that lying, deception, flattery, superstition, false prophecy, false accusations, slander, gossip, false teachers and lies, teaching false doctrine causes bondages, all operate under this demonic strongman.

In (2 Chronicles 18:18-22) King Ahab was involved in rebellion against God through idolatry where he was worshipping demonic gods, listening to and obeying their prophets, instead of obeying God. Because of this, God permitted him to be deceived by a lying spirit who volunteered for the job, and, according to verse 20, the lying spirit "stood before the Lord and said I will entice him." And the Lord said "Wherewith." Verse 21: "And he said, I will go out, and be a lying spirit in the mouth of the prophets. And the Lord said Thou shalt entice him, and thou shalt also prevail: go out, and do even so."

This proves this was a demonic spirit because no angel of God could (or would) lie and it also proves that he was not forced to do this.

Because King Ahab was so hardened, so engulfed by what he had "given" himself over to (as in (Romans 1:24 and verse 28) where God gave them up to a reprobate mind which in the Greek means to be rejected and a castaway), God permitted the lying spirit to work falsely through the occult prophets. King Ahab was in the same spiritual position as in (2 Thessalonians 2:10-12), "Because they received not the love ((1 John 4:18) says God is love) of the truth that they might be saved. And for this cause God shall send them a strong "delusion" (a false belief or a lie) that they should believe a lie: That they all might be damned who believe not the truth, but had pleasure in unrighteousness." It's not the will of God for anyone to go to Hell (1 Timothy 1:15), but if a person determines that they will not obey, and they determine to go to Hell then there is nothing more that God can do because of their own free will choice.

In (2 Peter the 2ⁿᵈ and the 3ʳᵈ chapters), Peter is warning us about false apostate teachers who are teaching lies. In (Revelation 21:8), liars are one of the ten groups who will be cast into Hell. In the chapter on the high ranking demonic spirit Beliel, one of his jobs is to slander God's people. In (John 8:44), Jesus tells us that Satan is the father of lies. One of the names of Satan is the accuser of the brethren. And Jesus also said in (John 8:44) that if you lie then you are a child of Satan. Because when you lie you allow what the demonic spirit is speaking into your spirit man; you are being enticed and you are yielding to the temptation as in (James 1:14-15). This also means that you are coming into agreement and covenant with the demonic spirit because (Romans 6:16) says you are a servant of "whoever" you obey. In this case, it is Satan and the demonic.

To overcome the temptation of the lying spirit you must allow God to transform your mind with his Word as in (Romans 12:1-2). In (John 17:17), Jesus tells us to be sanctified through God's Word. When you feel the temptation to tell the lie whether it is to keep yourself out of trouble or to make yourself look better or is to slander someone you dislike, do as (James 4:7-8) teaches us: "Submit yourself to God. Resist the devil, and he will flee from you. Draw near to God and he will draw near to you."

I've known people who have a problem with gossip. The bible condemns this. How many times have you heard someone say, "Well John said that Mary told their friend that Alice did this horrible thing." And when I heard it, there was no truth in it. Or the facts were so distorted because it's gone through so many people that very little truth remained. Basically they were telling lies on the other person. They were slandering their name and reputation with false accusations. This is purely demonic. We as Christians should

174

never do this to another brother or sister.

Tell Satan when you are tempted that you will read the Bible and pray. And if he doesn't stop, then you memorize some Scripture. If you will do this every time as a warfare strategy, he will leave because you are resisting him.

The Spirit of Heaviness

Many times, the bible states Jesus came to free those who were oppressed by Satan and the demonic. Jesus used the same Greek word for rebuking evil spirits that he used to rebuke sickness. The meaning was to down, under, "to hold power or under domination of Lordship." (Acts 10:38) says that Jesus went about healing all who was oppressed of the devil. The word "oppressed" means to weigh heavily on the mind, and to keep down by cruel unjust use of authority. This is to hold back, suppress, limit, confine, and restrain someone mentally and emotionally. The spirit of heaviness is a demonic strongman whose manifestations include oppression, depression, sorrow, grief, hopelessness, loneliness, inner hurts, rejection, self-pity, suicidal thoughts, and, overall, a defeated and negative attitude. (Galatians 5:22) tells us that love, joy, and peace are 3 of the fruits of the spirit, the exact opposite of the spirit of heaviness.

Have you ever known a person who seems to be consumed by these characteristics? People who constantly see the negative in everything? They may be under the influence of this spirit. This spirit brings a depressive heavy feeling of oppression and depression; sometimes it can be so strong the person may need to be delivered because they can't get free on their own. The aim of this spirit is to destroy faith in the person.
Sometimes it is possible for it to affect several people at once. It can steal the peace and joy of our salvation, our love for God and others; it can isolate you from others, and if left untreated, it will steal the purpose God has called you to do and shut you down physically,

mentally, spiritually, and paralyze us emotionally.

Many people have attempted to accomplish something, maybe in ministry, in business, or in a relationship. When it either failed, or did not turn out as "they" thought it should have, Satan jumps on with heaviness, depression, and oppression. They may be convinced that they missed what God was saying, causing them to doubt that they can hear from God. This may cause fear of trying anything else again. Many times, because the person does not realize that it is a spiritual battle, they give up and Satan wins.

I faced this once a few years ago. I was going to go into a business venture with someone. I prayed for God's leadership, giving it to Him, that if it wasn't His will that He close the door to it. Everything kept working in the direction, I had peace over it. But in my eyes, it failed because it didn't turn out like "I" thought it would. I beat myself up over it; I allowed Satan to beat me up big time over it for a long time. I would pray and say, "God, I don't understand. It didn't work out like I thought it would." I was under the influence of heaviness and didn't realize it.

Finally, one-day God spoke to me and said, "How do you know it didn't work out the way I wanted it to?" I said, "Well, God, we didn't make any money, the partner ripped me off, I put all this money into it, and it flopped." God said, "Well, didn't you have peace over it when you prayed." I said, "Yes." He said, "So, what's your problem?" I said, "But I put all this money into it." He said, "Didn't I give all the money back to you?" And he had, because, as a miracle, the same exact amount of money came back to me from another source, and to this day there is no answer for it except coming from God. So, I said, "Yes, you did." He said, "So, what's your problem?" "But God it didn't turn out like I had it planned." "But how do you know it didn't turn out the way I had planned, giving the partner a choice of his own free will to choose right or wrong, you listened to me and obeyed me, so what's your problem?" "Well, God, I don't guess I have a problem." The business partner had died in a motorcycle wreck almost immediately after ripping me off; I guess he made his choice.

Another time, in ministry I was to conduct a church service. I knew I was feeling led to ask a certain person to lead worship, and I didn't want to, but I obeyed God and asked them anyway. They turned me down. Immediately a very heavy depression fell on me. I had never been depressed before then; it was a new experience for me. It had me so emotionally torn down that I didn't even want to go to church. As a matter of fact, that next Sunday morning I went to the river still in that deep depression. It took a lot of praying, reading the Word, recognizing the Spiritual battle that it was, and telling Satan to get his grip off my mind and spirit in the name of Jesus to get me free. I had to make a conscious decision to fight it and win before I was going to be able to come out of it.

The medical world sees this as just a mental problem, and it is, trying to treat it only by medicine, but it is caused by a demonic spirit, so it is a spiritual problem. They don't see it as a trick of Satan, to be carried out by demonic spirits.

(Isaiah 61:1-3): "The Spirit of the Lord God is upon me; because the Lord has anointed me to preach good tidings unto the meek; he has sent me to bind up the brokenhearted, to proclaim liberty to the captives, and the opening of the prison to them that are bound; to proclaim the acceptable year of the Lord, and the day of vengeance of our God; to comfort all that mourn; To appoint unto them that mourn in Zion, to give unto them beauty for ashes, the oil of joy for mourning, the garment of praise for the spirit of heaviness; that they might be called trees of righteousness, the planting of the Lord, that he might be glorified."

If you are experiencing symptoms like this, then you may be oppressed by this spirit.

The way to get free is to first acknowledge it and come out of denial.

I began praying, (Hebrews 4:16) says we can come BOLDLY TO THE THRONE OF GRACE and tell God what we need. Don't be shy, timid, or feel like you have no rights, as if you don't deserve it. You are a child of God, and a heir of God, and a joint heir with Jesus Christ. You are to be as (Daniel 11:32) says: "The people who do know their God SHALL BE strong and do exploits." And as (Romans 8:37) says that through God you are even MORE than a conqueror. How can it be possible to be even MORE than a conqueror? Because Jesus said in (Luke 10:19) that HE has given US ALL power, over ALL the power of the enemy, and nothing shall by ANY means harm us. That's how.

Then put on the garment of praise as a warfare strategy against this spirit. Satan hates our praise to God. The more we pray and praise, the more empowered God's angels become to work on our behalf in the spiritual battle against the demonic spirits coming against us.

A few years ago, God revealed this to me in a dream. I saw a demonic spirit who was busy working on something with his hands. He knew that I was watching him, but he would not look at me. As I watched the Holy Spirit began to narrate what I was seeing. "Satan himself has orchestrated a plan of attack against you and this is the mid-ranking spirit assigned to carry out that plan against you. (At that time I did not know this information and had no idea what a mid-ranking spirit was.) As I began to watch him I saw what looked like deep gashing scars from wounds on his body that had already healed over. I thought what are those scars from? The Holy Spirit said, "Those are battle scars where it was defeated by angels in conflicts of spiritual warfare, and the defeat was due to the prayer of the saints praying the word of God." When I heard that I felt an anointing rise up inside of me so strong like I had never felt before. God's word begins to flow out of me with a very loud voice in prayer and praise directed toward Satan and the demonic spirit. Scripture that I didn't know I still remembered was flowing almost uncontrollably. Then I woke up, it wasn't just a dream because as I awoke I was praying these scriptures very loud. I fall back asleep and continue the dream. I watched the demonic spirit begin to back away; he would not turn his back to me as he backed completely out of sight. I then heard the Holy Spirit say, "He is gone for a season."

Praise exalts and glorifies God no matter what the situation may be. It is putting our trust and faith in Him. It's looking beyond the battle by faith. And it invites God into our lives. The Bible says that God inhabits the praise of his people. That means we do not have to get our praise all the way up through the spiritual wickedness surrounding the earth, but that God will come down to where we are and will began to touch us from the inside out, saturating us with His power and anointing, and we will rise up with his Word in our mouth, commanding Satan to leave and never come back. Wow I got excited there for a moment.

As a strategy of warfare we must use the sacrifice of praise. This is when because of the situation we do not feel like praising God. When Jonah was in the belly of the whale I'm sure he wasn't so filled with joy being there that he began to praise God. But in (Jonah 2:9) he said, "I will give the sacrifice of thanksgiving." In (Acts 16) Paul and Silas begin to give the sacrifice of praise, song, and worship and it brought freedom from prison. Anytime you begin to praise God when you don't feel like it, you will end up feeling as if you can't stop.

(Jeremiah 34:11):" The voice of joy, and the voice of gladness, the voice of the bridegroom, and the voice of the bride, the voice of them that shall say, PRAISE THE LORD OF HOST: FOR THE LORD IS GOOD, FOR HIS MERCY ENDURETH FOR EVER: and of them that shall BRING THE SACRIFICE OF PRAISE...For I will cause the captivity to be "reversed and returned" to be as it was at first says the Lord."

As a strategy of warfare, attack this spirit through praise and worship using God's word. Force yourself to do this even though you will not feel like it at first. God will cause the depression, the oppression, the grief, the suicidal thoughts, the despair, the loneliness, the hopelessness, the rejection, the hurt and the sorrow to reverse and return to Satan where it came from, which means you don't have to accept and carry it any longer, because it's not yours. It is not God's destiny and purpose for you, because God doesn't want you to be in bondage any longer. Jesus paid the price for that on the cross and destroyed it to annihilation when he said in (John 19:30), "IT IS FINISHED." So, it belongs to Satan and not to YOU.

(2 Corinthians): "Where the spirit of the Lord is there is liberty, freedom."

(John 8:36): "Therefore if the son makes you free, you shall be free indeed."

Spirit of Bondage

Some of the manifestations of this spirit include being held captive by Satan through addictions to sexual habits, drugs, alcohol, gambling, stealing, food, codependency, nicotine, broken heartedness, compulsive behavior, control, doubting salvation, controlling embarrassment, false burdens, strong feeling of constant guilt, an inability to break free, oppression, hatred, spiritual blindness, feeling unworthy, and that's just a few. Mainly anything that is a sin that you do not have the physical human strength to stop doing by yourself puts you under this spirit.

The word "bondage" means slavery and being subjected to force; this is when a person is under strong demonic influences where the demonic spirit coming against them is speaking the temptation into their spirit, constantly bombarding them.

(Romans 8:15): "For you did not receive the spirit of bondage again to fear, but you received the spirit of adoptions by whom we cry out, Abba, Father." Paul was saying that you have not received the spirit of slavery to continually relapse to the same addictions over and over, fearing you will never be free. Instead, you have received the spirit of son-ship in which the adopted children have all the same legal rights as the children born into the family.

I worked in a ministry that deals with helping teach people how to be free from, as we say it, life's hurts, habits, hang-ups, and addictions. All four of these things are common problems facing not only Christians today but also the unbelievers. Satan uses the bad experiences that he created to destroy people's lives. The things we went through as a child, the physical, sexual, mental, and emotional abuse. These types of abuse normally are not out-grown, it doesn't just go away, and no, time doesn't heal all wounds. In fact, time may allow the problem to fester and grow into hatred and resentment. At times, it may become a generational curse, allowing the same abuse to be passed down to descendants in the family blood line.

We see these bondages in alcohol, drugs, gambling, pornography, and sexual addictions where the parents, grandparents, aunts, uncles, and siblings struggle with the same bondages. We have even dealt with people addicted to the occult and witchcraft, where grandparents were also involved in witchcraft, an example of a generational curse. Sometimes I see people who do not realize the bondage or the emotional pain they are in because they have been there so long it is now a fixture in their life, much like a piece of barbed wire that the tree has slowly accepted into it, becoming a part of the tree. Often when this happens, people are afraid to let go of it because they cannot imagine their lives without it. This is bondage. Satan wants to use the spirit of bondage to destroy our purpose, our calling in ministry, our faith in God, our ability to fight against Satan and the demonic and our overall ability to be set free.

As a strategy of warfare to destroy the spirit of bondage, you must first do a survey of your life. As a strategy of warfare write down all the bondages that you struggle with, that you know God is not pleased with. Write down all the places and the people who help lead or enable you into temptation and committing the sin. And then remove that from your life. Stop going around the areas where the temptation could be. Begin memorizing Scripture to use in battle against the struggle. And probably one of the most important things, find an accountability partner. This is someone that you can trust. Be honest with them about your struggles, and about your past. Someone who is spiritually mature who doesn't care if you call them in times of temptation, so they talk and pray you through it. And when you find your accountability partner, CALL BEFORE YOU FALL!!!!

Spirit of Poverty

Where many of the demonic spirits in this chapter are mentioned in the Bible by the names given to each one in these sections, the spirit of poverty is one that I have not found mentioned by this name. But it is very clear that there is a great amount of demonic activity at work in this area to keep the human race, especially the believers, in bondage. By this bondage they can hinder and control the work the believers are commissioned to do in reaching the world for God.

Some people may say, "I don't believe there is a demonic force at work in poverty." It is this simple, if there are actions working against God, the believers, the church, and the human race, then there are demonic forces that are doing it, and nothing else. It's not just "life." This is one of the tactics of deception that Satan and the demonic use to hide their involvement.

This type of activity is part of the warfare that will affect a person mentally, emotionally and spiritually because it will steal God's blessings. The attack of these three areas will affect the person physically as well because they can't believe what God says in his Word. They are controlled by confusion as well as fear; they do not realize the reason the blessings are completely stopped, and their prayers are not being answered is because of this attack and it has to be broken.

The demonic spirits working in this area come through opened doors. It could be that somewhere in the generations past that an ancestor was dishonest, a cheater, and a thief or swindled people out of what was rightfully theirs. It could be that they themselves have given into the temptation of sin. This can open a door for a generational curse to come upon the descendants in the family blood line. The descendants may not have a clue what happened in the past, but they have grown accustomed to living in constant lack. They never have enough money to pay the bills; no matter how much money they make, it just disappears. The mental battle is lost at this point because now there is a demonic stronghold that has been created that is controlling them. In (Mark 11:23), Jesus said that we shall have "whatsoever" we say and believe. Jesus quoted (Proverbs 23:7) when he said that as a man thinks in his heart so is he. So, when these people constantly think and know that they are defeated then they are defeated.

People like this who are under this demonic attack will often justify their lack by making excuses like, "I'll never get ahead, and I never do. If I ever get ahead something will break down and take the money." This is creating word curses and speaking death over your life and blessings according to (Proverbs 21:18). They are critical and jealous of people who are blessed like friends, pastors, or anyone who teaches prosperity, often making statements like, "Those preachers make too much money, they shouldn't even get paid. They've got to be doing something wrong or dishonest to have a house and car like that; I know I can't have it. I can't imagine tithing to the church, because I can't afford it, after all the church has too much money as it is so they don't need mine. I felt like I should have given some money and helped, but I might need it for myself."

They see giving to the church as throwing money away. They are afraid to give even under the direction of the Holy Spirit. They can't possibly see them sowing into a ministry. They don't see God as their source; they see the tax refund, their jobs, or the lottery as their source. There is no way they will just give something away, as Jesus said, give, hoping for nothing in return, because they do not understand the principle of giving freely to be blessed. They think that receiving something free, even if a little shady, is always better than giving, because, after all, if you give it away you lose it. They live in fear of losing everything they have because they do not believe that they can be blessed by God, or that He will do what His Word says He will do. This fear causes them to constantly worry about money, and will cause mental anguish.

The strategy of warfare is to give God the tithe and offerings to be blessed as in (Malachi 3:8-10). God says that we have robbed him by withholding our tithes and offerings. He goes on to say that the windows of Heaven will be opened above us through obedience.

Spirit of Fear

Some of the manifestations of this spirit are fears and phobias, nightmares, being tormented and controlled by thoughts of defeat, anxiety, stress, distrust, doubt, rejection, dread, inadequacy, indecision, inferiority, and lack of trust. The spirit of fear creates bondage in a person's life. It can be a paralyzing torment and can manifest itself through worry, anxiety, stress, apprehension, depression, panic attacks, feeling out of control, indecisiveness, anxious and nervous, chronic fatigue, physical problems, being emotionally drained, avoiding people, addiction to drugs for coping, physical and mental sickness, migraines, nightmares, agitation, apprehension, overly sensitive, shyness, sleepiness, a feeling of unworthiness, and phobias. There are 210 phobias recognized by psychiatrists. It has been estimated that as many as 80% of Christians are oppressed by this spirit. The spirit of fear will stop Christians from being used by God in witnessing, teaching, praying for people, being used in the spiritual gifts, and using the natural God given talents such as vocal and musical gifts and ministering the Word of God. (Proverbs 11:9) says that through knowledge the righteous will be delivered. The fear of failure has controlled many Christian's outcomes in life. No Christian has ever received the spirit of fear from God, it came from Satan.

The spirit of fear is another stronghold in Satan's arsenal. Fear is also False Expectations Appearing Real. Fear stops prayers from being answered. Satan created fear not God. Fear is the opposite of faith. Fear manifests negative results, just as faith manifests positive results. Fear Stops God from working for you. Fear is listening to Satan instead of God. Fear is a spiritual force that expects bad things to happen. Fear can cause someone to make quick, rash decisions. Fear distances us from God. (2 Timothy 1:7) God has not given us the spirit of fear, but of power, love and a sound mind. "Power" means the ability, legal authority, force, strength to supply with a source of power given to do great things. (Daniel 11:32): "The people who do know their God shall be strong and do exploits." (1 John 4:18) says God is love. And all that gives us a sound mind.

Jesus said in (Luke 21:26) that in the last day's men's hearts would be failing them for fear. This shows how powerful fear is to the human race, that it alone can destroy someone's life. Heart disease is the leading cause of death and some of the reasons are fear, stress, and strain. Long-term stress can cause the body to age and deteriorate more quickly than normal, which will lead to a shorter life span. As people try to cope with fear, it can lead to tobacco, alcohol, drug abuse and addiction which can lead to even more heart and health problems. It can affect blood pressure, restricting blood flow, causing hypertension, diabetes, strokes and heart attacks. Other effects that fear has on the human body are: headaches, diarrhea, shortness of breath, anxiety attacks, depression, heart palpitations, sweating, change in eye movement and facial expressions, grinding teeth, and mental anguish. It causes doubt and people have been, literally, scared to death.

There have been many medical studies conducted where fear, anger, jealousy, spite, and resentment have affected the human body.

Holding on to negative emotions like these can and will have a definite effect on your body, your mind, your will, and your emotions. There are chemicals the human body produces because of fear as a coping mechanism. And if fear is experienced over and over for long periods of time, and not dealt with, it can lead to sickness and chronic health problems, even death, because these chemicals can suppress the body's natural immunity. Phobias can even be more harmful to us physically, mentally, emotionally, and spiritually.

As a strategy of warfare to destroy the spirit use God's Word and prayer as a weapon. Memorizing Scripture can dispel fear, and saying what God has said about your freedom from all of Satan's bondages over you can free you. (Revelation 12:11) says that we are made over-comers, victorious and conquerors by the blood of the lamb (Jesus Christ) and the word of OUR testimony.

For years I allowed Satan to control me through fear. Being from Alabama, I have a rather strong southern accent. For many years I knew that God wanted me to preach and teach his word, but I would not because of my accent. I wonder how many people I never reached because of this fear. After deliverance from fear I no longer care if I have an accent. If I get a chance to preach I go and God's word never returns void.

Deaf and Dumb Spirit

Manifestations are dumbness, deafness, insanity, seizures and suicide. (Mark 9:25-26).

Spirit of Infirmity

Some of the manifestations are chronic and lingering illnesses, cancer, epilepsy, blindness, mental illness, retardation, viruses, allergies and overall physical weakness and in (Matthew 15:22), a Canaanite woman came to Jesus about her daughter who the Bible says was "grievously vexed" with a devil. The word "grievously" means to be miserably possessed. The Greek word for vexed is "daimonizomi" which means to be exercised or controlled, disturbed, annoyed, distressed, and afflicted by a demon. If this does not prove it is demonic, then nothing will.

(Luke 13:11): "And, behold, there was a woman which had a spirit of infirmity eighteen years, and was bowed together, and could in no way lift up herself."

She had a demonic spirit which had taken possession of her body for 18 long years. It is very clear the spirit had caused her great pain and suffering. I believe there are people today who are possessed with this spirit of infirmity, while others may not be possessed but are "oppressed" by the spirit of infirmity as in (Acts 10:38): "How God anointed Jesus of Nazareth with the Holy Ghost and with power: who went about doing good, and healing all that were "oppressed" of the devil; for God was with him."

In this verse, the word "oppressed" means to be overpowered and to exercise hard control over, and to use power against someone. Someone who seems to never be able to get well, where they are constantly attacked by one illness after another, this is an indication of this spirit. I just want to say as a reminder here that (Acts 1:8) says that we shall receive power after the Holy Ghost is come upon us, the same power that God anointed Jesus with. Jesus said in (John 14:26) that we would receive the comforter, which is the same Holy Ghost that God anointed Jesus with.

And in (John 14:12) Jesus said that we would do the same miracles that He did, and He also said in (Mark 16:17-18) that these same signs would follow US who believe so that we can cast out the spirit of infirmity and see people set free. All accomplished by the same anointing and the same power of the Holy Ghost.

Satan has created a huge lie to protect the work of the spirit of infirmity. He has people thinking that it is God who sends sickliness and disease on His children. But these same people who think it is "God's will" for them to suffer, and that God has put disease on them to teach them humility, or that God uses sickliness to "teach them a lesson," they won't hesitate to go to the doctor or the hospital to try to get rid of what they believe is God's will for their life. If this lie were true, this would be getting them out of God's will. You wouldn't think of hurting your own children, or injecting them with a hypodermic needle with harmful bacteria just because they forgot to clean their room, or to make them learn to be better children, would you? You wouldn't think of breaking their leg just to make them thankful for the other good leg. You wouldn't think of giving them cancer just to make them humbler. No, and to think that God afflicts His children with sickness, that which His son Jesus died on the cross to destroy, is pure spiritual immaturity, spiritual deception, and even stupidity.

Jesus said in (Luke 13:16): "This woman who SATAN has BOUND, these eighteen years;" this proves that it is Satan, and not God, who sends sickness. What part of this do people not understand? As I said previously, Jesus used the same Greek word to rebuke and cast out evil spirits as he used to rebuke and heal sickness because they are one and the same.

There are many things that can open the door for the spirit of infirmity to come into a person's life. Generational curses are one way when people have not learned to be set free. Rebellion and disobedience to God, and even witchcraft, will open the door to it. (Psalms 66:18) says: "If I regard iniquity (sin, rebellion) in my heart, the Lord will not hear me." Jesus said if you do not forgive others then God will not hear your prayers.

In (1 Corinthians 11:27-29) Paul was teaching about taking the Lord's Supper. He said anyone who eats, or drinks unworthily shall be guilty of the Lord's blood because this is part of salvation provided on the cross in the shedding of his blood. And Paul said

188

this will bring damnation upon them. In verse 30 Paul says for this reason many people are weak, sick and even dead. The (11th chapter of 1 Corinthians) Paul tells us of many of these reasons. Verse 18 says strife and envy with others, verse 21-22 its alcoholic problems, irreverence, disrespect. Verses 27-30 tell us taking the Lord's Supper in unbelief, not realizing the importance, taking it as an unsaved person, and taking it with known, unconfessed sin will open the door for this spirit.

Another way the spirit of infirmity works on the person is by speaking excessive fear into the person's mind and spirit, causing their will to accept certain illnesses such as cancer, heart problems or strokes. Some people love the attention they receive from their illnesses.

As Jesus said in (Matthew 12:29): "That we have to bind the strongman." In (Matthew 16:19) Jesus gave us the power to bind and loose the powers of heaven and earth. You have to know your power and authority that Jesus gave us in (Luke 10:19). You also have to know the power of attorney to use His name (John 14:14) to ask for whatever we need and to command the strongman to be bound in Jesus' name. Binding is like spiritual chains and shackles to Satan and the demonic.

(Matthew 16:19): "And I will give unto you the keys of the kingdom of heaven: and whatsoever thou shalt bind on earth shall be bound in heaven: and whatsoever thou shalt loose on the earth shall be loosed in heaven." Keys are a symbol of authority and ownership. Giving you the power to go and come as you please and not being restricted in any way. "Whatsoever you shall bind on earth." The word "bind" means to hold or restrain by legal oath, restraint or contract.

We have a contract, agreement and covenant, with Jesus for this power over Satan right here on the planet earth. "Shall be bound in heaven." In the Greek, the word heaven also means "air."

(Ephesians 2:2) says "according to the course of this world," and it says that Satan is the prince and the power of the "air." Word in the Greek is "kosmos" meaning the world system that is run by Satan and man. The "air" is the spirit realm around the atmosphere of planet earth where the demonic spirits dwell and operate. This verse is not referring to binding things in the heaven where we will spend eternity with God. Heaven is a real place, not a realm. The word "realm" means a kingdom and a sphere. So when you bind the demonic, the spirit of infirmity in this case, from operating on the earth, they are bound in the air, the spirit realm. You take legal access away from them and you hold the key. Be careful not to do something that will loose them again, where they regain legal access. Sin, and the words that you speak, like gossip, slander and being negative, will put you under a curse, giving them an open door of legal access to attack you.

Like binding, loosing can be done on earth and will affect the spirit realm, the air. The word "loose" means not being confined or restrained and to release and be free. This refers to loosing someone being held captive in bondage by the demonic strongmen operating in the spirit realm. Jesus quoted (Isaiah 61:1-2) in (Luke 4:18-19) when he said he was anointed to release the captives and to set them free, and He gave us that same power. When we loose the healing and releasing power of God that Jesus has already given and provided to us, THEN we will be defeating Satan.

As a strategy of warfare, be specific, tell God what you need. Ask for prayer in the name and authority of Jesus Christ as in (John 14:14), with the laying on of hands in faith, being anointed with oil as in (James 5:14) and (Mark 16:17-18). Have the people praying for you agreeing with you according to (Matthew 18:19), ordering the demonic principality who ordered the attack against you to be bound and release the attack on you, loosing the healing power of God to saturate and fill you from the inside out. Then believe you received what you have prayed for as in (Mark 11:24).

Spirit of Error

Some of the manifestations are false teachings and doctrines, being unteachable, being unsubmissive, defensive and argumentative attitudes, confusion, lies and deception. This spirit works in collusion with many other demonic spirits to bring about these manifestations. For example when a false teaching that healing does not take place today is taught, it then opens the door for the spirit of infirmity to be received. When a false teaching that the occult, horoscope, fortune tellers, astrology, are good, it opens the door for the spirit of divination. When people are taught that pornography, sex among the unmarried, drugs, and so on is ok, then it can open the door to the spirit of bondage and a perverse spirit.

(1 John 4:6): "We are of God: he that knoweth God heareth us; he that is not of God heareth not us, hereby know we the spirit of truth and the spirit of error."

(2 Peter 2:18-19): "For they speak great swelling words of vanity, they allure through the lust of the flesh, through much wantonness, those that were clean escaped from them who live in error While they promise them liberty, they themselves are the servants of corruption: for of whom a man is overcome, of the same is he brought in bondage."

The spirit of error is on the rise through false teachers, false doctrines that are being taught, through cults and religions, some that we see in our hometowns every day. They often deny Jesus as the son of God and the redemptive work of His shed blood on the cross. Some deny the reality of an eternal punishment in Hell for those who never believe. The lying spirit is very active in these false religions.

I knew a minister a few years ago who said God had given him an explanation of the book of Revelation. His revelation of Revelation was totally different from anything I had ever heard. I decided to stick with what my Bible said.

Many times, false teachers will use just enough of the Bible to hook people, while leaving out the main points of salvation, healing, or acknowledging God as the Creator. Satan will allow people to believe what almost sounds right. But if it denies the shed blood of Jesus and his work on the cross with his resurrection. If it denies Jesus being the only way to God and Heaven. If it places a human being as the mediator between God and man. If it teaches that you can pray to some dead saint from 300 years ago for answered prayers and safety. If it teaches that it was the spirit of your dead uncle Tom and aunt Sally that rescued you when you were in trouble, then it is false teaching from the spirit of error, denying Jesus as savior, and God as our father, creator and supplier and is designed to carry people to hell. Some false doctrines would have us believe that we are gods. Some would have us believe that God can be found in some object. False teachers also work through the occult, which teaches the worship of Satan and demons instead of the worship of God. We know that the spirit of Antichrist works by counterfeiting the gifts of the Holy Spirit which deceives many people.

Jesus said in (Matthew 7:21-23) that many would say haven't we done this miracle and that miracle in your name, and Jesus will say: "Depart, I never knew you." Through this, the spirits of divination, familiar spirits, and seducing spirits which cause deception, lies, attractions and fascinations with the demonic and occult, operate, being empowered by the spirit of antichrist who operates in the works of Satan as the counterfeit and exact opposite of the Holy Spirit. (1 Timothy 4:1) says that some would depart from the faith giving heed to seducing spirits and doctrines of devils.

These people are so consumed by the Spirit of error that their minds are spiritually blinded to the truth. In (2 Corinthians 4:4) Paul said the god of this world (Satan) has blinded the minds of the people so they would not believe the truth. Paul also said in (Romans 1:28) because of this they would be turned over to a reprobate mind. Some become possessed by this spirit. This is why we see people in government positions and liberals passing laws that defy sanity. When the spirit of error begins speaking into the spirit of a person as in (James 1:14-15), and they begin to listen by their own lust; and by their own will, they begin to open a door, giving legal access for this demonic spirit to feed more lies to them. Their thinking becomes so twisted that it allows their mind, their will, and their emotions (which make up the soul) to be controlled. This affects their lives physically, mentally, spiritually, and emotionally.

(Romans 6:16) says that we are the slaves and servants to whomever we obey. Have you ever seen a person who is totally convinced that they are right in believing something so ridiculous and wrong and, yet they think everyone else is wrong?

(2 Timothy 2:25-26): "In meekness instructing those who oppose themselves; if God peradventure will give them repentance to the acknowledging the truth; and that they may recover themselves out of the snare of the devil, who are taken captive by him at his will."

The only way to be set free from this spirit is through prayer and God's Word, simply believing it. Begin with the basics of Jesus' teaching in the 4 gospels, the plan of salvation, living as He teaches us, then move on to the rest of the New Testament, studying what Paul taught about God and the Christian life. Bind the spirit of error in the name and authority of Jesus Christ from operating in you and loose the spirit of truth over your mind, your will, and your emotions. Stop reading any information that is contrary to the Bible. Begin praying for God to renew and transform your mind as in (Romans 12:2).

Remember your thinking didn't get messed up overnight and probably won't be repaired overnight, but if you're constant and diligent, God will heal and give you a sound mind as in (2 Timothy 1:7). As a warfare strategy begin to memorize Scripture, using it in prayer and praise every day. Pray for God to renew your mind through the leading of the Holy Spirit. Study the books of Ephesians, Colossians, and Philippians and begin praying the same prayers that Paul prayed. It will change your life.

When dealing with someone influenced by the spirit of error, do as (2 Timothy 2:25) says and instruct them in meekness. (Galatians 6:1) tells us to restore them "gently;" we have to have patience if we're to help them recover.

Perverse Spirit

This spirit causes a wide range of attacks. Some of the manifestations are sexual perversions and sexual addictions. They include: homosexuality, lust, incest, sexual abuse, molestation, pornography, child abuse, pedophilia, fantasy lust, and breaking the spirit of a person with evil thoughts. It causes rebellion against God and uses false teachers, creating doctrinal errors, twisting God's Word to deceive people.

As I stated before I believe the spirit of error works closely with the perverse spirit. I also believe because of the work these spirits do, that both are heavily involved with idolatry. I also believe if you take part in anything that is used in idolatry worship that you are coming into agreement and covenant with all the demonic spirits involved, even if you are not performing the entire ceremony. I say this because Jesus said if you're guilty of even the smallest offense then you are guilty of the entire offense.

(Isaiah 19:14) K.J: "The Lord hath mingled a perverse spirit in the midst thereof, and they (plural, more than one spirit) have caused Egypt to err in every work." The amplified Bible says the Lord has mingled a spirit of perverseness, error, and confusion within her leaders. (James 3:16) says, "Where envying and strife there is confusion and every evil work."

Egypt was set so hard against God in demonic idol worship, sexual

194

perversion, charmers, using familiar spirits, divination that God condemned them in his Word. God said the nation that forgets Him will utterly be destroyed. God had sent Moses to them with a message, but Pharaoh hardened his heart each time and the sin continued. For this reason, God removed his hand, allowing the perverse spirit and the other spirits that were working together to create problems through the entire empire.

(Romans 1:28): "And even as they did not like to retain God in their knowledge, God gave them over to a reprobate mind, to do those things which are not convenient." This spirit must be given an open door of legal access to work.

The perverse spirit in the above Scripture affected Egypt on a leadership level from Pharaoh down. Pharaoh represented the entire nation which gave the demonic an open door to operate. The same thing happens today through government leaders who are being led by these spirits. This is why laws are passed protecting same sex marriages and taking prayer out of schools and government. We may not be able to pray out loud, but I know of school bus drivers who pray quietly for every student on their buses. Satan can't stop that!!! Jesus said the days of Noah, which included severe sexual perversion, would be repeated in the last days. Sodom and Gomorrah were also known for intense sexual perversion. In both examples homosexuality was the main offense. Judgment came to both for this sin.

The sexual appetite and the lust for pornography are never satisfied because they are under demonic slavery. It starts out simple, and the desire leads to an addictive habit and can lead to even more perverse acts such as sexual abuse, rape, and even murder. This sin will distance us from God and can even render us useless to Him. This is Satan's plan.

When we see parts of society boldly "coming out of the closet," and it is accepted by society, then we know there is more demonic activity taking place. The more of this behavior that we see, the more demonic activity must be taking place.

Please do not misunderstand me; I do not hate the homosexual, or the sexually perverse person. I worked in a ministry that reaches out to these people, that teaches them how God can help them recover and be set free. This spiritual freedom normally does not happen instantly; it is a step-by-step process. The church world just a few years ago had no tolerance for these people. They did not want them in their churches because they were SINNERS. Well, yes, they are, and they often know it. Church is where sinners need to be!

A lot of churches have gotten away from spending time on their knees. Many have traded their prayer meetings for bowling parties. They have moved away from praying in the Spirit for those who need prayer—the sinners. Many church members forget that spiritual freedom (from their addictive behaviors) for some people takes longer than it takes for others. As I said before, we must instruct them in meekness, restoring them gently, and be there for them as accountability partners when they are struggling with temptation. This is how they become free.

You must first bind the perverse spirit that is attacking your mind, your will, and your emotions in the name and authority of Jesus Christ. You must take measures to stay away from the places and things that bring about the temptations. This might include the computer, book stores, strip clubs, and even some friends if they enable you. You know the places and things where they are. Then, find an accountability partner you can trust of your same sex, who is spiritually mature, and who has won victory in the same area. You must also spend time with God in prayer and Bible reading daily. Do not be discouraged if you feel you are not making much progress at first; you may slip from time to time, but if you stick with you it you will have victory.

Pornography was the hardest bondage in my life to break. I was sincere; I didn't want to do it. I would promise God that I'd never do it again and I would do it all over again. Don't promise God you will never do it again; He doesn't require you to do that simply because if you do fall then you may be tempted to lie to Him or to yourself. I had to realize that I could not do this by myself; victory would only come with God's help. I had to turn all my will and my control over to Him.

As a strategy of warfare, I told Satan that when I was tempted I would pray. Then if he continued I would read the bible. Then if he didn't stop I would memorize some scripture. And THEN if he didn't stop I would find someone to witness to. Well over the next few years, I did a lot of praying, read a lot of the bible, memorized a lot of the bible, and found some people to witness to. By all this I was building a spiritual foundation. After a while I realized I was stronger and was no longer struggling with temptation.

Spirit of Whoredoms

This spirit has manifestations that include: adultery, unfaithfulness, fornication, uncontrollable sexual perversions, immorality, idolatry, exhibitionism, fantasies of lust, masturbation, pornography, homosexuality, incest, seduction, soul and body prostitution, dissatisfaction, transvestism, and various excessive appetites.

(Hosea 4:12): "My people (habitually) ask counsel at their stocks (idols) and their staff (divining rods and oracles of instruction) which declareth unto them: for the spirit of whoredoms hath caused them to err and they have gone (into idolatry) a whoring from their God." Not only was this worshipping idols, but they had made the thing they lusted after a god and idol to themselves.

This verse says, "My people," if God's chosen people could be guilty of these sins, then we need to realize we can be guilty of this, too. The spirit of whoredoms, which Webster's dictionary describes as prostitution, is working strong in idolatry, where all kinds of sexual perversions were involved. Taking part in these perversions, even though you are not fully involved in idolatry; makes you guilty of this sin. This can open up generational curses for your descendants if you are involved in sexual perversions, fornication, and adultery because of the soul and spirit ties that are created. This opens the door of legal access for attack from all the spirits who are involved. There are spiritual attacks planned against you, and your church, on a very high level. The spirit of Jezebel, (Revelation 2:20) was guilty of seducing men into fornication. The spirit of perversion, the lying spirit, the spirit of bondage, the spirit of error, and the spirit of antichrist are involved in this, working together to bring you, your descendants, and your church under the bondage of generational curses, at the least.

When a person relies on drugs or alcohol to help them cope instead of God, or they rely on another person for peace, joy and strength instead of God, then they "have gone a whoring" (spiritual prostitution), and they are committing spiritual adultery and idolatry.

(Galatians 5:19-21): "Now the works of the flesh are manifest, which are these; adultery, fornication (sexual immorality), uncleanness, (the Greek word here is "akatharsia" and means whatever is the opposite, homosexuality, lesbianism, bestiality, and all forms of sexual perversions), lasciviousness, (lustfulness, sexual lewdness, incest, pornography, filthy thoughts) Idolatry, (doctrinal error) witchcraft, hatred, variance, (arguing, sowing discord, disputes) emulations, (jealousies) murders, drunkenness, reveling (rioting, parties with loud and wild music and activities), and such. This spirit is very strong in the pornography industry and causes many to struggle in this area. The battle takes place in the mind, the will and the emotions. The spirit of whoredoms also works through all these with each one giving it an open door of legal access.

(Hosea 5:4): "Their deeds do not permit them to return to their God. For the spirit of whoredom is within them, and they do not know their God." This is an example of the spirit working with the spirit of error. The people were deceived and then believed the wrong information, their minds were taken over and controlled by error to the point they went into apostasy and became reprobates from God as in (Romans 1:28).

We can see the effects of this spirit working in everyday life in the way men and women dress. It is normal now to see women and young girls dressing where there is more skin showing than what is covered. This makes it impossible within a man's own power and ability to not look and think lustful thoughts. Only with God's power can you not do it. These thoughts create a battle in the mind, the will, and the emotions. Many times, this leads to sexual abuse and molestation. We see this happening in the lack of morals, where most television programs are about witchcraft, sexual immorality, and how they can cheat someone. We see this in the changing of laws for liberals and against the conservative way of life. This is a very strong principality and it is leading the thoughts of the ungodly.

In (2 Corinthians 10:5), Paul tells us to cast down every imagination of our thoughts. This means to destroy and demolish all false religious teachings, mythology, metaphysics, philosophies, and everything that is set against God. Verse 4 tells us that all of this will create spiritual and mental strongholds. When we allow these perverse thoughts of sex, pornography, drugs, alcohol and other things to dominate our thoughts, it will create these strongholds. Each time you allow it, you are giving more and more of yourself over to it, giving Satan control.

The word "stronghold" means a place having defenses and fortifications. You are either building defenses for God or for Satan and the demonic. You do this by your choices and what you allow. Some people may say, "I can't help it, the thoughts are there all the time."

As a strategy of warfare as I have said before, you must spend daily time with God in prayer, Bible study, praise and worship. God's Word can break through this spiritual attack. But you have to do your part. Turn the television off ungodly programming and have the movie channels taken off your cable/satellite package. Stay away from book stores that would supply ungodly material. Stay away from places of entertainment that supply ungodly viewing. If you don't it only feeds the lust and you will never be free. You must clean up what comes out of your mouth, and what goes into your eyes and ears. Stop going to the places and to the people that enable you to continue in any perverse behavior.

Spirit of Haughtiness or Pride

The word "haughty" means to have and to show great pride for yourself and contempt for others and to be arrogant. Manifestations are pride, bragging, stubbornness, gossip, scorn, controlling, criticism, domineering, egotism, competitiveness, contentiousness, overbearing, stubbornness, superiority, self-righteousness, smug attitude, and mockers.

(Proverbs 16:18): "Pride goes before destruction and a haughty spirit before a fall." Satan was the first to fall because of pride and haughtiness. He said "I" will be like the most high in (Isaiah 14:14). We need to always depend on God and not our own ability. I like what my pastor says, "God, if you don't, I can't." (Job 41:34) says Satan is a king over all the children of pride. He was the first to commit the sin of pride in (Isaiah 14:14). (Proverbs 11:2) says that when pride comes, then comes shame. (Proverbs 13:10) says that pride brings contention and strife between people and nations. (Proverbs 29:23): "A man's pride shall bring him low: but honor shall uphold the humble in spirit." (Proverbs 29:1) tells us rebellion against God and leadership shall be destroyed. The book of Proverbs uses the word haughty in conjunction with the word "scorner" where they rejected the gospel as in (2 Timothy 4:3). (2 Timothy 3:5) describes it as "Having a form of Godliness, but denying God's power."

(Romans 1:22): "The reprobates were commending themselves as being very wise when God said they were fools." (Luke 18:11-12) tells about the pride and the arrogance of the Pharisee who was bragging on himself in fasting, praying, and paying his tithes. But it was only for show and not from the heart. (1 Samuel 15:23) tells us about the sin of rebellion, witchcraft, sin and idolatry. (Jeremiah 49:16) in the amplified Bible says: "Your object of horror, your idol has deceived you, and the pride of your own heart has deceived you." This refers to the Edomite God Asherah, who was a monstrous demonic idol god that caused confusion and deception. Paul said in (Colossians 2:18) to let no one defraud, trick or deceive you through pride and in worshipping angels. Again, the spirit of error is probably involved here also. So when you put all of this together we see that an excessive, ungodly pride and arrogance comes from none other than the demonic working under Satan's orders, who is the father of all pride, lies, confusion, strife, contention and rebellion over all people and all nations of the world.

We also find that pride is the main ingredient in the fall of all people and every empire. We see conquering empires from centuries past that were in rebellion against God due to idolatry, destroyed and nonexistent today. But look at Israel. Israel is still flourishing today because of God's blessings. (1 Peter 5:6) tells us to "Humble yourselves therefore under the mighty hand of God that HE may exalt you in due time." When we give God the praise, the worship, the reverence, the intense love, the admiration and the devotion that He deserves not just in church, but in our daily lives, then that will take care of the pride problem. Because then, and only then, we will not be giving any worship anywhere else because true worship of God is an intense humbling experience.

The Spirit of Antichrist

By this term, although there will be an actual man, the spirit of antichrist is an actual demonic spirit at work today. This spirit coordinates the functions of many demonic spirits to deceive and to teach false doctrines. In (1 John 4:3) the spirit of antichrist was very active; it has been active since the beginning of time. It is the spirit of antichrist that empowers the demonic forces to work through the occult. This spirit is against God, Jesus, His teachings and His doctrine, the miracles of God, the divinity of Jesus as God's son, opposing and harassing saints with attacks and persecution, denies the work of the Holy Spirit, and spreads false teaching.

The antichrist spirit will affect the church today if it is not detected and cast out. It will try to destroy the anointing, try to prevent the gifts of the Holy Spirit from being active, and cause churches to focus more on material things, such as extravagant buildings, than on reaching people for Christ. It will cause some saints in the church to say, "We don't need "THOSE" kind of people in OUR church." It will try to destroy friends, families, and ministers. It will cause confusion, frustration, faultfinding, and cause church splits due to unforgiveness between Christians. It will try to take over leadership of the church in order to continue this work.

I believe at a minimum the spirit of error, spirit of python, lying spirit and the spirit of Jezebel, all work together in this attack. In the last day's the spirit of antichrist is trying to use the spirit of python in churches to prevent the great outpouring of the Spirit from taking place that is prophesied in (Joel 2:28). (Timothy 4:1-2): "Now the spirit speaks expressly, that in the latter times some shall depart from the faith, giving heed to seducing spirits and doctrines of devils; speaking lies in hypocrisy; having their conscience seared with a hot iron."

The spirit of antichrist has always been here to empower and equip the unbelievers in pagan worship, idolatry, New Age cults, secular humanism, the atheist and the occult. The spirit of antichrist is the fuel and the controlling force behind all these false religions, denying the true work of Jesus. It is teaching that man is God and has the power to save himself; they leave Jesus out of the picture.

Familiar Spirit

Familiar spirits are demonic spirits used in the occult practices of astrology, automatic writing, black magic, channeling, charmers, good luck charms, clairvoyance, conjuring spirits, casting spells, consulting the dead, mind reading, palmistry, mediums, necromancy, soothsaying, spirit guides, witches, warlocks, sorcery, horoscopes and Ouija boards. They also work as reconnaissance and surveillance much as a military recon unit would gathering information by spying. They learn everything they can about people for many different reasons. The information they gain is used by the entire network of the demonic. The information is given to the four levels of demonic warfare, the principalities, power, rulers of darkness, and the workers spiritual wickness. They use this information against the human race in accusations to try in gaining legal rights of attack. They custom design temptations and attacks on individuals based on the information they receive. They use this to attack families, churches, ministries, and create strongholds. By spying on individuals they can determine how strong a believer is, where their weaknesses are, and even their strengths. This is another way they custom design attacks. They work with the spirit of divination and feed the fortune tellers with all the information they use to deceive. People are deceived because the fortune teller or the medium in a haunted house or on a police case has details that no one told them. That's no surprise. These familiar spirits have been there years in the past; they have gathered information of the people who lived in the house before. They know the horrific crimes that have taken place there and the people who committed them. They know your grandparents and your uncle bob. They know the sexual abuse you went through when you were 10 years old. So, it is no surprise that the fortune teller can tell you about it. They have records on every individual that has ever lived on the face of the earth. This is how people are deceived into thinking the haunting of a house is a civil war soldier who never passed over because they have unfinished business. Or that it is the spirit of a young lady who was murdered who has never passed over because she is still trying to figure out what happened to her. And history reveals the lady lived in the house and looks exactly like the spirit that has been seen.

To start with (Luke 12) tells us the rich man died and in hell he opened his eyes. No hesitation, no delays, no wondering around to settle any unfinished business, but a direct, instant relocation to eternity. They do not come out of hell to roam the earth again. The haunting of a house is nothing more than a demonic spirit with all the information from the familiar spirits to imitate whoever they want to. They use this deceit to keep people blind to the truth.

The spirit of antichrist uses the familiar spirits with this information to counterfeit the gifts of the Holy Spirit, through the occult to deceive people away from God and to serve "other gods" as in (Deuteronomy 13:13) The Holy Spirit of God using someone working through the gift of knowledge and prophesy can reveal things that only God can tell you. All of this is condemned by God because it falls under idolatry. The use of any of these will open doors to demonic attacks, and even possession, because you are coming into agreement and covenant with them. Involvement in these can and will cause demonic manifestations in your home, or as what many people call a haunted house. I have on several occasions been asked by someone to come pray over their home which was inhabited by demonic spirits. This is not an area of ministry that I chose for myself, but apparently God chose it for me.

The Tormentors

Repeated unforgiveness, soul and spirit ties can bring on generational curses from many different directions. In (Matthew 18:34) Jesus said that God would turn the servant that was unwilling to forgive his fellow servant over to the tormentors.

The word "tormentors" means a source of great pain or anguish, a great source of anxiety, to cause great physical, mental, spiritual, and emotional pain, to annoy and to harass. The word "annoys" means to hate and to irritate by action. The word tormentors can also be traced to the word demon that causes all this torment.

Several years ago, I knew where an old man lived who had severe mental problems. He would be in his yard sometimes in fierce anger, chasing people down the road with his belt in his hand as they passed by his house. Other times he would be standing in his yard laughing and pointing at people passing by. Now, you have to understand all my life I have been (and still am) a practical joker. So, naturally, I would go out of my way to go by his house just to harass him to chase me because, like everyone else, I thought it was fun. After a while, God began to teach me the things that I am now writing about.

One day, as I was passing by doing the usual harassment, the Holy Spirit spoke to me: "You're not harassing the old man, you are harassing the spirits inside him and that is causing them to torment him." With that conviction of the Holy Spirit, I asked forgiveness for my actions and never did it again. Was I tempted to do it? Oh, sure I was, remember I'm a practical joker. Hey, God gave me this personality; just ask my wife, my sons, coworkers, people at church, the dog, the cat. Ok, I admit it; no one is safe around me. But I do try to control it.

Territorial Spirits

Geographic areas of the earth are ruled by territorial principalities that can bring that area under a generational curse, based on the level of obedience to those spirits the people offer them.

The Canaanite god Baal had several localities named after him: Baal-peor, Baal-gad, Baal-hermon and others, which suggest that Baal was the ruling principality, or spiritual owner of that geographical area. Since Baal was the god believed to bless fertility, agriculture, animals, and the people, it was thought that if they named an area after him, he would take notice to their reverence and bless them.

In the (18th chapter of Leviticus) it mentions many different types of sexual sins that God calls abominations. The word "abomination" means a strong dislike, to hate, and to loathe. He says this will bring a curse. The 27th verse says even the houses and lands where these sins took place were defiled. The word "defiled" means "to make filthy or profane;" filthy means "obscenity," "profane" means disrespect for sacred things. In our society today, there is more disrespect for God, the Godly, and our rights than ever before in our lifetimes.

But that is no surprise because Jesus said this would happen. He said they would hate us because they hated him. This hate comes from these territorial spirits who are causing spiritual warfare against us.

We see from (Ephesians 1:22, Ephesians 3:10, Ephesians 6:12; Colossians 1:16 and 1 Peter 3:22) that there are different ranks of authority in these territorial spirits of the Satanic-demonic kingdom. If you do not believe that Satan has a kingdom, remember what Jesus said in (Matthew 12:26): "and if Satan be divided against himself how shall his kingdom stand." Jesus admitted in that verse that Satan does, in fact, have a kingdom. When Jesus was fasting for 40 days, Satan came to Him, showing Him all the kingdoms and said, "if you will bow down and worship me all these kingdoms I will give to you." He was not just talking about the earthly kingdoms such as Rome and Jerusalem. Knowing what we see in our earthly realm reflects what is the spirit realm Satan was offering Him the demonic kingdoms that ruled over those earthly territories.

I believe this shows that when the people of a geographical area, as a majority or a whole, give their wills over to the control of the demonic spirits that are in control of that area, negative effects take place in that area. Giving over one's will constitutes worship to those demonic spirits and brings the people and the land itself under a generational curse.

We can see this in places like Las Vegas and San Francisco, through gambling and sexual immorality. We see it in New Orleans where the witchcraft and voodoo spirits are strong. We also see it in countries like Haiti where demonic worship is rampant, and India, where sexual perversion is very strong.

I know of a town near where I grew up that had a very tainted past. It was always a very economically, spiritually and morally depressed town. People have told me that they could feel a heavy spiritual oppression as soon as they hit the city limits, and that this feeling went away as soon as they left the area. One minister I knew, not knowing how well acquainted with this town I was, told me about this town and how God had opened his eyes while he drove through it. He said that he saw what looked like gargoyles sitting on the tops of buildings and telephone poles. It was the same town. On a funny, but truthful note, the running joke was that "everyone" in this town had the same Uncle Bob; he was the "same" because he was related to everyone on both sides of the family. Go figure that one out.

"Molech," god of the Ammonites, whose name means "king and ruler," was the fire god. He had gained so much power and control over the people of Ammon that he required newborn babies to be sacrificed and burned to death in his arms and the people obeyed him. This is the same god as "Chemosh" (meaning subduer) of the Moabites. He had gained power and control over the people as well. This was shown through devotion, sacrifice and worship to him. By this, he had the ruling power over that geographic area.

Could it be that he is responsible for the abortion industry today, giving him devotion, sacrifice and worship just as the Ammonites and the Moabites did thousands of years ago? This gives him more and more territory, all of which is under his power and control. In Leviticus and Deuteronomy, we find that demonic worship brought about curses and opened doors to the demonic, giving them free legal access to continue afflicting future generations by the same power and control. This is something to think about. You will find all these same sins have followed man throughout history.

The word "principality" means a prince or a chief that rules over a territory. The Greek word for principalities is "archas" which refers to the top ranking demonic positions over geographic regions of the earth. (Ephesians 6:12) in the amplified Bible uses the word "despotisms" as meaning basically the same thing but explains it a little deeper. "Despotism" means a system, or government, with a ruler having absolute authority over; a form of government system ruled by a tyrant dictator, and a master of slaves. (Ephesians 1:20-21) says that we are seated with Christ on heavenly places far above all principality and power.

The word "powers" means one with influence over other "nations," a person or thing having influence, force or authority, legal authority and vigor, force and strength. Here it is referring to demonic spirits who are second in command below the principality that has power over geographic regions, broken down to smaller areas, with others under their authority to carry out commands and strategies against the saints. The word "powers" in Greek is "exousia" and means delegated authority. The word "delegate" means a person authorized to act under the rule of another's representation, to entrust power and authority to another of higher authority. They are given orders to be carried out for all kinds of evil and warfare against the saints.

The Methods of Demonic Attacks

Demonic forces want you to blame others for the problems that you have created yourself. You didn't get into this mess overnight, and the answer doesn't always come to you overnight. Having worked in a recovery ministry, I've seen many people who would not keep with the program because they didn't immediately see results and freedom. We must grow in God and his Word, and this is what brings the freedom.

The demonic want you to believe the situation is bigger than God by focusing on the problem instead of what God's Word says. Find Scripture relating to your problem and memorize it; use it in prayer and praise. This will build your faith level and will bring the answer.

If you do not use God's Word and prayer, Satan can bring confusion to the situation. "Confusion" means disorder. You will be in turmoil over the right decision and that can lead to a hasty decision which will create even more problems, bringing about more confusion. Remember, when you are in confusion about something, it is not of God. Do nothing until you have prayed about it and have received peace from God on what to do.

Chapter 20

Jezebel

The Jezebel spirit is a strongman spirit that uses other weaker spirits, who are working under its authority, to carry out its plan. The Jezebel spirit is named after the Sidonian princess Jezebel who married King Ahab and was responsible for having many of God's prophets killed. This is a good description of what this spirit wants to do. This is also a religious spirit that works in many churches to destroy the ministry. We can also see this spirit in the workplace where it can control and attempt to ruin the lives of many believers. Many times, the person being used will have an unbelievable control over weak-minded superiors.

As a Star Trek fan, I'm reminded of the Borg. The Borg was a collective of many individuals who had been taken over. Their former lives, and their ability to think for themselves, their own desires, were no longer their own. They operated as one unit for the sole purpose of control and domination by destroying lives and civilizations to grow the Borg collective.

In much the same way the spirit of whoredom, spirit of perversions, divination and witchcraft, spirit of error and many others demonic spirits work with Jezebel, making up the total collective of all these spirits that makes the Jezebel spirit so strong.

The spirit of Jezebel is mentioned in both the Old and the New Testament and is present at the end times. There are thousands of years between these two periods of time, proving the spirit of Jezebel did not die when the woman Jezebel died.

(Revelation 2:20): "Nevertheless I have a few things against you, because you "sufferest," (meaning to allow, permit, not to restrain, to let one do as they wish) that woman Jezebel, who calls herself a prophetess, to teach and seduce my servants to commit sexual immorality and eat things sacrificed to idols."

The spirit of Jezebel and Beliel work together because they both have a common goal, to seduce God's servants to commit fornication, death, to deceive through false teaching and to draw God's people away from God to serve idols. Remember what we studied on Beliel in (Deuteronomy 13:13)? One of his goals is to draw people away from God to serve other gods; in other words, other demonic spirits. Beliel also promoted sexual immorality of all kinds, as does the spirit of Jezebel. The spirit of Jezebel has been responsible for the fall of many churches and ministers.

The word "fornication" refers to a brothel; the word "seduce" means to tempt to wrong doing, to entice into having illicit sexual intercourse. From there we get the word "whoredom" which the dictionary says means prostitution; "debauchery," which means seduce, to lead astray morally, to corrupt, and to orgy. This is in common with Beliel and many other demonic spirits worshipped as idols who promote extreme sexual immorality with their worship.

In (1 Kings 16:31), Jezebel was a real woman who in this verse becomes King Ahab's wife. The name "Jezebel" in Hebrew means "without cohabitation." Jezebel will not tolerate, or "coexist" with, someone it cannot dominate. (1 Kings 16:31) is the first mention of her in Scripture. Jezebel's father was a high priest of Beliel. She was also a worshipper of Baal. Jezebel used sex to get everything that she wanted. It was her power. She killed God's prophets, and controlled them through fear. In (1 Kings 21:8) she forged letters in Ahab's name and sealed them with his seal, sending them to the elders in the city.

I know a Jezebel who has tried to come in the name of the pastor saying, "Pastor isn't going to like this, he will shut down this entire ministry," which was a lie, because I already knew the pastor's heart in the matter. A Jezebel will try any kind of seduction to gain control and power, using manipulation and intimidation.

King Ahab, her husband, was totally dominated by her. She introduced the worship of Ashtoreth, who was the female counterpart of Beliel, supposedly the wife of Beliel. Ashtoreth was the Canaanite's main female deity. They believed she was embodied in the moon. The idol was a female with a crescent moon on her brow and was set up in temples. She was worshipped with the most perverted forms of sexual immorality and perversions imaginable. These were performed by priestess-prostitutes offering their services. There were also male prostitutes there, committing sodomy. This goes hand-in-hand with the characteristics of Beliel. Many Israelites turned from worshipping God to worship Beliel and Ashtoreth, all because of Jezebel.

The spirit of Jezebel can come to us through witchcraft and rebellion, where it is at work today in churches and in the world system. She can control through flattery, seduction, tears, emotions, hurts, wounds, poor health, excessive need for attention and sympathy, and by her words.

This spirit wants to destroy the entire body of Jesus Christ, the Church, and wants to operate in the presence of believers, obtaining positions of power and influence. These positions can include Pastors and their assistants, church secretaries, music leaders and other church members. Sometimes, those under this spirit will work their way up close to the pastor so they can push their way into a higher position. This spirit often works through women, but can operate in men, too.

The Jezebel spirit steals your peace. It brings strife and confusion into the church. Paul said, "For where strife and confusion are there is every evil work." It can bring sickness, discord, and adultery into the church. I was once over a single's ministry in a certain church, and it amazed me how much premarital sex was going on, not only between the single people but also between those who were married.

A friend of mine who was in ministry at another church told me of the level of deception in his church. Some of the people went on outings where adultery and skinny-dipping would take place. This is exactly the description of (Revelation 2:20). All of this can bring curses and generational curses.

One way this spirit tears down ministers and ministries is this: A person feels the call of God for a certain area. This is a real and genuine call of God, where their call is very clear. They start out their calling seeing great things happen, they are very excited, but at some point, someone begins to criticize them, telling them they are not doing things right. These criticizers are sowing discord and causing doubt. "Well God hasn't called "you" to preach." "Well you don't do it like Brother so in so does." You may not have the same anointing that brother so in so has. God may have given you different insight in the word than another minister. They begin to start internal fights, not even knowing they are being used by the demonic. After a time, the person who was called will begin to doubt his or her abilities and start doubting God as well. If the person walks away from their calling, the demonic spirit has won.

In the story of Nehemiah, as he was rebuilding the city walls, he encountered the enemy coming out daily, trying to discourage him, so he would not accomplish the task. But Nehemiah kept working, ignoring the demonic accusations against him. He kept his focus on the call God had given him.

The human Jezebel we have to be aware of is power-hungry and control-hungry. She respects only another Jezebel who is stronger than she. She feels all others are inferior to her. No one is as wise as she. They are usually very gifted and talented people. This is part of their power to influence and deceive people, which is how they get into places of authority. They are very faithful attendees, great supporters, and volunteers. They are often over-achievers which can cause them to be admired by the weak, often causing others to never achieve their goal because of criticism. They sometimes lack a social personality, but are very outspoken and aggressive; always adding their opinions of how "they" think things should be run. The weak minded will easily fall under their control and, many times, will be the first to defend them.

These people will begin planting verbal seeds of discord; they threaten, manipulate, discourage, and entice people to gain control. They use doubt, slander and gossip about the pastor, the church, and other leaders to tear down churches, families, friends and relationships. This is why you go into a town and you have 15 different churches of the same denomination within a mile and half of each other; it is because Jezebel tore them all apart. It tears apart individual ministries inside the church as well. I have seen this happen. When she is in the church, the movement of God is hindered. Freedom, happiness, peace, and joy are replaced with confusion, disharmony, and a striving, spiteful spirit. The attendance and tithes begin to decrease. But, there is more.

There is also a decrease in new salvations. The church becomes dead and dried up because the Holy Spirit is not allowed to have His freedom. The church and pastor lose their vision. It can even cause the pastor to be burned out and want to get out of ministry completely. This is the goal of Jezebel. It brings criticism and false accusations against ministers. This was also the effect that the real woman Jezebel had on Elijah.

I believe the Jezebel spirit works through political liberals and the feminist, because for Jezebel the marriage to Ahab was political. It was to gain control of Israel through Ahab using false religion. I believe that we see this in federal government today. I've said this at the beginning of this chapter, but I need to repeat it. Her goal is to do the same work as Beliel, who is the higher authority, as in (Deuteronomy 13:13), causing men to be led away so that they worship other gods (demonic spirits). This draws them into error, dragging them into bondage, which brings curses upon them.

Look at how the liberals have taken prayer and God out of the schools. How they have allowed homosexuality to run rampant, bringing Godly marriage under attack. Homosexuals are drawn into influential positions as politicians and entertainers to make it look more socially acceptable. The Jezebel spirit is working with Beliel behind the proliferation of internet pornography, using this to bring believers and non-believers into bondage and curses. Jezebel uses this to bring people into adultery and whoredom, which means prostitution. "Prostitution" means faithless and unworthy, engaging in promiscuous sexual activity. This has direct connections all the way back to the Old Testament. In many Scriptures this is shown to be one of the main activities of idol worship; namely, sexual orgies.

Another word that comes into this is "debauchery," which means to seduce from chastity, to be led away from virtue, to morally corrupt, and orgy. Jezebel and Beliel work in collusion together to promote sodomy, homosexuality, incest, rape, immorality and perversion all kinds. Jezebel and Beliel both drive men and women with an appetite for sex that cannot ever be satisfied. This spirit is behind the "spas," or what was once known as massage parlors, and we find them in abundance around the country. We see them opening in many places. These spas are often disguised as legitimate places for massage therapy, but are nothing more than places of prostitution. Inside are hot tubs, and "whatever" sexual extras that you want to pay for and I do mean whatever. Your money is the only limit. In the chapter on idol worship I have traced this activity back to idol worship.

There was one of these spas on my way to work and home. I would pass it every day and say, "In the name of Jesus, you are cursed by your own sin and you are closed down and out of business." Shortly after that, it burned to the ground, but they rebuilt it. Later, the sheriff's department raided it and today it is closed permanently. Never give up praying.

Beliel's works include idolatry and so does Jezebel's.

215

(Deuteronomy 13:13) and (Revelation 2:20) proves this and links them together.

This spirit also wants to physically kill just as the real woman Jezebel did to the prophets of God; it wants also to discredit the servants of God. It wants to gain power through recognition; it loves to be praised, internally worshipping herself. She can't stand for others getting attention over her, and will try preventing others from getting that attention. She must have control in her home, must be worshipped by her family, and needs to be their goddess.

She is very bossy, domineering, demanding authority, and offended (to the point of rage) if her authority is questioned. She yields to no one. Many times, she wants to command people who are not under her authority. Once a woman that I did not know, but owned the property next to mine, came to my door telling us what we were and weren't going to do. She was told to stay off my property and never come back. Later we tried to help a couple who were temporarily homeless. We have rules to live by in our home. She begins telling us, "Well if I want to do it, I'll do it, I don't care what you say." "If I don't want to help clean the house, then I won't clean." They were told to find another place to live, and I put all their belongings outside. Sound harsh? Well I will not allow the Jezebel spirit to have a foothold in my home or on my property.

I've known several in ministry like this and usually they are very good at hurting and offending people by their words, not caring who or how bad they hurt someone. She won't allow anyone to come between her and the object of her desired control without an attack, trying to destroy their reputation and undermining their authority.

Once, at a particular church, I witnessed the pastor having to dismiss a Jezebel from the congregation. These people do not care who they step on to get where they want to go. They submit only to gain control. This person had gotten their hand into almost every ministry in that church, and ended up being dismissed from at least two other churches after that. These people often want to control the finances since finances control the church's vision. Weaker people will, without even thinking about it, blindly submit to Jezebel's every demand. Weak people will think the Jezebel is superior and smarter than anyone else, and the Jezebel loves it.

The Jezebel spirit wants to dominate and emasculate men spiritually and emotionally. I have witnessed Jezebels doing this in public. I have watched some men cower before them. This spirit hates men and wants to destroy them, especially when she can't control them. She is attracted to weak men. Ahab was weak, as are a lot of men who give into this spirit. They become slaves of the woman who says, "no man is going to tell me what to do." They often control them through sex. There are two kinds of people in the world: those who rule and those who are ruled. A Jezebel wants to rule.

Jezebels hate anyone in authority over them because they are power hungry. Often, they are hard workers and that works well in their hindering others. Often are jealous of others getting more attention than them. Sometimes, they are a perfectionist, after all no one can do it as good as they can. If you don't believe me, just ask them.

Sometimes when there is more than one Jezebel in the same location they can be drawn to each other, if one is stronger than the others. I have seen this happen, and have had to work in ministry with a few people who were under the spirit of Jezebel. I had to keep a close eye on them, making sure that they did not get any leadership positions in the ministry where I was involved. I watched their facial expressions when it was announced that someone else was assigned a leadership position over them. And I saw one become very angry when they didn't get the attention they thought they deserved. The face said it all. I witnessed a new church being led away from the pastor's vision because of a Jezebel.

Elijah was a man of God who saw God perform many mighty miracles. God led him in the wilderness and protected him when

Ahab's armies were trying to kill him. He prayed and watched as God rained fire down out of heaven and killed the priests of Baal. But even with all of that, one earthly woman named Jezebel, possessed by a demonic spirit, intimidated Elijah. She caused him to be depressed to the point that he ran away into the desert, asking God to kill him. This sad request based on just one threatening message. Jezebel had, and still has today, a very powerful demonic anointing. Elijah allowed her to steal the focus of his vision, lose faith in God, bring fear and confusion, caused him to want to leave the ministry and almost cost him his life.

If you look at ministry today you can see the same thing still happening when ministers become weary in the battle. But staying in the battle is the way to win, even if you're in the desert. The desert isn't the best place to be, but God sent Jehu to avenge the prophets Jezebel had killed. Jezebel was killed when she was thrown out of an upstairs window and eaten by dogs.

You see if you are in a desert-place God can send a Jehu to you. Begin to fast and pray whether you feel like it or not. When Jesus was in the desert wilderness during his 40 days of fasting, Satan came to him to tempt him. But Jesus defeated Satan once and for all when He said on the cross, "It is finished" in (John 19:30). But people overlook this. Jesus already had the power, He promised it to us in (John 14:12a): "Verily, verily, I say unto you, he that believeth on me, the works that I do shall he do also." In (Luke 10:19) He said, "Behold, I give you power over all the power of the enemy." He had already given this power to the 70 disciples. But although he was the son of God, Jesus still had to achieve this power, so He could give us an example of how we could achieve it also. Or it would be impossible for us to have it. When did this happen? In the desert, while being tempted during the 40-day fast when He did not yield.

If we want this power, we must follow His example. Starting with a 40-day fast is a good way to do it. You can make your desert a new beginning and overcome the Jezebels.

Chapter 21

Breaking Soul Ties and Closing Open Doors

In (2 Corinthians 6:14-15), it says, "Do not be unequally yoked together with unbelievers, for what fellowship has righteousness with lawlessness? And what communion has light with darkness? And what concord has Christ with Beliel? Or what part hath he that believeth with an infidel?"

None of these things can co-exist together at one time in the same place in unity. The Bible doesn't use the term "soul tie," but it speaks of souls being knit, joined and connected spiritually. The meaning here is to be glued together. In the demonic world, soul ties can serve as bridges to link two people to pass demonic garbage through. Soul ties can be created in different ways. Soul ties can create the possibly for one person to manipulate and control another person. In (Matthew 18) Jesus told a story about the servant who did not have mercy on his follow servant. He would not forgive him, so in verse 34 his master had him turned over to the "tormentors," the word "tormentor" means one who torments. The word "torment" means great pain or anguish, a source of pain, anxiety, to cause great physical, mental, emotional, and spiritual pain, anguish, to annoy and to harass.

Looking at this in a spiritual sense, if you have unforgiveness toward a person, and that person just happens to be oppressed, tormented physically, mentally, spirituality or emotionally because of sin they themselves have committed, then they've opened a door, and given demonic spirits the legal rights (which I'll get into later) to torment them; then the unforgiveness that you carry toward them can create a spiritual soul tie between you and them, thus giving the same legal access to the same demonic spirits attacking them to attack you also. Your unforgiveness can create a spiritual soul tie that can bring sickness and oppression into your body. This may be one of the leading reasons that keep people from being healed, physically, mentally, and emotionally. With unforgiveness, God will not hear your prayers.

In (Ephesians 5:31) we see that when two get married a soul tie is formed. They become one flesh, joined together. (1 Corinthians 6:16): "Know ye not that he which is joined to an harlot is one body and shall be one flesh." This is another way that soul ties are created. Adultery, fornication, and sex outside of marriage also creates a soul tie to all the soul ties that they've had in the past. The demonic spirits tormenting or affecting all those partners of the past now can have a legal right to torment you. Spiritually looking at a person with many unforgiven partners would reveal many different people attached to them. This is why soul ties must be broken in Jesus' name.

A soul tie can also be formed if a person is so close to another person that they take their advice over God's Word. In (1 Corinthians 6:16) the word "joined" means to connect, to become a part or member of something. This is spiritual transference. When a person comes under the curse of a soul or spirit tie with another person, they are joined spiritually to this person. Satan and the demonic now have free legal right and access to attack the second person. Many times, this transference will take on the form of attack in both people. This is how people have the problems they have that affect their health, their souls, their minds, their will and their emotions.

Objects given to you through sinful or occultic relationships, occultic items used in ceremonies, books on the occult, certain video games, Satanic and demonic movies, and charms can have a demonic spirit connected to them that can cause curses and soul ties. This leads to demonic vows which also causes soul ties and gives the enemy legal control and access into your life.

(Leviticus 18:27) says that lands and houses can become defiled from these types of sins. (Leviticus 18) lists many different sins that God said are an abomination to him. People involved in these abominations can be linked together by soul ties. One of which included worship of a demonic god named Molech, whose name means king; he was the fire god. He is recorded as one of the warrior demons. He is listed as one of the chief generals of Satan's demonic army. The characteristics of Molech are not that far from those of Beliel, so I believe this is one the demonic spirits in collusion with Beliel. Remember "collusion" means a secret agreement for fraudulent purpose or conspiracy. Worship of this god included sexual perversion, prostitution, and human baby sacrifices. Does this sound familiar today? What about abortion? I believe it is very possible this is the demon controlling the abortion industry today. Did you ever think of abortion as sacrificing to a demonic god?

Molech is also associated with the feminist movement (Jezebel), and both are in collusion with Beliel. Wow, these practices and associations "will" cause spirit soul ties and "will" set generational curses into action, funneled and passed down to future family generations. Examples of how this might occur when being linked with those participating in a séance, Satan worship, rebellion, emotional cutting, blood covenants, playing with witchcraft, Ouija boards, joining cults, witch covens, etc. All these can defile a home or a piece of property and create soul ties with those involved. Even if a horrible murder or severe physical, drug or sexual abuse has taken place in a house and property, it can set up a demonic memorial, a perpetual remembrance in the spirit realm that can open a doorway to demonic activity. If you allow yourself to become linked spiritually with these people, you are now tied to them. This can lead to different forms of manifestations in that house or on that property. In cases like this, when a new family moves into the house, the demonic spirits may not manifest immediately. They may "lay low" and observe that family to see what they are about. If the demonic believes it can control that family because they (the family) do not know God, they will attempt to do so. Therefore, you need to be careful when buying a house or property. Pray about it.

My family and had begun experiencing these kinds of

manifestations about 15 years prior to this writing. At first it scared me silly. As it went on, God began to give me dreams of what I was facing and how to fight back. His answer came to me in a dream:

I saw a demonic spirit walking up to me very slowly; it started getting down on all four feet into a pouncing position, as an animal does when it is getting ready to attack. It was growling and looked very angry and mean. As I looked at it I didn't feel any out-pouring of the Spirit, but I felt no fear. As a matter of fact, I felt about as dry spiritually as a bowl of dust, but I knew what I believed. I very calmly spoke: "In the name of Jesus." When I said Jesus' name it fell on its belly with the greatest look of fear on its face. It began to back away and would not turn its back to me. This gave me strength.

In another dream God gave me during this time, I saw a demonic spirit. It knew that I knew it was there, but it refused to look at me. It was very busy doing something with its hands, but I could not see what. As I looked at it I heard the Holy Spirit say: "Satan himself has orchestrated a plan against you, and this is the mid-ranking spirit who was sent to carry out that plan against you." As I looked at it, I noticed that there were deeply gashed wounds on its body that had healed over. I began to think: "I wonder what caused all those wounds?" Then I heard the Holy Spirit say: "Those are battle scars, where it was defeated by angels in conflicts of spiritual warfare. And the defeat was due to the prayers of the saints praying the Word of God."

In the dream I felt the anointing come over me as never before and Scripture began to pour out of me as a prayer. The demonic spirit began to back away in fear, refusing to turn its back to me until it was out of sight. I woke up and I was praying very loudly and forcefully, but it never woke my wife up who was laying there beside me. I realized then it doesn't matter if it is a dream or not, the Word of God and the authority He has given you still works.

Over time, however, the manifestations began to increase. When we bought the house that we currently live in the manifestations began to kick in shortly after we moved in. I didn't know why this was taking place. Now, I have about 10 eyewitnesses who saw and heard the same things I am about to describe.

We began seeing dark shadows and white smoky figures flying around our 14-foot living room ceilings and moving through the rooms and through the walls. Once, I saw a dark figure which was blacker than pitch that had two red eyes. All the kitchen cabinet doors started opening and closing by themselves repeatedly. Things began sliding across the kitchen counter top by themselves. Once, the front door opened very fast with no one there, and when I went to close it, the dead bolt was still extended out, which means the dead bolt had come through the wall. One night something kicked my bed very hard. The same thing happened to my oldest son, doors opening and closing repeatedly with no one there.

One night I woke up and saw the house was on fire. When I got up and began to put the fire out, the fire mysteriously vanished instantly, and nothing was burned. We would hear laughter and voices coming from empty rooms. Footsteps could be heard upstairs where no one was, and we also heard loud stomping through the house as if someone was wearing combat boots. Our beds would begin to shake as if we were experiencing an earth quake.

On another night something grabbed my son's foot and tried to pull him out of bed. The house would be engulfed with strong, putrid odors, like the worst body odor times 100 that you've ever smelled. Sometimes it would be a strong sulfur smoke smell; sometimes only I could smell it, sometimes only my wife could smell it. At times, two or more people could smell it, but never everyone at once. We could do nothing to get rid of the smell, nor could we find where it was coming from. There would be small patches, maybe 4-foot square, in the house where there would be no smell, just fresh air. But, take one step over and there it was again. Then, after maybe two hours, it would instantly vanish, with no trace of it having been there.

One day we came home and found a meat cleaver that we did not own lying on the floor. Things would disappear around the house, and sometimes they would reappear later with no explanation. One night I woke up and felt an eerie presence in my room. I just rolled over and turned my back to it, unconcerned about it, because I was not afraid of it; I just wanted to go back to sleep. Well, I guess I must have ticked it off, because I heard what sounded like a 250-pound man do a body slam against my bedroom wall. I knew what was leaving the room at that time. I knew it was demonic manifestations and something had opened the door and given it legal access and had created a spirit tie there. I was not afraid, I knew that it could not hurt us; it could only try to scare us.

You see, I knew in my spirit that there would be a time for battle, so I decided that I would just watch it, and learn from it whatever I could. We began to experience strife between everyone in the house, which we had never had before. We had always been very close. Although I knew what was going on, I was fighting thoughts like: "Why am I even here in the middle of all these crazy people, putting up with all this fussing? I need to be out of here and somewhere quiet and peaceful." That is not me. The battle was beginning to get stronger and more personal. Now I was getting ready to fight.

One night I was home by myself while everyone else was at a ball game. It started to happen again, only this time I heard the Holy Spirit say: "It's time." I got up and immediately felt the Holy Spirit come upon me very strongly. I begin to pray in the spirit, taking charge in the name and authority of Jesus Christ. I said to the principality, which oversaw originating this attack: "This is my home, my property, and my family. You are not welcome here. Now, in the name and the authority of Jesus Christ, get out and stay out."

The Holy Spirit began to take over and pray through me as I was led through the house while He did the rest of the praying. I came to a certain closet in the house, and I knew that this was the doorway between the physical and the spirit realm. Although I wasn't praying in English, I knew the Holy Spirit was commanding the doorway to be closed. And it was closed! That was the last time that any manifestations took place in our home. All the strife was gone. It was cast out that night and the doorway was closed, and the authority was taken back.

I found part of the source of the legal right that allowed it to come was from one of our sons. He had brought into our home, against our knowledge and our will, demonic books, video games, and movies. The items were very graphic, detailed material, and occultic in nature. We burned these items, and they did not want to burn even with gasoline poured on them. This took care of the problem for a while until he began bringing in more of the same items again.

After that the strife and attacks tried to come back. This time I immediately recognized what was happening.

One day I came in from work and everyone was in the kitchen fussing and arguing. I didn't say anything to anyone; I just turned and walked back outside. I didn't feel any great outpouring spiritually at that moment, but I knew the power and authority God had given me. I very calmly said: "To the main, head principality who oversees originating this attack against my family, in the name and the authority of Jesus Christ, this is "my" family, "my" house, and "my" property, you are not welcome here. Get out of "my" family, get out of "my" house, and get off "my" property in the name of Jesus, and don't come back." After that I walked back into "my" house, where "my" family was gathered. Two minutes later, as I walked back in the house, they were laughing, hugging and joking with each other. Before getting angry with your family members take action against the real cause of the problem. Not against them.

Later, I found buried in my family-ancestor history that there had been a direct connection to Satan worship. A blood-line ancestor of mine had owned a casino. I'm sure all the usual things involved in casinos were probably involved there. In the same exact location of the casino was documented proof that Satan worship had taken place at that location. I talked to an eyewitness of a ceremony there. Another person told him that both animal and human sacrifices had taken place in this general area, with a good chance it was with this same group. I believe soul ties from all this is what opened the door to what we experienced. (Leviticus 26) tells us to repent of the sins of our fathers, (or past our generations.) This is because we do not know what is in the past that can affect us now. By taking this action, we can cut off the enemy's hand against us.

Breaking ungodly soul ties is the key to deliverance. Ungodly associations cause demonic spirits to be transferred from one person to another. You must break every ungodly soul tie to be delivered from Beliel's control. Beliel uses soul ties to gain legal access that has been given to him through sin. (1 Corinthians 6:15) directly connects Beliel with unrighteousness, darkness, infidels, and idolatry. It is not strange that the first reference to Beliel in the Old Testament ties him to idolatry

Beliel is the enemy of the church and the family. Beliel will try to control the church and our families through soul ties, which will also affect us through strife, envy, contention and sexual impurity. All these will stop the movement of God's Holy Spirit, and will stop physical, mental, and spiritual healing until repentance is made.

Soul ties can also be created by vows, commitments, and agreements. In (Numbers 30:2), Moses talks about binding your soul with a vow.

The words that you speak have spiritual power that can open a door, tying you to demonic control of your life. I have an entire chapter on words. (Proverbs 18:21) says death and life are in the power of the tongue. (Matthew 12:37) says for by your words you will be justified or acquitted, and by your words you will be condemned and sentenced. Speaking death and defeat over yourself such as "I wish I could die," "nothing ever works out for me,." "if anything's going around I always catch it and get sick," gives Satan an open door of legal access to afflict you because you asked for it.

In a town next to where I grew up a man's daughter was diagnosed with a certain type of cancer. The father said more once that he would gladly accept the cancer on himself if it would leave his daughter. In what looked like a miracle at first, the cancer in the daughter went away. However, shortly after that the father was diagnosed with the same exact cancer. Seems strange? Coincidence? No, not at all. God could have healed this man's daughter. Jesus died for that. The father did not have to take the cancer on himself. Jesus already did that for him. But the man accepted the cancer by his own words, from his own mouth, and he died from it; he was condemned to death by his own words. How sad.

We also learn from (Exodus 20:5) that generational sins from past relatives (generational curses) are also a form of soul ties. Rejection of a parent, or a person that you have given extreme, underserved authority over your life, can cause a spirit of rejection to oppress you from that point on, which can also be a type of soul tie.

Chapter 22

Satan's Strategy of Emotional Hurts

Emotional hurts are the hurts that we have experienced throughout our lifetime from circumstances, events, and people that have caused us deep emotional pain.

(3 John 2) says: "Beloved, I wish above all things that thou mayest prosper and be in health "even as" your soul prospers." This verse gives scripture reference to material and financial prosperity as well as physical health. But most people overlook the two words "even as" your soul prospers; as in being equal to, or directly proportioned one to the other. If your soul is a mess, then the rest of your life will also be a mess. The health of your soul is directly proportioned to, and equal to, the health of your physical body, your mental health, your emotional health, and your daily relationships with everyone that you come in contact with.

If you are secretly harboring the pain, the hurts, and the emotional traumas that people have done to you, or said to you, or if you are holding on to the failures you may have suffered in the past, then you are in denial. Denial is a coping skill and a defense mechanism to keep you distanced from feeling the pain or wound.

According to (3 John 2), we know that there are blessings that are waiting to be poured out on God's people. But if we are not growing spiritually, then every part of our existence will suffer and hinder the blessings that God has for us.

We are made up a three-part being: the body, the soul and the spirit. Your soul is made up of your mind, your will and your emotions. Your mind involves your thinking and your reasoning ability. Your will involves your ability to make right and wrong choices. God tells us to make a choice between being blessed or cursed.

Our minds will always try to operate against our spirit, opting for the curse. Our spirit is always trying to operate on what God says. The demonic speaks into us the temptations that we struggle with; they want our emotions involved, which involves our beliefs, attitudes and feelings. We greatly desire the thing that we are being tempted with because it is operating off of our lust, and this will affect us from operating as God has designed us to operate.

It is our mind that "wills" the way for our emotions, and our "will" follows what the mind/emotions tells us to do. The only way that we can get our mind to operate and think correctly is to do what Paul said in (Romans 12:1-2) where we are to be transformed by renewing our minds through God's Word and prayer.

While researching for this chapter, I found quite a bit of information proving your physical health is directly related to the health of your mind, your will, and your emotions. This goes back to (1 John 3:2), that your health prospers as you soul prospers. If you believe that you're going to be sick with a certain disease just because it runs in your family, then guess what? You have just accepted it. If you believe that you're a failure, then you will be a failure.

Your body responds to the way your mind thinks, feels and acts. This is called mind/body connection. If you're stressed, anxious or upset, your body can respond by trying to tell you that something is wrong. Satan and the demonic can use this on a person to weaken their faith. High blood pressure, or an ulcer, may develop after going through a very stressful event in your life. Just some of the problems you can face include: back pain, change in appetite, chest pain, extreme tiredness, body and joint aches and pain, insomnia, sexual problems, shortness of breath, upset stomach, weight loss or gain and many others. Poor emotional health can weaken the body's immune system. This can also make it easier for the addiction of drugs and alcohol abuse to develop. If there is a problem, first recognize it and admit it, to yourself, to God, and to someone you can trust. Having an accountability partner, who can be there to hold you up and pray for you during the hard times, is a good idea.

At the time you are saved, born again, the (8th chapter of Romans) tells you that you receive the Spirit of Christ and since the Spirit of Jesus Christ is perfect, with no sin, darkness, and no emotional wounds, then your spirit-man is made perfect, too. (2 Corinthians 5:21) says that we are made in the righteousness of God in Christ Jesus.

But your soul (your mind, your will and your emotions) are not made perfect or we would be sinless perfection, not having any struggles with temptations. That is why Paul said that our flesh and spirit are constantly in battle with each other. (2 Corinthians 10:5) tells us to cast down imaginations, and every high thing that exalt itself against the knowledge of God, and bring into captivity every thought (your mind) to the obedience of Christ, (your will). This Scripture shows that there is a process of healing taking place to bring our mind, our will and our emotions into a place of healing and submission to Jesus Christ, which affects us emotionally.

I remember growing up in a certain Pentecostal denomination whose slogan was, "being saved, sanctified, and filled with the Holy Ghost." Well that is very true and real. But the problem was this denomination thought that once those three steps were accomplished that you had "arrived." And to them anyone who wasn't saved, sanctified and filled with the Holy Ghost was according to "their" standards were not acceptable. This is being spiritually prejudiced. Prejudice is a sin and a bondage. It can also be a generational curse. After these three steps were accomplished you were no longer supposed to have any spiritual problems, you were automatically free and healed of all of them. They did not teach anyone how to walk out their deliverance on a daily basis. After all why should they, when you weren't supposed to have any problems anyway. And you did not dare let any of them know that you were struggling with a spiritual problem. If you did, they would not do, as Paul instructed in Galatians to pray and restore such a one "gently," no, you were ostracized as a "sinner."

But the truth is all of us have experienced circumstances, situations, traumas, hurts and people who have deeply hurt us, leaving us wounded. These wounds are in our souls. This affects what we think; this will affect how we see ourselves, how we see the situation that we are in, which can affect the outcome that we have. Thinking the wrong thoughts can cause you to make the wrong decisions. It can cause divorces, missed opportunities, dread, panic attacks, failed attempts and treating other people wrong, because like the old saying goes, "hurt people, hurt people." It starts with your thoughts. Dwelling on your pain will allow Satan to build up a snare in your mind that will further control your mind, your will and your emotions.

You now have a choice to make. But since your mind is freely thinking the wrong thoughts, it is easier for you to make those wrong decisions, which are to move forward with the wrong thoughts that you have. This affects your ability to choose right from wrong.

Paul said in (Romans 7:18): "For I know that nothing good dwells in me, that is in my sinful nature, for I have the desire to do what is good, but I cannot carry it out." The amplified says: "I have the intention and urge to do what is right, but no power to carry it out." Paul is saying the will is there, but it is so overpowered by the lust, that without God it is humanly impossible to not give into it.

When people have been hurt, or their souls wounded by other people, they begin to speak to other people out of the pain and bitterness of those wounds. (Job 7:11) says: "I will not refrain my mouth, I will speak in the anguish of my spirit, I will complain out of the bitterness of my soul." The word "anguish" means to cause great mental, physical, emotional, or spiritual pain or agony. Job was sure feeling anguish, a great wounding emotionally in his soul at that time. In one-day Satan, not God, had killed all his children; he had lost his house, lost all his wealth, and lost his animals which was a great part of his wealth. Later, he was inflicted with painful boils that covered his entire body; the only thing he was left with was his life and a fussing, griping, complaining, mean and hateful wife—the one thing he would have probably rather been without at that moment.

To explain how this anguish from (Job 7:11) is created, and how it affects us, we must understand how Satan works through people. People begin to speak in a hateful way to others, in ways they do not deserve. The wounds are beginning to control them. These people are the ones in the family, or in the work place that are known as the ones you do not talk to because they will bite your head off, chew it up and spit it back at you for no reason. About 2 days a year they are in a good mood and are a likeable person. Those 2 days a year is probably their real personality. The other 363 days a year they are speaking out of the pain of the soul. Fear is afraid of being hurt again. The unforgiveness of those wounds says, "nobody will ever hurt me again" so they make sure they hurt everyone else before they get a chance to hurt them.

This leads up to how the emotional wounds are formed. They are usually formed by sin. Someone may have sinned against you. Maybe it was by verbal, physical or sexual abuse, being betrayed in a relationship like adultery or a close friendship, rejection from a parent or someone that you have allowed authority over you, false accusations, abandonment, maybe being belittled all your life, or many other ways. Many adults in their 40's, 50's, and 60's, are still being controlled by children that made fun of them way back in high school. Satan uses this to create strongholds in their minds for a lifetime of defeat. There's a good chance that it was not your fault. But still "you" may have to repent because their sin will cause you to sin. "But, that is not fair; I didn't do anything to deserve it." But what happens is this, when they sin against you, it can cause you to have unforgiveness, hatred, resentments, bitterness and the sin that you have to work on getting over and forgive them. This will create

233

soul and spirit ties that will create generational curses.

As a strategy of warfare to battle this, we must spend time with God in prayer to ask Him to bring back our memory of all the events in our lives that have caused us physical, mental, emotional, and spiritual pain so we can ask forgiveness for sins we have committed, as well as to ask forgiveness for those who have wronged us. Only then can we begin to get healing for all of the emotional wounds that have been controlling us.

Prayer: Father God I ask you to reveal to me all the wrongs that I've done, and the wounds caused to me by others and forgive me for my unforgiveness to them. Apply Your blood to me now and to my wounds for your healing. I ask You to apply the power of Your resurrection and the total work of salvation that You died and rose from the dead to give me. I receive it now in the name of Jesus. Amen.

Chapter 23

Satan's Strategy of Strongholds

The word "strategy" means the science of planning and directing military operations.

Satan uses the past mistakes, failures, and guilts of what we've done wrong, along with our own worry and concern of what people think about us, hurts from our entire lives, shame of things that have been done to us that was not our fault to attack our minds in his spiritual warfare against us. He does this to build strongholds. He constantly reminds us of our failures as he tries to convince us that we are defeated. He tries to make us think that everyone else remembers these things about us, and that they remember those failures every time they see us. These lies, over a period of time, become the stronghold that will dominate us. The truth is that most people do not remember what happened, and the rest don't care. And the ones who do remember and hold it against you after God has forgiven you don't matter. Jesus said as a man thinks in his heart SO IS HE. That is why Satan and the demonic battle your mind for control. This is a form of demonic influence.

This demonic influence of thought is always contrary to God's Word and to God's will. We do not need to waste our time thinking about it or our past. If this demonic influence is accepted fully, it can open the door to demonic oppression. When the oppression occurs, the person is in bondage physically, mentally, emotionally, and spiritually. Jesus said in (Luke 4:18) that he was sent by God to deliver those who are oppressed by Satan. That is reason enough to realize what is going on, and to do as (James 4:7) says and resist the devil so that he will flee from you. The word "flee" means to run away from, or to try to escape from. If we use the authority Jesus gave us in (Luke 10:19) then he will flee from us. The word "authority" means the power and the legal right to command and use power.

It's All in Your Mind

Funny, but true when talking about mental strongholds: it IS all in your mind. Let me give you an example of how a mental stronghold can also become a spiritual stronghold.

As we have learned in another chapter, demonic spirits speak lies into your mind and it is up to you to listen and obey them or not. Maybe you have a rebellious teenager, who is always telling other people or posting on Facebook about how mistreated they are by you and others. You've given this teenager everything they need, a home, a car to drive, food to eat, you buy their gas, they go out on dates, and basically most of what they need and want comes from you. But just because you ask them to clean their room or help around the home, they balk and say they are mistreated. Here's what is happening:

In the spirit realm, you and your teenager are under a spiritual attack. There is a demonic spirit who is constantly speaking into your child's mind, saying things like: "They are always on your back about something." "You shouldn't have to do ANYTHING you don't want to do." "All they ever do is gripe at you all the time." "Aren't you tired of them telling you what to do?" "You can't stand living here at home any longer; you need to leave and get out on your own." "You'll be better off if you just run away where no one can tell you what to do." "What right do they have telling you what kind of movies and video games you can have?" "Yeah, play that music that praises Satan, play the video games that feature Beliel, there's nothing wrong with it." "Your parents are so stupid, just one drink or one joint will not hurt you!" "You know you need some harder drugs now; try some meth."

The next thing you know your child 40 years old, has lost everything he or she has to a life of drugs and alcohol addiction, are in and out of jail or prison, and they often honestly wonder how this happened to them. You, the parent, may be wondering the same thing. Working with people in the recovery and deliverance ministry for years, I have had this happen many times.

Another example: a woman who was betrayed in a marriage gets remarried to another man. She constantly fears her new husband will also betray her. The new husband is faithful and has given her no reason to distrust or accuse him. So, why does she fear?

It might be that there is a demonic spirit constantly speaking into her mind and spirit, telling her lies such as: "You know he will do the same thing to you." "He's seeing someone else." "You know you can't trust him, he's just like all the rest; they are all the same." "You need to sneak and check his phone, his Facebook, and his car because you know you can't trust him." "He's hiding something from you." "It's only a matter of time; it will happen again." "You know when he's with you, he's thinking about her." "You know you will end up divorced and living by yourself." And about that time a misdirected text message comes from a wrong number that reads, "where are you, I'm at our meeting place." At that point Satan's plan is concreted. There is no convincing the other spouse there is nothing going on. And more thoughts are created.

When these types of thoughts are continually planted into the mind and spirit, the person becomes programmed to operate as if these thoughts are all true. The person begins to act as if the perceived offenses are really taking place. They conform to the Satanic-demonic strongholds. The word "conform" means to bring into agreement, to be in agreement, and to act in accordance with what someone else says. When we say, or believe, what Satan and the demonic says about us, we are confirming what Satan's word says about us instead of what God's Word says about us.

This is why Paul told us in (Romans 12:2): "And be not conformed to this world: but be transformed by the renewing of your mind, that you may prove what is the good and acceptable will of God." The original Greek word in this verse for conform means to conform to another's example. Why would we want to conform to Satan's example by repeating his word over us? The original Greek word for "transformed" in this verse means to be transfigured by a supernatural change. The word "transfigured" in the Webster Dictionary means to change so as to GLORIFY someone. (Psalms 50:23) says: "He who brings an offering of praise honors and glorifies me: and he who orders his way or conversation aright [who prepares the way that I may show him] to "him" I will demonstrate the salvation of God." The word "salvation" means having forgiveness, healing, deliverance, protection, safety, being rescued, being avenged, and much more.

Who are you going to glorify: God or Satan? You do it by choosing whose word you agree with and obey. This creates a covenant and a stronghold of power with the one you obey. How can we do this? (Romans 12:1-2) says, "And present ourselves as a living sacrifice, making our bodies holy, being acceptable to God in his service." How can we do this if we are not transformed and transfigured by his Word?

Strongholds of oppression, if fully accepted, can come in the form of demon possession as (Mark chapter 5) says where the person is accepting and obeying what is being spoken into their spirit by the demonic spirit. A good example is Ananias and Sophia (Acts chapter 5) who listened to and obeyed the demonic by lying to the Holy Spirit. That cost them their lives, both physically and spiritually. A stronghold can also come in the form of obsessions such as OCD. Satan wants to control us by getting our attention focused on our hang-ups and our struggles instead of realizing where the struggle is coming from.

Satan uses both mental and spiritual strongholds to steal, kill, and destroy you physically, mentally, emotionally, and spiritually. (2 Corinthians 10: 3-5) in the Amplified says: "For we walk (live) in the flesh, we are not carrying on our warfare according to the flesh and using mere human weapons. For the weapons of our warfare are not physical [weapons of flesh and blood], but they are mighty before God for the overthrow and destruction of strongholds, [Inasmuch as we] refute arguments and theories and reasoning's and every proud and lofty thing that sets itself up against the [true] knowledge of God; and we lead every thought and purpose away captive into the obedience of Christ (the Messiah, the Anointed One)."

The King James says to "cast down the imaginations." Meaning to throw off or shed with FORCE.

The dictionary says a "stronghold" is a place having a strong fortress and defenses. In spiritual warfare a stronghold is exactly that. Deception that has taken hold of a person's mind is a difficult thing to break. Strongholds are built on Satan's lies, and the mind believes this incorrect thinking. As I have already stated in the paragraph above, this can begin in your childhood and continue throughout your adult life. Many adults, even those in their 50's, 60's and 70's, are still defeated because of what someone spoke over them as a child, being told repeatedly how stupid, ugly, and sorry they were. Satan had people placed throughout their young adult lives to continue this verbal abuse, setting them up for one failure after another to confirm this. You become programmed by these lies and begin to operate off them as if it is normal operation, but it isn't! These are lies!

Thinking contrary to the truth of what God says in His Word about you and your situation is destructive. We can be misled by wrong teachings and false doctrines that we have been taught in church. These falsehoods weaken what God can do in your life. These lies can nullify God's Word in your life, because you are not able to receive, believe, or act on what God's Word says. As we move away from God's Word, we move closer to Satan and the demonic, allowing them to set up strongholds and fortresses. A fortress is a fortified place. The word "fortifies" means to strengthen physically, emotionally, spiritually, and mentally. It also means to strengthen against attacks and to support. Note: Being an accountability partner for someone is playing the supporting role for them.

Verse 4 says we have to fight them spiritually and to "overthrow" the strongholds. The word "overthrow" means to overcome, to conquer, and to bring to a destructive end. The King James says, "pulling down of strongholds." The word "pull" means to pluck out, to rip, to tear, to bring to a stop and to move ahead. The word "refutes' means to prove to be false or wrong. The way we prove if something is true or false is to see what God says about it. Whatever situation you are facing, go to the Bible, write down all the verses you can find pertaining to your problem, and use those in prayer and praise every day.

When You Are Feeling Defeated

Have you had, or are having now, thoughts like these:

Nothing ever works out for you.
You've always been a loser, and you always will be a loser.
Well, if anyone is going to make a bad investment it'll be you.
You'll never be able to get ahead financially; a bill will always come along.
You're too stupid to do anything right.
You will never accomplish anything with your life.

If you begin believing these lies, you will be coming into agreement and conforming to what Satan and the demonic are saying about you. As a strategy of warfare your defense is in Scripture. Say out loud:

(2 Corinthians 5:7): "I" walk by faith not by sight (or by feelings).
(2 Corinthians 2:14): God always causes "ME" to triumph in Christ.
(Philippians 4:19): "MY" God shall supply ALL my needs by his

riches in glory.

Pray: God, I thank you for your word that I will believe and trust. Your Word will govern what I believe for my situation and NOT my feelings. Through your power, I will not believe what Satan says about me, but I will believe what your Word says. And just because things do not go as I had planned does mean it didn't go the way that you had planned. I trust you. I thank you that because of my faith in you I will NOT be defeated, and I will triumph in Jesus Name. Amen.

When You Feel Fear Trying To Grip You

When Satan says to you:

You don't need to go out; someone will try to rape you.
You know someone is going to try to break in your house as soon as you leave.
You know your children will end up as addicts, and there's nothing you can do about it.
You don't need to go on vacation, you know your car will break down in the middle of nowhere, and then someone will rob you.

We have all had these types of thoughts that come from Satan. We can fight back by saying out loud:

(2 Timothy 1:7) For God has not given us "ME" the spirit of FEAR but of power, love and of a sound mind.

Pray: God, I thank you that I do not have to fear because I walk in YOUR power and YOUR strength. I thank you that every promise of the (91st Psalm) is over my home, my property, my automobiles, my children and over my life, and I will not allow Satan access to my life through fear. God, I trust you and receive every promise of your delivering power in Jesus' name. Amen

I Feel Like a Weak Christian

When Satan says:

You are not worthy to be a Christian.
You'll never be as good as brother so-and-so or sister so-and-so.
You know sister so-and-so can see right through you; she knows how bad you are.
You will never have a gift from God.
You know you're no good.
You couldn't pray your way out of wet paper bag.
You'll never be good enough to be on the prayer team.
You can never work in the church because of all the bad things you used to do.

(Luke 10:19) says: Behold I give unto "YOU" power.....over all the power of the enemy and nothing by any means of attack shall harm you.

Tell yourself that you will not think on words of defeat, powerlessness, or failure. Do not allow Satan a place to dwell in your mind or to accuse you of being a weak Christian. God's forgiveness for those who are saved is complete. Do not allow Satan to steal that from you.

Pray: God, I accept the power that you've made clear in your Word; that you have already given me power over Satan and any thoughts and feelings of weakness that he causes in my mind. I will use my life, my mistakes, my failures as a spiritual tool in reaching the lost and the weak, and teaching them to overcome in Jesus' name, Amen.

While we are at it, let me tell you something about all those bad things you used to do. It's called a testimony. (Revelation 12:11) says that we are made overcomers by the blood of the Lamb and the word of our testimony. Your testimony says to others, "I've been there before, and I am not there any longer. If God did it for me, He

242

can do it for you."

Your testimony can give a person hope and faith. There is power in the word of a shared testimony. After all, the stories we read in the Bible, Daniel in the lion's den, Moses parting the Red Sea, Peter, Paul, and Silas being delivered from prison in the book of Acts, the blind man being healed in Matthew, all these stories are a testimony of what God did for these people.

When You Are Facing Sickness and Healing Seems So Far Away

When Satan tells you:

You will always be sick.
Your whole family is sick, and that's why you are sick.
Even if you get well, you'll have a relapse.
You won't live to be very old.
You are sick because God does not love you.
Don't ask for God to heal you, He won't listen to someone like you!

Defend yourself with Scripture:

(Isaiah 53:5): With his stripes we are healed.
(2 Peter 2:24) NIV: He himself (Jesus) bore our sins in his body on the cross, so that we might die to sins and live for righteousness; "by HIS wounds you have been healed

Pray: I know that all I have to do is ask in Jesus' name for my healing, and it is just as simple as accepting salvation, because healing is a part of my salvation package and You said that "If we ask "ANYTHING" in Your name, Jesus, it shall be done. Amen

When You Put Money and Life Before God

When Satan says to you:

Serving God can wait; you need to earn a paycheck.
Missing church is not "that" important; go to the lake, enjoy yourself.
You cannot afford to pay tithes to the church.
Missionaries don't need "my" money; others can pay for that.
I'm too busy to serve God; let others do that.
I'm too good to help with the church feeding program.
If I give to the church, I'll suffer lack in my own family.
It's MY money and I want to keep it!
It's MY time and I want to use it for ME and MINE!

Defend yourself with Scripture:

(Matthew 6:33): But seek first the kingdom of God and his righteousness, and all these things will be given to you "ME" as well.

Pray: God, help me to take the gifts you have given me, no matter what they look like, to others to glorify You and not me. Help me to always remember that You are the source of all good things and You can multiply them as You did the loaves and the fish in feeding the multitude. I pray for discernment in recognizing the leading of the Holy Spirit's will in every decision I make and to follow your peace, guiding me to the correct decision. In Jesus' name, Amen.

You Don't Know If God Will Answer Your Prayers

When Satan attacks with thoughts such as:

Pray all you want but God will not hear or answer you.
You are not good enough to receive an answer from God.
You don't know how to pray correctly.
Who are YOU to ask God for anything!
God does not love you; He doesn't even like people like you.
Praying to an invisible God is stupid; there is no God to hear your prayers.

Defend yourself with Scripture:

(Jeremiah 33:3): Call on me (God) and I will answer you, and show you great and mighty things.
(John 15:7): If you abide in me and my words abide in you, ask what you will, and it shall be done.
(John 14:14): If you ask anything in my name I will do it.
(Psalms 37:4): Delight thyself also in the Lord: and he shall give you the desires of your heart.

Pray: God, I believe that you will give me my heart's desire simply because you have promised to do it, in Jesus' name, Amen.

When You Doubt God's Desire for You to Prosper

When Satan comes at you with:

You will never get ahead.
Your family has always been poor, and so will you.
You will never get out of debt.
You are too stupid to prosper.
Good things are for good people, not for people like you!
What's wrong with you! Christians are supposed to be poor and hungry.
Why would God bless and prosper YOU?

Defend yourself with Scripture:

(Jeremiah 29:11): For I know the plans I have for you, declares the Lord, (plans to prosper you) and not to harm you, plans to give you hope and a future.

(3 John 2): I wish above all things that you may prosper and be in health "EVEN AS" your soul prospers.

Pray: God, I know according to your Word if I seek your will for me above my own that you will bless my life in every way, financially, physically, family and most of all spiritually. And that you will prosper me, accordingly as my soul prospers. God, I trust you and commit my life to you to fulfill your plan and purpose in me. In Jesus' name, thank you, Amen.

When You Feel Like You Have No Hope

This is a common attack that Satan makes on us:

You will never get through this!
Just give up; it's no use trying anymore.
No one is out there to help you.
This is God's punishment for your past sins. You cannot fight God.

Defend yourself with Scripture:

I love the verse above, (Jeremiah 29:11), there is no better confirmation of God's plan for his children.

(Proverbs 23:17): There is surely a future hope for you, and your hope will not be cut off.

The word "hope" here means a feeling that what is wanted will happen, and a desire accompanied by expectation.

Pray: God, I thank you that you have a definite plan for my life. You made me one of a kind. You made plans for me before I was even born that only I can fulfill. You have given me the power to fulfill those plans. I ask you to lead and guide me every day toward your purpose for me. Give me the discernment to recognize your plan and to not let it pass me by. Help me to fulfill your plans for me. I know your plans for me are for my good, and I want to do your will. In Jesus' name, Amen.

When You Have Been Wronged By Someone And You Want Revenge

This is another favorite tactic that Satan uses:

You know they did you wrong, now get even with them.
You should never speak to them again.
Well, you should go tell everybody what they did, that will show'em.
I will never forgive that person.

I used to get revenge when someone did me wrong, and I was really, good at it. Many people suffered a lot of expense because of my revenge. God had to break that in me. God said in his Word, "Vengeance is mine, says the Lord." I learned it was better to let Him do it.

Someone owed me about $700 once and said they would never give me my money. I begin to think of several things I could do to them for revenge. Then I believe God spoke to me, saying, "Let me handle it." I said, "But, God, I want to get even." It was as if He said to me: "Do you want to get even, or do you want your money back?" So, I finally turned it over to God. About a week later, the money arrived in the mail. Turn your issues over to God and let Him handle it for you.

(Luke 6:28): Bless them that curse you, and pray for them which despitefully use you.

(Romans 12:17): Do not repay anyone evil for evil. verse19: Do not take revenge…It is mine to avenge; I will repay, says the Lord.

Pray: God, you know the wrong that has been done to me, and the hurt and anger I feel. I really want to get revenge and even the score. But if I do, I will be stealing something that belongs to you because vengeance belongs to you, not me. I give it to you. I pray for the one who has done me wrong and ask you to save and bless them. So that by following your word and showing them love they can see you in me, and by doing so I take away Satan's power and control over my life by not allowing hatred and strife in my life. This I pray in the name of Jesus. Amen.

When You Feel Controlled by the Same Temptations Over and Over

Satan loves to accuse us of failing:

You'll never be able to quit the drugs.
You'll never be able to quit the drinking.
You'll never be able to quit looking at porn.

You may face the same temptation repeatedly, and you may fail several times. You cannot give up. When you give up, Satan wins. When you fail, go to God and admit it. Ask Him for forgiveness and ask Him for strength. If you stay in faith, you will win this battle with God's help and power.

(1 John 1:9): If we confess our sins; he is faithful and just to forgive our sins.

Pray: God, I ask you to forgive me of all the sins I've committed and help me to stand strong in Jesus name Amen.

When You Doubt God's Love For You

Satan loves to use this one on us:

God does not love you.
You are not worthy of being loved by God or anyone else for that matter.
Why would God love someone like you?

Defend yourself with Scripture:

(1 Peter 5:7): Casting all your cares upon him for he cares for you.
(1 John 3:1) (NIV): How great is the love the Father has lavished on us that we should be called the children of God. (And that is what we are).
(John 3:16): For God so loved the world…(and that includes YOU).

Pray: God, take all these problems out of my hands and put them into your hands. I give them to you. By faith I will accept your love because your Word says you love me. And I thank you that you're my father and that I am your child. I trust you with my life for protection, strength, help and accept every work in the gift of salvation that you have provided for me. In Jesus name, Amen.

But I Don't Want to Forgive Them For What They Did to Me

(Ephesians 4:32) And be kind one to another, tenderhearted, forgiving one another, even as God for Christ's sake hath forgiven you. That's a command. Not a suggestion. God, I ask you to help me forgive the wrong done to me. Not holding grudges. Help me to desire to be able to get to the point where I can pray for the ones who have wronged me. By that I will be taking the first step to forgiveness recovery, in Jesus name Amen.

Why Do I Need to Admit My Wrongs?

(1 John 1:9): If we confess our sins, he is faithful and just to forgive our sins and to cleanse us from all unrighteousness.

Pray: God, I thank you for the promise that if we confess our sins you will hear us. God, I confess what I did wrong, and I ask you to forgive me for it. In Jesus name, Amen.

When Your Mouth Gets Ahead of Your Head

Many people, and this includes Christians, have no idea how

powerful their spoken words are once released from their mouths. Our spoken words can bring about positive effects, or they can bring about negative effects. The Bible is very clear about this, and it is worth remembering what God says about foul language and cursing.

(Ephesians 4:29) Amplified Bible: Let no foul or polluting language, nor evil word, nor unwholesome or worthless talk ever come out of your mouth, but only such speech as is good and beneficial to the spiritual progress of others.

Pray: God, I ask for your help to keep my witness for you pure and holy. Always show me how to glorify you in my speech and keep me from saying anything that displeases you. In Jesus name, Amen.

The Spiritual Stronghold of the Mind

Because of the many strongholds that Satan builds many people come away with the wrong view of God. They may end up not seeing Him as the loving Father that He is, but rather as a mean, cruel task master ready and waiting to crush us at the slightest mistake. This type of thinking can cause a person to stay at a distance from God, preventing them from having an intimate relationship with God. Fearing to have a close personal relationship with Him destroys our faith level, putting distance between the Lord and us, and keeping us from drawing close to Him. This thought process will have us thinking that God doesn't care about our needs. This will make some people afraid of God. Satan wants you to have an unhealthy fear of God because that destroys faith and drives you into Satan's hands.

I suffered from this many years ago. I was raised in a church where everything was a sin. Now, I'm talking about things that were man-made traditions, not God's. For example, according to some of those in this church picking your nose was considered a sin. Honestly, where does the Bible say that? We were taught from a young age that if a boy even noticed that he liked girls that meant that he was a sex maniac, a sinner. This type of teaching was driven into you. Because of this, we (the kids of the church) felt extremely guilty from an early age, not understanding that we were just experiencing God-given feelings and not taught how to deal with those feelings or with the guilt. After all, the adults in the church were married and had children; I don't suppose this applied to them. This caused great mental-spiritual battles in our heads. We were taught that if you even felt a temptation (even though you did not give into it), God would "get you" because if your heart was right, you would not have been tempted in the first place, it proved that you were evil. Worse still, we were taught that God would take your name out of the Book of Life and that you would lose your salvation completely and that you might not ever have a chance for forgiveness so that you could come back to Him. ALL of this was a lie, straight out of Hell.

Because of the way I had been taught, my view of God was distorted and wrong. Once I grew up, I began to do worldly things because of the strongholds Satan had over me. I was 98% convinced that God had abandoned me and did not love me because of the things I had been doing. I was convinced that forgiveness was out of reach for me and that God would never take me back. I was convinced that I was a spiritual outcast from God forever, and that He now hated me for what I had done.

But! I had a 2% chance of hope within me that maybe, just maybe, what I had been taught was wrong. I can't describe the agony and despair I felt as I wrestled with this. I tried to pray for almost 3 years and felt like I wasn't getting anywhere. I had no one I could turn to. I sure couldn't go to the church people I knew; they'd shoot me with their spiritual shotguns and leave me for dead if I came into their presence with a spiritual problem. So, I cried, I begged, I pleaded, and I prayed some more. Of course, God was there all the time, but the stronghold was so strong I didn't know it. I couldn't feel Him or His presence because I did not believe. Jesus said he that comes to him must believe.

One day after praying, I said: God, even if I never feel Your spirit again, and even if You never forgive me and never take me back, I will never give up trying, and You will never get rid of me and You will never get me off Your back, and I'm not giving up, and that's a promise. Then, on a really bad day, I felt I couldn't take much more of it. I picked up my pistol and as I looked at it, it was as if I heard a voice saying: all it will take is just one shot and all of this will be over. The thought was very tempting because I just couldn't take much more. As I picked the pistol up and got it halfway to my head, I remembered my promise to God and I said, "NO, I PROMISED GOD! I'M NOT GIVING UP."

Some days later, I was driving down the interstate, having another really bad day, and that voice came back. It said: "YOU SEE THAT CONCRETE PILLAR HOLDING UP THE OVERPASS? STOMP IT TO THE FLOOR AND HIT IT AT 100 MPH AND ALL THIS WILL BE OVER." I said: "NO, I PROMISED GOD; I'M NOT GIVING UP."

And still another time, I had a bottle of narcotic pain pills, and the voice said: "TAKE THE WHOLE BOTTLE. GO TO SLEEP. THERE WILL BE NO MORE PAIN. IT WILL ALL BE OVER. GO ON, TAKE THEM." I said: "NO, I PROMISED GOD! I AM NOT GIVING UP! NOW SHUT UP." (I was always a little hard-headed).

One night, I don't know if it was a vision, a dream, or in person, all I can tell you is I was there when it happened. I saw myself kneeling, praying in a dark room. A tall, broad shouldered man, dressed in white from the shoulders down to the floor, walked into the room. The next thing I knew I was no longer watching, I was now there kneeling on the floor. The room lit up as he walked over to me; he knelt beside me and put his arms around me. He never said a word; he just wrapped his arms around me and held me tight. He totally engulfed me as he did. At that moment, I felt God's love as I had never felt it before, pouring through me like an open flood gate. I knew everything was forgiven and that God did love me. And I knew that I had met Jesus one on one.

That one stronghold of seeing God as a mean God that hated me, of being convinced I was a spiritual outcast from His presence, was instantly destroyed. I knew God loved me, and that He was with me. I was (and still am) convinced of that.

Greater love has no man than this that a man gives up his life for his friends. (John 15:13).

Jesus loves you so much that He said in John 10:18: No man takes my life from me, I lay it down of myself.

He gave His life for you.

(1 John 4:9) TLB: God showed how much He loved us by sending His Only Son into this wicked world to bring to us eternal life through His death.

(Zephaniah 3:17) RSV: The lord, your God...will rejoice over you with gladness, he will renew you in his love; he will exult over you with loud singing.

The word "exult" means to leap, to rejoice greatly, and glorify. Wow, God loves us so much that He rejoices over us greatly. Does that sound like a God who is out to "get you" with anger and revenge? No, it does not!!!

But understand this: Satan wants you to feel guilty. Guilt can destroy relationships and your self-confidence, causing low self-esteem, and will make you feel powerless. Suffering from low self-esteem will make you feel like a sinner instead of feeling like a child of God. It will distance you from God.

If you have asked Jesus to forgive ALL your sins, and you have truly repented of them, then you fall into "the saved by grace group." And the apostle Paul said in (Romans 8:1): There is therefore now no condemnation to them which are in Christ Jesus, who walk not after the flesh but after the Spirit.

(2 Chronicles 30:9): For the Lord your God is gracious and merciful, and will not turn away his face from you, if ye return unto him.

Realize that He wants an intimate relationship with you. He is not a Father God who hates you.

(Psalms 103:12): As far as the east is from the west, so far hath he removed our transgressions from us.

Realize that if your sins are forgiven that you have "NO" past. He doesn't remember it anymore. There is a story that I've used many times to illustrate this point. A man was praying one day, "God, I just don't understand. You said that David was a man after Your own heart, but Your Word says that he was an adulterer, and a murderer. How could someone like that be a man after Your own heart?" God answered the man with this, "I don't know what you're talking about, and I don't remember David doing any of those things." Why did God not remember those sins? Because David was a man who knew and understood God's mercy and forgiveness. He knew how to access it and how to move forward in praise, and not let guilt rule his life.

Low self-esteem is one of the weapons that Satan and the demonic use against you to build strongholds. It will cause you to live a defeated life. It will cause you to feel unworthy to ask God for anything in prayer. It will cause you to constantly look down on yourself. Paul said in (2 Corinthians 5:17): "Therefore if any man be in Christ, (saved and sins forgiven by faith in the shed blood of Jesus Christ and asking him to forgive you.) He is a new creature: (a child of God) old things are passed away; (all of your sins, your total past forgiven never to be remembered again by God) and behold all things are become new. (You have a new, clean future ahead of you.)

Yet, many people suffer feelings of shame, causing them to look at themselves as a failure because of their past, instead of seeing themselves as (Philippians. 4:13) says: "That I can do ALL these things through Christ who strengthens me." And (Romans 8:37): "Nay, in all these things we are more than conquerors through him that loved us." In all what things? The hurts, failed business attempts, bondages that we haven't been able to get free from, the guilt complex from sexual abuse which was not your fault, but that Satan has convinced you it is. You wonder what "you" did that brought the physical abuse on you from your parents. Here's the answer: YOU DID NOTHING. Stop feeling guilty about it. This will cause you to fear supervisors and anyone in authority over you with a sense of guilt. You should respect them as a leader but not fear them.

If Satan can make you feel worthless through fear and guilt, you will never be able to achieve and carry out God's will for your life because you will see Him the same way. You will feel like God isn't going to answer your prayers because you are unworthy, and you don't deserve it. But because of His love, grace, and mercy for us, we can have it.

You see, all of this is in a spiritual and mental battle of the mind, intended to defeat you. (Ephesians 3:12) says, "In whom we have boldness and access with confidence by the faith of him." The word "bold" means daring and fearless. The word "access" means the right to enter and to use. God gives us the right to come before Him in prayer with boldness, with liberty to speak, and ask for what we need without fear. Jesus said in (John 14:14): "If you ask anything in my name I WILL DO IT." He cannot get any plainer than that. In (John 5:14-15): "And this is the confidence that we have in him that if we ask anything according to his will, he heareth us. And if he hears us, whatsoever we ask, we know that we have the petitions that we desired of him."

Chapter 24

Distractions

"Oh! I'm just so busy I don't even have time to stop and rest; I need two more days in the week just to break even!!!"

Have you ever said those words? I know that I have.

The words "distract," and "distraction" mean to draw the mind away in another direction, divert, diversion, to confuse and to cause great mental distress. In other words, a battle of the mind.

Satan can cause distractions to keep us from realizing where he is attacking, exactly where the attack is coming from, what he is attacking, and sometimes even when he is attacking. Distractions can be things or time-consuming situations that keep us from being able to spend time in Bible study, reading, fasting, and praying; all the things that we get our strength from. Satan and the demonic know how to make all these things happen subtly, much like placing a frog in comfortable water and slowly bringing it to a boil to the point it boils the frog to death. The frog doesn't realize he is dying so he doesn't jump out to freedom. It is often the same with us. Only after the fact do we realize that we have not been spending time with God. Usually, this is after a recognizable attack has blindsided us to the fact that the Holy Spirit may have been able to warn us about it had we been in tune with Him as we should have been.

Sometimes distractions can cause the wrong decisions to be made by not praying for God's guidance. Or by the wrong decisions from the soul wounds we have. These can cause us to travel years in the wrong direction in a bad marriage, debt we can't pay, or serving a prison sentence.

If you're standing on a mountain, it is hard to get a picture of the size of that mountain. But if you get back some distance away then you can see what you are facing more clearly and can see exactly how to pray.

An example of a distraction is what happened when I had a rental house. I had a really bad experience, lost a lot of money, and had severe damage to my house. I knew there had been a lot of negative things going on there. To name a few partying, drugs, prostitution and witchcraft. I knew when the renters finally moved out that I needed to pray over the house and ask God to cleanse it. I was so distracted by the mess of garbage inside and outside, distracted by all the physical damage to the house, which was all I could think of. I had to work hard repairing the damages, basically rebuilding the entire inside from floor to ceiling of every room.

I worked from the last week of April cleaning up tornado damage on both houses from the massive storms that roared through the south on April 27th, 2011, all the way through the year, until almost Christmas. During this same time, my oldest son was sick for almost five months and almost died. Also, my wife was diagnosed with cancer of which God healed her totally. I was still involved in a weekly ministry, and working a full-time job on top of that. But I didn't have as much time to spend in Bible study, prayer, and alone time with God as I had been used to and wanted to. I was not trying to be slack, but the work had to be done, and since they were both my houses, and I couldn't afford to pay someone to do all of it, it fell on me. I guess I could have used the 3 or 4 hours of sleep I was getting a night for it. I didn't realize the ground I had lost at first until I slowed down and only then I could feel it.

One day as I was working some friends stopped by. As we talked on the porch, I noticed one of them go to the front door which was standing open. He stopped, turned his head slightly, then he stepped just inside. As he stepped back onto the porch he said, "You have not cleansed this house; there are spirits in here, and an Ouija board was used here." I said, "You're exactly right, and I should have prayed and cleansed it, and I should have detected that." He said, "Don't feel bad that you didn't detect it because you were being distracted and overloaded by the condition of the house and all the work that you have to do, and everything that has hit you. Satan was using that as a trick to keep you from detecting it."

As I walked through the house, the Holy Spirit began to speak to me, he said: "Begin filling the house with praise, inviting in the presence of Jesus to fill the entire structure, the subfloor, the walls, the ceiling, and all the space in between beginning with the lowest floor, casting out every evil spirit there. Then move upstairs, doing the same thing."

I followed those instructions exactly. I began with praise to God, and then I began to ask Jesus to fill the entire house with His presence, asking Him to fill the space between the flooring joist, the space between the ceiling joist, each space between the wall studs, and the crawl space below the house. Then I commanded every demonic spirit there to leave and to never return. Then I went upstairs and did the same thing. There was a remarkable difference in the atmosphere in that house after that. I learned a very valuable lesson. And it has been peaceful there ever since.

Another example of a distraction happened during this same time. My oldest son, Josh, began to get sick. I recognized the symptoms; 23 years ago, his mother had the exact same symptoms. It was cryptococcal meningitis. His mother was sick for six months and never fully recovered. The doctors told us that "if" Josh lived he would be brain damaged. He deteriorated to the point that he did not know any of us, or who he was, or where he was. It wasn't looking good in the physical realm. But I had total and complete peace that God was going to heal him, even though we were not seeing any change for the better. At what seemed to be at the worst point on Sunday morning, about 11:00 am, I began to see a noticeable change in his condition for the better. I did not know that at that very moment my entire church was having prayer for him. It took about

3 months for him to recover. Josh's immune system had never been right since birth; it had always been low. God healed him of the meningitis.

The distraction came in because even though I was praying, covering my family in healing and protection, and my church was also praying for Josh; I had spent less time than usual in studying the Word and seeking God on a personal level. More and more, I was relying on my church family to pray while we were taking care of him. It was like I was on a spiritual diet and didn't know it. I lost spiritual weight during this time, and I did not even realize it, or the toll it had taken on me spiritually, until it was all over. I had to spend time putting that weight back on through Bible study and prayer. This taught me to watch for the distractions that sometimes can't be avoided, but to make sure that I reserve daily time for God.

Before this story took place, I was talking to a young woman who had recently gone through a divorce. She was telling of all the problems that her ex was causing her; it seemed to be just one thing after another. It was running her ragged spiritually and keeping her heart torn up. I immediately saw this as a distraction to keep her away from time with God and told her what this was. Her eyes lit up and she said, "Yes, you're right. I see it." But you see it took someone else to tell her that.

Distractions can also come in open spiritual warfare. A lady that I know had decided to sing in the praise and worship group in a ministry that was changing lives. Immediately, she began to experience one thing after another. First it was a spiritual attack on her home. This was defeated by some of the warfare strategies that had worked for me in my home. Then, when that attack failed, her marriage was attacked. This, too, was also recognized as a demonic spirit working through, or influencing, her spouse and it was defeated. When that attack failed, her children were attacked. All of these were distractions to keep her from operating in the ministry as God had called her to do.

Satan can also use this sort of attack, mentally and emotionally, to make you feel you are inadequate and a failure. Satan wants to attack your mind because your mind is a part of your soul. Your soul is made up of your mind, your will, and your emotions. Your mind will affect your whole being. If he can control those three he will have control of you. (Be sure and read the chapter on soul wounds).

Paul said in the (7th and the 8th chapters of Romans) that our spirit is always at war with our flesh, our mind, our will, and our emotions. Paul also tells us in (Romans 12:2) to be not conformed to this world: but be transformed by the renewing of our minds, that we may prove what is good, and acceptable and the perfect will of God. It's through this that God can reveal His will for our lives. If Satan can keep your mind in turmoil, he will be able to steal, to kill, and to destroy any chance you have of finding God's will because you will be too confused to recognize it.

Other examples of distractions that can set up demonic strongholds are strife and confusion. Many people do not recognize when they are being set up. Let's say you have not had a good day at work. You walk in the door of your home, only to find your spouse is giving you that "Don't say a word to me" look. If asked, the spouse doesn't know why he or she feels that way, but it feels like a driving force inside of them. And because you have had a bad day, that force is working on you, too. An argument begins. The kids start screaming, and this agitates both of you even more. Perhaps some things get broken, and, in many instances, physical, verbal, and emotional abuse may occur which will create mental abuse. In the extreme, which is all too common, the police are called, and people go to jail. All the while, the kids are watching, and they are emotionally and mentally torn. And you still don't have a clue what just happened.

Allow me to explain. You, and your family, have been singled out for a demonic attack of strife and confusion. (James 3:16) says where strife is, there is confusion and every evil work. You opened the door and welcomed it into your home when you obeyed and began the argument. These two, strife and confusion, always work together and will open the door for many other demonic spirits to join the attack. They will continue to feed the conflict they have just created. Over time, they will have total control of the situation if you do not cast them out of your home. Their goal here is to kill, to steal, and to destroy the lives of your family; a family that God has put together. This will also create generational curses of abuse and broken marriages if it is not destroyed and cast out.

Here is a rebuke I have used several times that works every time.

I am speaking to the principality that is responsible for originating and sending this attack. This is MY home, MY family, and MY property, and YOU are not welcome here. In the name and authority of Jesus Christ, get out of MY home, get out of MY family, and get off MY property, AND STAY OUT.

Try it; it will work for you also.

Chapter 25

Emotional Strongholds

When I think of emotional strongholds I think of the past hurts that caused them. Many times, people who are emotionally unstable, irritable, easily offended, tense, verbally offensive to others for no reason, and easily unnerved are usually that way because of past hurts. These hurts affect the soul, which is the mind, the will, and the emotions. This causes turmoil and commotion in their lives. Hurt feelings can cause unforgiveness and feelings of bitterness, fear, and emotional damage; feelings of rejection or abandonment that can totally devastate our spiritual lives and our relationship with God. This will affect our relationships with others, because we will treat them out of our hurt and bitterness. Job said: "I will speak out of the bitterness of my soul."

(Isaiah 43:18) says: "Forget the former things; do not dwell on the past." We cannot ignore the past but have to face it and stop denying what happened. God can take the strongholds in our minds, the lies told to, us by Satan, and destroy them through his Word by working through these steps noted in this book.

(John 10:10) tells us that Satan is come to kill, steal, and to destroy our lives. He wants to kill our faith in God who can help us. He wants to steal the purpose that God has for us. And it is Satan's desire to destroy our lives and happiness. Jesus Christ is the solution to these attacks. He (Jesus) said in this same verse: "I have come that you may have life, and have it more abundantly."

When we yield ourselves to God, He can take these strongholds, the habits, the addictions, the fears and defeated thinking and remove them from our lives. He can do for us what we cannot do for ourselves.

The Stronghold of Anger

263

The stronghold of ANGER is a big one. It can present itself as a simple problem with losing one's temper or it can present itself in a much more violent way. Anger, regardless of its level, must be dealt with quickly. When anger is not dealt with, it can (and will) fester into a spiritual cancer that will destroy your relationship with God. With anger comes unforgiveness and that can cause God to not hear your prayers. It can also destroy relationships with friends and families. This makes anger one of the great weapons in Satan's arsenal.

Ask yourself: "What, or who, has caused me to have anger inside me?" Pray and ask God to reveal to you the causes of your anger. Write down everything that He reveals to you. Pray for God's forgiveness over each situation; go to whoever you can to make amends, if possible. You cannot be free until you do.

The Stronghold of Guilt

Guilt can be another stronghold that can destroy the lives of people and hold them in bondage. God uses guilt in the form of conviction when we have sinned. Satan, however, will use guilt in the form of condemnation to keep us in bondage even after God has forgiven us. Satan wants us to beat ourselves up over our past sins; the same sins that God has forgiven and forgotten.

Ask God to forgive you out loud so Satan can hear you as well. Then ask yourself, "What do I feel guilty about?" Write down the first thing that comes to your mind. I used to feel so guilty that I'd cry myself to sleep at night, promising God I'd never do it again. But I would do the sin again over and over, usually the next day, because I had not dealt with the root cause. What you can do if you are in this same place is to find Scriptures that tell us what God says about forgiveness and the power He has given us to use. Then pray and praise and give thanksgiving to God.

The Stronghold of Fear

Fear is another stronghold in Satan's arsenal. Fear can be expressed as:

False
Expectations
Appearing
Real

Fear stops prayers from being answered. Satan created fear, not God. Fear is the opposite of faith. Fear manifests negative results, just as faith manifests positive results. Fear stops God from working for you. Fear is listening to Satan instead of God. Fear is a spiritual force that expects bad things to happen. Fear can cause someone to make quick, rash decisions. Fear distances us from God. (2 Timothy 1:7) "God has not given us the spirit of fear, but of power, love and a sound mind."

"Power" means the ability, legal authority, force, strength to supply with a source of power given to do great things.

(Daniel 11:32): The people who do know their God shall be strong and do exploits.

(1 John 4:18) says God is love and this gives us a sound mind.

Write down the things from the past and present that have caused you to fear. Face and deal with those events. Find scriptures that fights against the cause of the problems that you are facing. Begin several times a day using these scriptures in prayer and praise against the situation that you are fighting. Begin telling Satan that he is a liar. That God's word does not agree with what he is saying. That God is in control of your life. And STAND your ground and don't give in, then you WILL begin to see victory.

The Stronghold of Depression and Oppression

Another stronghold that destroys many people is the stronghold of DEPRESSION. This stronghold is one of Satan's strongest weapons. It can lead to many problems that can hinder you from being able to see God as the loving Father that He is to us. It will destroy our faith level. It can break up relationships, marriages; it can cause many different physical, mental, spiritual, and emotional problems. It also cause's loneliness, missed opportunities, anxiety, dread, panic, sleep and appetite problems, social withdrawal, problems with concentration, drug and alcohol abuse, and the results of depression go on and on.

When depression, which affects about 350 million people worldwide, is present, the spirit of heaviness is always in operation. Depression and oppression work hand in hand. The word "depress" means to press down, sadden, discourage, weaken, and to lower in value. The word "oppress" means to weigh heavily upon the mind, to worry, and to keep one down by cruel and unjust tyranny. If this does not describe the work of Satan and the demonic to steal, to kill, and to destroy, then what does?

The Stronghold of Possession

Another stronghold that Satan tries to deceive people with is possession. Satan often wants people to believe that they are possessed by demons. Many believers struggle with this even though they should not.

(1 Corinthians 6:19-20a) in the Amplified Bible says: "Do you not know that your body is the temple (the very sanctuary) of the Holy Spirit Who lives within you. You were bought with a price."

That price is the blood of Jesus Christ.

The word "possessed" means to totally own, dominate, and to

control. This is total agreement and covenant. I DO NOT BELIEVE a born-again Christian, in a daily relationship with, bought and paid for by the blood of Jesus, can be demon possessed. Jesus said in (Luke 16:13): "No man can serve two masters."

If we look at (Romans 6:16), Paul said you are a servant and a slave to whomever you yield yourself to obey, backing up what Jesus said that you cannot serve two masters. You can only agree and covenant with one. The Holy Spirit (who is Holy) lives in the born-again, blood-bought child of God and will not dwell in the same temple with a demon that is being yielded to and obeyed. He does not tolerate sin, so how could He tolerate co-habitation with a demon?

Chapter 26

Satan's Counterfeits

Webster's Dictionary defines the word "counterfeit" as: made in imitation of something genuine so as to deceive, to pretend, and a sham, a fake or fraud.

I believe that Satan has a counterfeit for everything that God has. Not some, not a few, but everything. Satan's purpose in doing this is to cause confusion and to deceive the elect, meaning the chosen and elected, if possible. Satan wants to offer believers a false sense of security and love. For everything that God has done for us Satan has counterfeited. This includes teaching, preaching, spiritual gifts and spiritual people, signs, and wonders and even miracles. Yet there are many people who do not believe this, or understand the vast spectrum this encompasses.

Some people have ignorantly said, "Well, to say that Satan counterfeits God is say that he is equal with God." Nothing could be further from the truth and nothing could be closer to ignorance and insanity. Jesus said in (Matthew 7:15): "Beware of false prophets, which come to you in sheep's clothing, but inwardly they are ravening wolves. Ye shall know them by their fruits." What is this except counterfeiting God's ministers in order to deceive?

In (Matthew 13:24) we see that Jesus sows the good seed of the word; in (Matthew 13:25), Satan sows tares to destroy the word. In (Matthew 13:38) it says the good seed are God's children, and the counterfeit are the children of Satan. In (Philippians 2:13), God works in us, God's children; and in (Ephesians 2:2) the prince of the power of the air, who is Satan, works in the children of disobedience. In (Matthews 24:14) we read about the gospel of Christ, but in (Galatians 1:7-9) there is another gospel, the gospel of Satan and Paul said anyone who preaches it is to be cursed. Sounds like a counterfeit to me.

In (Luke 6:13) Jesus has his own disciples and apostles; in (2 Corinthians) Satan has his own apostles transforming themselves into the apostles of Christ. (Revelation 7:3) says that God's angels will "seal" His children in their foreheads. (Revelation 13:16) says that the children of Satan will receive a "seal" in their foreheads. (John 14) says that Jesus is the truth; John 8:44 says Satan is the father of all lies. (John 8:12) says that Jesus is the light of the world; (2 Corinthians 11:14) says that Satan is transformed into an angel of light. In (Revelation 5:5), Jesus is the lion of the tribe of Judah; (1 Peter 5:6) says Satan goes as a roaring lion. (Matthew 24:31) tells of Jesus and his angels; (Matthew 24:41) tells of Satan and his angels. Jesus quoted Scripture in (Matthew 4:4-10); Satan quoted Scripture in (Matthew 4:6). Sounds like even more counterfeits to me.

All through the 4 gospels, Jesus performed miracles, and He said in (Mark 16:17-18) and (John 14:12) that we would also. In (2 Thessalonians 2:9) and (Revelation 16:14), Satan will also work miracles, signs, and wonders through his workers. In (Revelation 3:21) Jesus is seated on His throne; in (Revelation 2:13) Satan has one also.

(Colossians 1:18) says Jesus has a church; (Revelation 2:9) says Satan has his synagogue. In (2 Corinthians 11:2), Jesus has a bride; in (Revelation 17:16) Satan has a whore. (Revelation 21:1-2) says God has a city, the New Jerusalem; (Revelation 17:5, 18:2) says Satan has a city also, Babylon.

(1Timothy 3:16) talks about the mystery of Godliness; (2 Thessalonians 2:7) says Satan works in the mystery of iniquity. (John 1:14-18 and 3:16) says Jesus is the only begotten son of God to forgive sin and save the soul; (2 Thessalonians 2:3) says Satan has his son of perdition, meaning the loss of the soul.

(Ephesians 4:11-12) says: "And he gave some, apostles, and some prophets, and some evangelist, and some pastors and some teachers; for the perfecting of the saints, for the work of the ministry, for the edifying of the body of Christ." All of this is by the Holy Spirit working through us by His power and anointing. Satan has a counterfeit for this being powered by the "spirit" of antichrist, not the man antichrist; they are two different things.

Satan has his false evangelist, preachers, and apostles. (2 Corinthians 11:13-15): "For such are false apostles, deceitful workers, transforming themselves into the apostle of Christ. And no marvel; for Satan himself is transformed into an angel of light. Therefore it is no great thing if his ministers also be transformed as the ministers of righteousness; whose end shall be according to their works."

Jesus said, "Many shall come in my name saying I am Christ (or the messiah) and shall deceive many." Paul said in (Galatians 1:6-9): "I marvel that you are so soon removed from him that called you into the grace of Christ unto another gospel; which is not another; but there are some that would pervert the gospel of Christ. But though we or an angel from heaven preach any other gospel unto you than that which we have preached unto you let him be accursed."

What other gospel would this be that can cause a born-again child of God to be deceived to the point of believing something totally contrary to what they had first believed? (1 Timothy 4:14) says, "Now the spirit speaketh expressly, that in the latter times some shall depart from the faith, giving heed to seducing spirits, and doctrines of devils; speaking lies in hypocrisy, having their conscience seared with a hot iron." The Greek word for "depart" is "aposteeontai" meaning to slide back from; "giving heed to seducing, deceiving, and wandering spirits" in the Greek (I won't bore you with the word) means the teaching of demons. It also means the person has gone into apostasy. An "apostate" is someone who departs from the faith that they believe, that they know, that they have experienced and have understood, and the faith they have professed as a believer, and now comes to believe that the blood of Jesus Christ is not needed in their life for redemption.

I have found this in many of the cults and false religions I've studied. Paul said in (1 Corinthians 10:21), "You cannot drink of the cup of the Lord, and the cup of devils: you cannot be partakers of the Lord's Table, and the table of devils." In (Matthew 26) the last supper took place with Jesus and His disciples at the table, so we cannot take communion with both. The word "communion" means to have a possession in common.

Counterfeit Gifts

Every spiritual gift supplied by the Holy Spirit can be counterfeited by Satan and can influence and deceive Christians and non-Christians. This is accomplished by the spirit of antichrist working through the occult. In 1 (John 4:1): "Beloved, believe not every spirit, but try the spirits whether they are of God."

Paul teaches in (1 Corinthians 12) about the 9 gifts of the Spirit. The 3 mind gifts are the word of wisdom, the word of knowledge, and discerning of spirits. The 3 vocal gifts are prophecy, diverse kinds of tongues, and interpretation of tongues. The power gifts are the gift of faith, gift of healing, and the gift of working of miracles. I've already mentioned that Satan can empower those who have given their wills over to him to work signs, wonders, and miracles; counterfeiting the gifts of faith, healing, and miracles to deceive people.

He can counterfeit the gift of word of knowledge, which in (1 Corinthians 12:8) is the supernatural revelation from God of divine knowledge or insight into a situation that would be impossible by human means.

In (1 Corinthians 12:8) the word of wisdom is the supernatural revelation of wisdom to devise plans to solve impossible problem; insight into God's will, and purpose.

In (1 Corinthians 12:10) the gift of prophesy is a supernatural message from God in a known language that is outside of any human knowledge.

Many times, I've witnessed these gifts being used. The person being used by God would be able to tell things that they could not have known without God's knowledge being sent to them. This is the gift of the word of knowledge. These holy messages were sometimes for encouragement, confirmation of God's will, or for protection. Satan counterfeits this through the occult and witchcraft, using demonic spirits as familiar spirits who are "familiar" or have knowledge of the dead and through the spirit of divination. The word "divination" is defined as the practice of trying to foretell the future by the supernatural or occult through mediums and fortune tellers, instead of from the Holy Spirit. See the similarity? I heard of a man who was on a missionary trip in a far country. While in a church service a lady who knew no English begin to speak to the man in perfect English to call home that his daughter had been in an accident. After calling home he found the message to be true.

I witnessed a counterfeit gift in a person once. A woman who worked with a familiar spirit would have the individual hold an object in their hand as a charm. She would then tell them information that she could not have known by herself alone. Although the sign on her door did not say "fortune teller," "palm reader," or "medium," yet it was the same thing. She did not go about it with prayer, nor did she use God's word. She used a charm. God condemned the use of charms in his word. He said this was the actions of a witch. I took a lot of flak from many ignorant believers in a couple churches who were faithful followers of this woman when I said while preaching that she was a witch. I have a saying, if it waddles, and it quacks, then it's probably not a possum dressed up in a duck suit, it's a duck.

Here's the Proof

In (Acts 16:16-18) there was a girl who the Bible says was possessed with a spirit of divination. In the Greek, this means the spirit of python or Apollo. Python was a huge serpent that had an oracle on Mt. Parnassus where predictions or false, counterfeit prophesies of future events would take place. It was believed that anyone who pretended to foretell events would be influenced by the spirit of python or Apollo. This girl continued to follow Paul saying, "These men are the servants of the most high God which show us the way of salvation." What she said was true, but it was not from God. She was a fortune teller, or soothsayer. Today you would probably drive down the highway and see her sign, usually in front of a house, "sister so-and-so palm reader-advisor."

The King James Version reads "the" way of salvation. But the original Greek does not use the word "the"; instead it uses "a" which shows us "a" way of salvation. This would be promoting "Polytheism" which is the worship of many gods, and "Pantheism" which is the worshipping of all the gods of all different religions, trying to get the focus off Jesus Christ as the only way of salvation and onto the false god's. I have seen these false doctrines over and over many times in studying the beliefs of many different cults and religions. Satan and the demonic does not mind one bit showing you "a" way of false salvation if they can keep you from knowing "the one and only way."

They work with the demonic and familiar spirits. These familiar spirits are involved in "necromancy" which is divination by alleged communication with the dead. The demonic spirit speaks through the person who acts as a medium. The demonic can mimic the voices of the dead or the living. When the spirits are summoned they will show up because they are invited. When a person summons them by inviting them, they are coming into agreement and covenant with the demon and accepting all the spiritual bondages and curses

273

associated with them. Black magic and sorcery are also involved because this creates an evil, supernatural power and influence over people through what is spoken to them by the demonic spirits. And these are things that they normally would not know. A clairvoyant supposes to have the ability to perceive things that are not in natural sight, through spoken words, making it seem a great spiritual insight to the recipient. Satan uses this as a counterfeit to the word of knowledge, word of wisdom, and the gift of prophecy. Many times, this takes place in the name of God, or a god. The familiar spirits have gathered enough information on the people they are intimating to make people believe they are their long lost loved one. They know the events of the past, so it is nothing for them to tell you what you did a year ago.

In the occult world of the Greeks and Romans there were "oracles" in the worship of their gods. This took place in a so-called temple where the oracle consulted with the gods (demons, familiar spirits). This was divination. Oracles were thought to be portals through which the gods spoke directly to people. This sounds like channeling also which is demons speaking directly through a person. We have the Holy Spirit to speak directly to us and through us. This places oracles as another counterfeit Satan and the demonic have used throughout history.

The occult is being marketed to children today with books, movies, video games, television programs, games, and toys. This gets them used to it at an early age, so it will be accepted as common place as an adult. Then you have an entire generation who is programmed and deceived, making them ready to accept the coming of the antichrist. Again, I have taken much flak from believers who believe there is no harm in the Harry Potter and other similar books. If it makes witchcraft, black magic, astrology, and the occult which is clearly condemned by God in his word, look so great and innocent, then it is clearly a deception by Satan. Ask yourself this question, would a Satanist teach his followers Bible stories?

Jesus also speaks about those who would prophesy and cast out demons in His name, but who were workers of iniquity. Some examples of this in Scripture are: The so called "Reverends" we hear in the news who never mentions God, his love or his word. Rather they only stir up strife, hatred, and confusion. Anyone who does this is not a Christian by the definition of the word to be "Christ like." (Genesis 3:4-5), where the serpent predicts eternal life by eating the fruit of the tree. (1 Samuel 18:10), where King Saul prophesied with the help of an evil spirit. In (1 Samuel 28), when Saul went to the witch of Endor, and an evil spirit imitating Samuel came with a prophesy about Saul's death. In (1 Kings 22:6), King Ahab requires advice of the false prophets of idol worship. The entire (13th chapter of Ezekiel) is about prophesies. (Matthew 24:2; Thessalonians 2:8-12; 1 Timothy 4:1), and many scriptures in the book of Revelation tell of false prophesies of the last days.

In (1Cornthians 12:10) we learn about the gift of discerning of spirits, which is a supernatural gift or revelation from God to see into the realm of spirits to know ahead of time of their plans against God's children, and to discern the hearts of people.

A few years ago, I had a situation with a woman who the Holy Spirit revealed to me was a witch. While walking through a store our eyes made contact; she would not stop staring at me. She stopped where she was, and stood watching me. I continued to look at her as we passed. The Holy Spirit spoke to me what she was, and that the familiar spirit with her recognized God in me, and she knew it. Being the kind of joker, I am, I considered saying "BOO" when I walked past her, but I didn't. Kind of wish I had.

There have been many times that I knew the Holy Spirit had revealed something about someone to me only to find out that it was correct. This is the gift discernment. Does it happen all the time? No, it doesn't; I wish it did. Well, why doesn't it? Frankly, I don't know. But, whatever the reason, I'm sure if I was more in tune with the Holy Spirit it would probably happen more often. I believe He desires to use these gifts in many Christians today, but they do not recognize it; they think it is only in their minds and simply pass it off as just being of them instead of God.

When God's people who are ignorant stray into these areas of the demonic that seem very harmless at first, they open spiritual doorways of free legal access to the demonic to work havoc meaning destruction, devastation and ruin in their life. Divination is leading people to call on Satan for guidance instead of God. (Micah 5:12): "I will cut off witchcrafts out of thine hand; and thou shalt have no more soothsayers."

Charmers and chanters mentioned in the Bible would probably be the hypnotist that we have today; used to reveal things we don't know. This is made to seem harmless, but it is extremely spiritually dangerous. This allows the mind to be left open or unguarded, opened to suggestions outside of God's hand of protection, and allows an open doorway to the demonic. It can cause many spiritual problems. God teaches us that we are to meditate on Him and His Word. (Romans 12:2) tell us to be transformed by the renewing of our minds through God's Word and prayer; then He can reveal to us through the Holy Spirit what we need to know.

The ability to contact familiar spirits, through witchcraft, spirit mediums, clairvoyance, use of psychic powers, transcendental meditation which is often unknowingly using the name of a demonic spirit to meditate on, is calling out to that demon to guide and possess. Many false religions refer to these as "spirit guides." Extra sensory perception, ESP, is using demonic spirits through what seems to be mental powers, like bending metal objects or moving objects, to perceive someone's thoughts. All these, along with hypnotist and channeling, carry curses that can be passed down as generational curses on the familiar blood line. The word familiar comes from the root word "family." Do I need to say more?

Counterfeiting Tongues and Messages

In (1 Corinthians 12:10) we have diverse (or various) kinds of tongues. This is a supernatural utterance given by the Holy Spirit in other languages which is not known by the speaker; sometimes used as a message to someone present, who may speak the language being spoken, as a message from God. Sometimes no one present knows the language. That's when the gift of interpretation of tongues comes in. This is the supernatural ability from God to interpret the language being spoken which the person does not know, but is a message from God.

I have been in church services and heard many times a message given in tongues, sometimes as encouragement to the people, or sometimes as a warning to someone. But you can always tell that it is Holy Spirit inspired because of the Holy awe that is present. Tongues can sometimes be a known language to someone else present, but it is a language that Satan does not know; only God knows.

But outside of the church service, in meeting with mediums of Satanic worship, a counterfeit for tongues can be used to deceive people. (Isaiah 8:19) says, "And when they shall say unto you, Seek, unto them that have familiar spirits, and unto wizards that "peep, and that mutter:" should not a people seek unto their God?" In the Hebrew, "peep and mutter" means to coo, chirp as a bird and chatter. The Amplified Bible says, "chirp and mutter." It means to make a noise by opening the mouth with sounds that are not able to be understood in low indistinct tones, or that sounded like chirps and whisperings which the idol worshippers thought were messages from the dead. I believe this is Satan's counterfeit.

(Jeremiah 27:9-10): "Therefore hearken not ye to you prophets, nor to your diviners, nor to your dreamers, nor to your enchanters, nor to your sorcerers, which speak unto you saying, ye shall not serve the king of Babylon; for they prophesy a lie unto you, to remove you far from your land."

Divination uses many different venues such as: Ouija boards, charms, crystal balls, horoscopes, tarot cards, automatic writing, palm reading, reading tea leaves and counterfeiting of tongues. All this is to steal, to kill, to deceive and to destroy. In ancient times, with the Greeks and Romans, this would come through priests, priestesses, and oracles. Both the Romans and the Greeks used a symbol of a python that meant that a priest or priestesses had the spirit of prophesying, performing through peeps and mutters.

The Bible shows us the work of diviners and necromancers in (Deuteronomy 18:1) and (1 Chronicles 10:13); mediums and clairvoyants in (1 Samuel 28); dreams from false prophets in (Jeremiah 23:16, 25, 32, and 27:9-10), and false prophesies in (Isaiah 8:19 and 29:4). Fortune tellers and soothsayers are revealed in (Micah 5:12) and (Isaiah 2:6); charmers, enchanters, and hypnotists in (Deuteronomy 18:11) and (Isaiah 19:3). Using magic in (Exodus 7:11, 8:7 and 9:11); using divining rods for water witching in (Hosea 4:12); astrologers, stargazers, and monthly prognosticators (horoscopes) are also shown in the Bible.

All these are used by Satan and the demonic as counterfeits to the gifts of the spirit. These were used by every major civilization around the globe that had no relation to each other personally, geographically, or historically. Some would say, "Well, there must be something to it." Yes, there is, it's demonic.

Pagan, non-Christian, religions throughout the world use the counterfeit tongues: American Indians such as the Peyote and Haida; Shamans in Africa, Greenland, Siberia; the Shago cult in Trinidad; the Voodoo religion in Haiti, and the Tibetan monks. The word "xenoglossia" is used for the true biblical gift of tongues as in (Acts 2:4).

For example, when in spirit trances the Peyote Indians were observed speaking Swedish. Tibetan monks were speaking French.

These were languages none of these people knew. Now for you who do not believe what I am saying, if these were not saved, born-again Christians then it didn't come from God.

Counterfeit Healings and Miracles

The gift of healing is God's power to heal all kinds of sickness and disease, without any human aid or medication other than prayer to God and faith in His promise. This is the power and authority that Jesus walked in. All you have to do is read the 4 gospels to see how many times Jesus healed people. He said in (John 14:12) the works that He did we can do also. He said in (Mark 16:18): "And these signs shall follow them that believe.....they shall lay hands on the sick and they shall recover." Then read (Acts 3:6) where the lame man was healed when Peter prayed for him. The working of miracles is the supernatural power from God to work through His power to intervene in situations that would otherwise be humanly impossible to have a safe outcome, or an instant healing, or a way of escape in times of danger.

There has been an increase in the occult, and of occult healings, that are a counterfeit for God's true healing for us physically, mentally, spiritually and emotionally (body, soul and spirit). God also uses doctors; He gives them knowledge. He gives us natural healing through what he has created. ANYTHING else comes from the occult and is demonic. Anyone who uses spiritual energies, charms, or crystals for healing, or where a spirit guide (or demonic spirit) is involved giving the diagnosis and the cure for sickliness, is condemned in Scripture. This uses spirits or mediums to contact the spirit realm through a familiar spirit, again a demonic spirit. Edgar Casey used what he saw in trances to diagnosis sickness. This did not come from God as He nor was prayer a part of it.

(Deuteronomy 18:10-12) says: "There shall not be one found among you that useth divination, (fortune teller) or an observer of times (horoscopes) or an enchanter or a witch, (medium, spiritists, caster of spells) or a charmer, (hypnotist) or a consulter with familiar spirits (demons) or a wizard or a necromancer (communication with the dead, channeling). "Channeling" is a New Age term for mediums, or spirit-possession, using spirit guides in the New Age medicine. The person allows the spirit to enter and possess them for New Age healing to take place. This is a form of mediumship. The spirit can perform psychic diagnosis or healing through a healer or a medium. They can also speak through the person's vocal cords to give spiritual, medical answers to questions (counterfeit for prayer to God). Edgar Cayce comes to mind here.

Automatic writing is also another form of channeling. The Bible warns against this, and under the law was punishable by death by God's command. One method is Reiki which uses spirit guides and the universal energy that flows through all things. It comes from the Japanese words "rei" meaning universal spirit and "ki" meaning energy. The word "reiki" basically means a balance of cosmic and energy force, or spirit energy. This is supposed to dissolve the bad physical, mental, emotional, and spirit energy from your aura or life force which balances and creates a harmony of environment with the body. Only God can bring healing physically, mentally, spiritually, emotionally, and of the soul. New Age healing is occultic. Satan uses this as a counterfeit to God's healing.

Another New Age medicine rooted in the occult is "vibration" or "hearing" therapy. "Healing with sound' is where the new agers believe that the entire body, and every organ in it, has a specific vibration attached to it. They believe the energy flow to the body and its organs can be interrupted by and thrown out of balance by unnatural sounds that we encounter in everyday life. Meditative New Age music is used to gain alternative states of consciousness and is supposed to soothe the soul and bring healing. They also use chants or sacred words (like in a trance or hypnotic state) to align and balance the energies. Trances like this, where the mind and spirit of the person are left open and unguarded, opens a door for the demonic to influence the person as spirit guides (demons) and advisors in making decisions. (2 Corinthians 11:14) says Satan himself (which means demon also) are transformed into angels of light. This seems so innocent and sounds so good that many people will be deceived.

Using crystals is another New Age healing method. The new agers believe that energy or vibrations exist in certain stones and crystals which are used in a variety of rituals like physical healing and meditation which makes it another of Satan's counterfeits for God's healing power and prayer. God condemned the use of amulets, magic stones, or gems and charms in His Word. Crystals supposedly have the ability to focus and direct psychic energies for healing, making them fall into the category that is condemned.

In (Exodus 7 & 8) God sent the plagues to Egypt in judgment. Pharaoh's magicians and sorcerers used enchantments by demonic power to perform these counterfeit miracles.

The Occult as Counterfeit Christianity

One of the main purposes of these counterfeit gifts used by Satan and the demonic is to use them as tools to give people dreams, visions, and revelations to receive messages for false teachings and doctrines that they need to begin cults and false religions. As the gifts of the Holy Spirit are used for God's Glory, the counterfeit gifts are used for Satan's glory. The gifts of the Holy Spirit are used to speak life into the lives of believers; while Satan's counterfeit gifts are used to speak lies and death.

In many false religions Satan uses just enough of the Bible to make those religions seem okay. Others teach a form of Godliness, but deny the power of God, (2 Timothy 3:5). Some even use the name of Jesus, but not as our savior and God's son, but only as a teacher or human prophet. Jesus said in (Matthew 24:5) that many would come in His name. But they all began with Satan and the spirit of antichrist. The main strategy of Satan and the demonic are to lead people away from God into bondage and deception as in (Deuteronomy 13:13).

Some of the cults say that man is basically good, a God, and has the power to save himself, or that we are a divine part of God. Sometimes their belief is "pantheism" which is worshipping all the gods of all different religions. And some say that God is equal with all the other forces in the universe. Sometimes their belief is "polytheism" which is the belief in many gods. Some beliefs are "deism" which believes in a natural religion that is based on morals and that God is not personally involved in our lives in any way. Some believe in "fatalism" which believes that everything that happens to us has already been decided, so nothing we do matters and does no good because we can't change what has already been decided. Some are "agnostic" which believe that we cannot know whether God exists. Some beliefs are "theism" which is the belief that "a" god or other gods exists. And, sometimes, it's "atheism" which believes that no God exists.

Many do not believe in an eternal afterlife, they believe you die and that's it. I watched a television preacher telling people not to worry about being in eternal punishment in hell if you die without having accepted Jesus. He said that when you arrive in hell you would be instantly burned up without feeling any pain and you would simply cease to exist. This is not the case in (Luke 12) where the rich man died and instantly lifted up his eyes in Hell, where he was in pain and torment. Some believe in reincarnation which says when you die you may come back as a rat, cricket, or maybe a skunk. Some believe there is no eternal punishment in hell, while others believe our life here on earth is the only hell that there is. Others believe you make it to heaven, but they leave belief in Jesus out as the only way to get there, relying on our own works of merit to get us there. (Ephesians 2:8-9) says: "For by grace through faith are we saved. Not by our works of righteousness which we have done, but by his mercy and grace we are saved." (Acts 4:12) says: "There is no other name given under heaven among men by which we can be saved."

Some believe that we were created by happenstance and an accident of nature. Christianity and the Bible says in (Genesis 1:26) that God created man in HIS own image, not created as a God, and that he has a sinful nature (Romans 3:23).

The occult says there are many gods to be worshipped. (Isaiah 45:5) says: "I am the Lord and there is no one else, there is no God besides me." The occult worships the earth as a sacred thing. The Bible says in (Genesis 1) and (Colossians 1:16) that God created the earth for His purpose to glorify Him. (Romans 1:25) says that they were condemned because they worshipped and served the created instead of the creator. The occult, when it acknowledges Jesus, says He is only an earthy man, a great teacher, but not the Savior. Christianity and the Bible says in (John 3:16) that He is the only begotten son of God who gave His life for our sins, was buried, and rose again from the dead the third day as prophesied, and that He is the promised Messiah. Did Mohammad rise from the dead? Did Buddha rise from the dead? NO! Only our Savior, healer and worker of miracles Jesus CHRIST did.

Demonic spirits know that Jesus is real, after all He defeated them. They know that God is real because He created them. They know that Jesus gave His life for our sins on the cross and gave us power and authority over them. Demon inspired false religions and cults deny this, so they can keep the human race in darkness of the truth.

The Antichrist as Satan's Counterfeit for Jesus, The Messiah

The apostle Paul said in (2 Thessalonians 2:9-10), speaking of the Antichrist: "Even him whose coming is after the working of Satan with all "power and signs and lying wonders." And with all deceivableness of unrighteousness in them that perish; because they believed not the love of the truth that they might be saved." In (Revelation 13:13-14), speaking again of the Antichrist: "And he doeth great wonders, so that he maketh fire come down from heaven on the earth in the sight of men. And deceiveth them that dwell on the earth, by means of those "miracles" which he had power to do." (Revelation 19:20): "And the breast was taken and with him the false prophet that "wrought miracles." The dictionary defines the word "miracle" as an event or action that apparently contradicts known scientific laws. The Antichrist will use signs, wonders, and miracles as a counterfeit to the gifts of healing and working of miracles to deceive people during the Tribulation as Satan's last chance to take them away from God and to carry them to hell. In (1 Kings 18:38) Elijah prayed to God and was answered with fire falling from heaven to prove to the Baal worshippers that God was the one true God.

The word "anti" means against, to operate against, the opposite and reverse. But the Greek word "antichrist" means to replace or in place of. Can you see how the Antichrist, beginning with Nimrod and ending with the Antichrist of Revelation, is all of this and Satan's counterfeit for Jesus Christ the Messiah? The title "Messiah" means the anointed one. The Antichrist will be called the Messiah and his image will be worshipped by many. This has been Satan's main goal since before his fall. But he is not anointed by God; he is empowered by the spirit of antichrist. All through Matthew, Mark, Luke, and John Jesus performed many miracles for God's glory and to bring people to God so they can go to heaven. The Antichrist will do this for Satan's glory to deceive people and to carry them to hell.

Since the beginning of time, Satan has tried to replace the worship of God with idolatry which is the worship of demons, many different demons as in (Deuteronomy 13:13). This is where the sons of Belial draw the people of their city to worship other gods. Throughout history this has continued through the occult practices as a forerunner being empowered by the "spirit" of antichrist as the counterfeit to the Holy Spirit. Picture this, many different civilizations that had no, or little contact with each other, some even in different centuries, worshipped the same demonic idol gods, differing only by name, promoting the same sins and focus. The gods of each civilization had either the same, or very similar, beliefs, and promoted the same types of sins, each with almost the same occult type beliefs, and each with a different name. For example, the Greeks and Romans worshipped Apollo, where the Egyptians worshipped Horus. The Celtics worshipped him by many different names. It was believed he was multi-talented, having the gifts of prophecy, healing, being the god of light and the sun, and could raise men from the dead, counterfeiting the gifts of the Holy Spirit. Above I mentioned the Oracles, the counterfeit for prophecy and word of knowledge. Oracles were involved in the worship of Apollo, but to show you how this same counterfeit made its way into other civilizations around the world we find them in China as far back as 1122 BC, in Celtic Polytheism during the dark ages around the 5th to the 12th centuries by the Druids and the Vates (which are prophets and soothsayers). In India in Hinduism, the oracle was known as Akashwani or Asariri which means "a voice from the sky;" which was believed to be a message of a god. It is found in Tibetan Buddhism, in pre-Columbian history among the Aztecs and the Mayas, who both practiced human sacrifice to the gods. It was found in Africa, in the Norse mythology, in the American Indians, and in Hawaii.

Baal was known to the Ammonites as Molech and was known to the Moabites as Chemosh, and to the Edomites as Dushara. Baal's female counterpart is Astoreth, Astarte and Asherah. Astarte was identified with Ishtar the Assyrian fertility goddess. Ishtar is pronounced eas-ter; this is where we get the pagan symbols of the rabbit and the egg at Easter. Astarte was also identified with the planet Venus, the brightest planet in the solar system also known as the bright and morning star. Astarte was also similar to Aphrodite, the Greek Goddess of love and beauty, and was almost identical to the very adulterous Roman Goddess Venus, who was unfaithful many times to her husband the god Vulcan.

All these religions believe basically the same things. These are only a few examples; it would take an entire book to log all of it.

Now all these were working to get world civilizations, many who did not know each other, many not even in the same centuries, into the same belief system, drawing these civilizations together into a one-world occult belief system or as (Deuteronomy 13:13) says: "The sons of Beliel drew the inhabitants of "their" city to worship other gods." It could not be totally achieved as a one-world order back then because they did not all have communication with one another at that time.

But Satan almost achieved the one-world worship of himself in the book of Genesis. The tower of Babel is where it almost happened. God confused the languages so they could not communicate with each other. Then as a measure of counter warfare, God caused the continental shift to take place. Yes, the scientists are correct. In (Genesis 10:25) it says, "in the days of Peleg was the earth divided." The Hebrew word "Peleg" means to shift, to split, and to divide. The Hebrew word for "earth" in this verse means continents, land, and earth. The continental shift theory really happened.

By this God was able to disperse the different groups of people around the globe where they could no longer have communication to come together as one to worship Satan, or the image of the beast as they will the antichrist in the book of Revelation.

Today, we have total worldwide communication through the internet, smart phones, and television. The occult has been on the rise since the 1960's, getting ready and building on this. Read the chapter on the great outpouring of the spirit in the last days. All of this is getting the world ready for the acceptance and worship of the "image" (idolatry) of the beast or the "man" the antichrist will use through this same occult system. This proves this is the entire plan of Satan and the demonic to continue idolatry to the end of time, bringing the entire world into a one-world satanic belief system, powered by the spirit of antichrist (the counterfeit and exact opposite of the Holy Spirit).

The entire purpose of idolatry throughout the Old Testament and history was to cause people to worship Satan (the created) instead of God (the Creator). This would be the ultimate idol god worship. God is against these worshippers of the counterfeit Messiah; He condemned it in Scripture, and Satan will be defeated. God will reign supreme and we will be with Him.

The "Spirit of Antichrist" in the World as the Counterfeit and Exact Opposite of the Holy Spirit

The Bible clearly says there is a specific person who will be the end time Antichrist, but the Bible also tells us of a "spirit of antichrist." These are two totally different and separate things. John said the spirit of antichrist was already at work back in his day.

Just as God's Holy Spirit is given to us to empower and equip us as stated in (Acts 1:8): "But ye shall receive power after the Holy Ghost is come upon you." The Greek word for power here is "dunamis" which is inherent power capable of reproducing itself like a dynamo. The Holy Spirit is sent to us as a comforter (John 16:7), to bring conviction for sin (John 16:8), as a guide (John 16:13), and to glorify Jesus (John 16:14).

The spirit of antichrist has always been here to empower and equip the unbelievers in pagan worship, idolatry, New Age cults, secular humanism, atheism, and the occult. The spirit of antichrist is the fuel and the controlling force behind all these false religions, denying the true work of Jesus. They teach that man is god and has the power to save himself; they leave Jesus out of the picture. (Acts 4:12) says: "There is salvation in none other except Jesus Christ." And in (1 John 1:22): "Who is a liar but he that denieth that Jesus is the Christ? He is the antichrist that denieth the Father and the Son."

Another lie of the spirit of antichrist can be found in The Humanist Manifesto which states that traditional, dogmatic, or authoritarian religions that place revelation, God, ritual, or creed above human needs and experience do a disservice to the human species. It says they find insufficient evidence for belief in the existence of a supernatural savior. They believe that no deity will save us, we must save ourselves. They believe that promises of eternal salvation or fear of eternal damnation in hell are both illusory and harmful, and that there is no credible evidence that life survives the death of the body. And they call THIS a "pathway to enlightenment." Paul said in (2 Thessalonians 2:11-12): "...that they would believe a lie and be damned because they believed not the truth." Someday they will change their minds, but they may be in hell by then.

(1 John 4:2-3): "Hereby know ye the Spirit of God: Every spirit that confesseth that Jesus Christ is come in the flesh is of God: And every spirit that confesseth not that Jesus Christ is come in the flesh is not of God: and this is that spirit of antichrist, whereof ye have heard that it should come; and even now already is it in the world." The spirit of antichrist is already here.

The antichrist spirit affecting the church today, if not detected and cast out, will try to destroy the anointing and try to prevent the gifts of the Holy Spirit from being active. It will cause believers to be more focused on their extravagant buildings than reaching people. It will cause those in the church to say: "We don't need THOSE kinds of people in OUR church." It will try to destroy friends, families, and ministers. It will cause confusion, frustration, faultfinding, and cause church splits due to unforgiveness between Christians. It will try to take over leadership of the church to continue this work.

I believe at a minimum the spirit of error, spirit of python, lying spirit, and the spirit of Jezebel all work together in this attack. (1 Timothy 4:1-2): "Now the spirit speaketh expressly, that in the latter times some shall depart from the faith, giving heed to seducing spirits and doctrines of devils; speaking lies in hypocrisy; having their conscience seared with a hot iron."

When the demonic spirits deceive people, as in (1 Timothy 4:1-4) to

288

form new doctrines or beliefs that are contrary to what the Bible teaches, false religions and cults are created.

The spirit of antichrist will work through whatever means it can to oppose Christian values and truth, not only in the church, but also through human governments which control society. When a government such as the United States allows all the other religions more rights than the Christians have this is the antichrist spirit at work. When Christians are not allowed to have a nativity scene in many areas because it might offend an atheist or Muslim, something is wrong. If a Muslim wanted to pray on the street of a major American city he would have the right to, but if we, as Christians, wanted to kneel on the street and pray, we would be told we would be arrested if we didn't get up and stop. The loss of prayer in the schools is a sign of this.

What about our rights and freedoms as Christians. No one cares if we are offended.

The spirit of antichrist is also a part of the demonic trinity. This demonic trinity is worshipped by witches and Satanist in their ceremonies. It consists of Satan as the false father, Beliel as the false son, and spirit of antichrist as the false Holy Spirit.

A Counterfeit Gospel

(2 Corinthians 11:3-4): "But I fear, lest by any means, as the serpent beguiled Eve through his subtlety, so your minds should be corrupted. For if he that cometh preacheth another Jesus whom we have not preached, or if ye receive another spirit which we have not received, or another gospel which ye have not accepted."

Paul said in (Galatians 1:6-9): "I marvel that ye are so soon removed from Him that called you into the grace of Christ unto another gospel: Which is not another, but there be some that trouble you, and would pervert the gospel of Christ. But though we, or an angel from heaven, preach any other gospel unto you than that which we have preached unto you, let him be accursed."

Jesus said in (Matthew 24:5): "For many shall come in my name saying I am Christ and shall deceive many." Jesus also said in (Matthew 7:21-23): "Not everyone who says, Lord, Lord shall enter the kingdom of heaven, but only he does the will of my Father in heaven. Many will say to me in that day, Lord, Lord have we not prophesied in your name, cast out demons in your name, and done many wonders in your name? And then I will declare to them, I never knew you, depart from me ye that work iniquity." (Acts 4:12): "Neither is there salvation in any other; for there is none other name under Heaven given whereby men must be saved."

There have been many throughout history, and today, who use ministry for personal and financial gain. Satan is using them to deceive people condemning them to hell. There are many religions that almost sound right and good to someone who does not know God's word. They teach Satan's deception but leave out the most important parts, Jesus giving His life and shedding His blood for our forgiveness. (Hebrews 9:28): "So Christ was once offered to bear the sins of many." Or they leave out the virgin birth of Jesus. (Matthew 1): "The virgin shall bring forth a child and his name shall be called Jesus." Teaching that Jesus was just a man and another great teacher as Mohammad, Buddha, or any one of many other teachers of the past, this makes them a counterfeit for Jesus. Or they leave out the Tribulation and the Rapture of the body of Christ; (1 Corinthians 15:52): "In a moment, in a twinkling of an eye; (1 Thessalonians 4:16-17) that we shall be "caught up together" in the clouds, to meet the Lord in the air, and so shall we ever be with the Lord." Some are teaching that only a certain small number will make it to heaven instead of "whosoever shall believe." Teaching that all you have to do is be a good person, just go to church on Christmas and Easter. I actually heard a television preacher say, "If you come down, fill out the card, and shake my hand you will be assured of a home in heaven if you die."

Many false preachers are being used by Satan as counterfeits to the real thing and are leading people to hell. Live however you want to as long as you go to the priest and confess your sins. That is a counterfeit for Jesus. (Hebrews 4:14) says that Jesus is our high priest and that WE can come boldly to Him, not an earthly man. Having faith in a man, the earthly priest in the Catholic Church, to obtain and forgive your sins will carry you straight to hell. Satan doesn't care what you believe as long as you believe the wrong doctrine.

We, the body of Christ, may not believe the same thing on every issue, but as long as we agree with what Jesus said in (John14:6) (I am the way), and that we must go through Him as the only door to God and heaven, we may not all agree where on the wall the door needs to be, but we all must agree that somewhere on that wall we need the same door to get through to the other side.

The Mormon Church

Funny that the apostle Paul would mention letting the angel from heaven be accursed for teaching the wrong gospel in (Galatians. 1:9) because that's exactly what happened in the Mormon Church. Joseph Smith supposedly meets an angel named Moroni. Smith said he has visions from God telling him that basically all other Christians and churches were wrong and an abomination to God. Mormons believe that the Christian church fell into apostasy after the apostolic age and stayed there until the Mormon Church was founded.

Joseph Smith was a misguided man that led many to believe a lie. The second major Mormon was Brigham Young, whom history says had an entire wagon train of people about 150, including women and children, murdered in cold blood.

Mormons think they are the only true Christians. They believe the

King James Version of the Bible to be defective and incorrect, and they do not believe that it is reliable. Joseph Smith set out to revise his own version according to his supposed revelations. For one example, he wrote a completely new section to the (3rd chapter of Genesis) writing that Satan came before God and offered to be sent into the world to redeem mankind, if only he could receive God's honor. When God refused to give Satan what he wanted, he rebelled against God. The title page to the book of Mormon reads: "THE BOOK OF MORMON-ANOTHER TESTAMENT OF JESUS CHRIST." They believe it to be as equally inspired as the Holy Bible. But my Bible says in (Revelation 22:18-19): "If any man shall add unto these things, God shall add unto him the plagues that are written in this book. And if any man takes away from the words of the book of this prophecy, God shall take away his part out of the book of life, and out of the holy city, and from the things which are written in this book." Sorry, Joseph Smith, you had your chance.

They deny the Trinity. They believe the Trinity to be 3 separate Gods, making them "polytheist," or the belief in many gods. In one of Joseph Smith's sermons he said taking what Paul said in (1 Corinthians 8:5) "as there be Gods many and lords many." If you read the 4th verse above it you will see that Paul was talking about idols which were demonic spirits, not God the father. But Smith said, "The head of the Gods appointed one of these Gods for us. The second leader of the Mormons Brigham Young also taught this. "How many Gods they think there are, I don't know." I'll stay with my God, the great "I AM."

They deny that God is a spirit and has to be worshipped as a spirit as in (John 4:24). Smith said, "The father has a body of flesh and bones as tangible as man's, the son also, but the Holy Spirit has not a body of flesh and bones." This teaching denies that God is omnipotent (all powerful), omnipresent (everywhere at once), and omniscient (all knowing). It would mean He is confined to one place, does not know all, and is not all powerful. This is not the God I serve.

Smith believed that God was once a living mortal man like we are and graduated to the position of a God; sounds like the Egyptian teaching of the pharaohs going to Osiris after death then becoming gods.

Remember the above section on the spirit of antichrist and how some of the same demonic teachings mixed with and blended into other cultures and civilizations in different centuries around the world. Another Mormon leader said, "As man is, God once was, as God is, man, may become." Doesn't that sound a little like the New Age teaching, that we are gods ourselves, we can save ourselves? This is satanic teaching to deceive people from God.

They do not believe that Jesus is eternal. They believe Jesus is the "spirit" child of God and his wife. They believe that God and his wife had many spirit children that had to come into the world to get a physical body. They think the only difference between Jesus and us is that He was the first spirit child of God and we came along later. The Mormons believe that everyone had a preexistent spirit that existed somewhere before they were born into the world. That is not scriptural.

They believe that Jesus' atonement, giving His life, shedding His blood on the cross was incapable and not sufficient to cover and forgive all sins. They believe these sins can only be atoned by those shedding their own blood. That sounds like the other religions that believe they must mutilate themselves for salvation; my Bible doesn't say that. The worshippers of Baal-Berith in the Old Testament were into self-mutilation, cutting themselves. I don't like self-mutilation, it hurts.

They believe that salvation is not a free gift by grace alone but also by works. If you work hard enough to obtain salvation, great, but if you don't, oh, well. Oh, and if you don't have a chance to get baptized or are not able to, you won't make it to heaven.

I don't have time to go through all religions and cults, and I don't have all that knowledge anyway, but what I want you to see is how almost right and close Satan makes it sound to the real thing, but missing the whole thing. This is just one example where you can see the Satanic-occult teachings through history creating counterfeit religions.

Counterfeit Trinity

Scripture tells us of the Holy Trinity: God the father, Jesus, and the Holy Spirit. But as stated in the above paragraph, the Satanic Bible tells of the demonic trinity that is worshipped during Halloween by Satanist and witches: Satan as the false father God, Beliel as the false son, and the spirit of antichrist as the false Holy Spirit. This is involvement in idolatry.

Counterfeit Armor

People do not think of Satan and the demonic as having their own armor, but they do. Webster's dictionary defines "armor" as any defensive or protective covering. In other words, it is something that you can hide behind and launch an attack from. Satan and the demonic use many different things as their armor. Fear and lies being two of the strongest pieces of armor they have. Anyone that you can control with fear is someone that you have complete mastery over, causing defeat and creating strongholds. Jesus said He was the truth in (John 14:6) and Jesus also said in (John 17:17) that the word of God is truth. Satan and the demonic use lies to spread deception and confusion through false doctrines. A good example is in the (3rd chapter of Genesis) where Satan lied to Eve, condemning the entire human race to sin.

We know we are the righteousness of God in Christ. According to (2 Corinthians 6:7) we have the armor of righteousness. Satan and the demonic use the armor of unrighteousness to fight us through our minds and thoughts.

Jesus said in (John 8:36) that anyone who He sets free is totally, and completely free. Paul said we are a new creation in Christ and that ALL our past is gone and forgiven. Satan and the demonic want to use the armor of false condemnation to keep us in bondage. They do so by constantly reminding us of our sinful past. They will make us continue to beat ourselves up, over and over, with these past sins that have already been forgiven. If you have confessed to God, and have asked Him to forgive you, then according to (1 John 1:9) you are forgiven, and God will never make you feel guilty over that again (Romans 8:1). Unless you do it again.

Satan wants to make you feel like you will never be good enough for God to use. If God waited until people were perfect before He used them, then we would not have the Bible, because He would still be waiting for a perfect person to write it. Read (Psalms 51) and rest in God's peace. Satan will use these false accusations to defeat you physically, mentally, emotionally, and spiritually.

(2 Timothy 1:7) says that God has not given us a spirit of fear. That sounds to me as if there is a spirit of fear. One of the demonic's most powerful pieces of armor is fear which is worry; worry is sin, and worry is anxiety. (1 John 4:18) says that fear has torment, and the word "torment" means a source of pain, and anxiety to cause great physical pain and mental anguish, and to annoy and to harass. "Anguish" means great mental and physical pain. "Annoy" means to hate and to irritate by repeated action. Jesus said in (John 10:10) that Satan and the demonic will kill, steal, and destroy you by this if you let them, but He said that He will give us abundant life. God rewards and operates through our faith in Him. Satan and the demonic will use fear to defeat us by fearing the future, fearing the unknown, fearing strangers, and fearing everything.

Another very powerful piece of Satan and the demonic's armor is distraction. Distractions can show up seemingly from nowhere, in different ways, and knock us off our feet spiritually before we know what is going on. And when this happens, it can also affect us mentally and emotionally. Sometimes they operate through people who take us off course from where God is leading us, or to cause us to make a bad decision. Sometimes when a new Christian is trying to keep away from the addictions and habits that had them in bondage there will be that one influential person to show up to pull them back into the destructive lifestyle they just left.

When a Christian begins to spend more time praying and digging into the Word, suddenly, everything that can go wrong does go wrong. This is done by the demonic to draw the person away from God. Things around the home begin to break down, one by one, all of which has to be repaired. Or someone in the home becomes sick and takes constant attention; even to the point the person doesn't have time to pray for the sick one. Or maybe an emotional situation such as a divorce or a death occurs, or a very intense church or relationship problem arises, and you find yourself just not feeling like praying or getting into the Word anymore. Wow, what happened? It's distractions. I have experienced all the above, and I can tell you that you cannot allow yourself to be drawn away from God. You must stand your ground and pray even if you don't feel like it, and you must read the Word even if it is just one verse. This way you are not allowing the enemy to win.

(Ephesians 6:13-17): "Therefore put on the complete armor, that you may be able to resist and stand your ground on the evil day of danger, and having done all the crisis demands to STAND firmly in your place. Stand therefore and hold your ground, having tightened the belt of truth around your loins and having put on the breast plate of integrity and of moral rectitude and right standing with God. And having shod your feet with preparation to face the enemy with the firm footed stability, the promptness, and the readiness produced by the good news of the gospel of peace. Lift up over all the covering shield of saving faith upon which you can quench all the flaming missiles of the wicked one. And the helmet of salvation and the sword that the Spirit wields which is the Word of God."

Paul tells us in (Galatians 5:1): "To STAND in the liberty and not be entangled in the yoke of bondage." Meaning to not be deceived by the false condemnations, the bondage of fear, distractions, false doctrines and covenants, and to be able to resist and stand. First, he mentions the belt of truth and having it tightened around your "loins." This refers to the stomach and groin area, the sexual areas, and the seat of the many emotions. Satan can use these emotions to control us. Sexual immorality has always existed, as we have already studied, especially in idol worship rites, and it is on the rise. The sitcoms and movies make immoral sex look good. When we see the provocative way, people are dressed on a variety of television shows. One day several years ago, before I got to the place I am now with God, I was channel surfing and came across a very well-known national talk show which is known for its trailer park trash content. Now this show was on a prime network channel. One of the guests was a stripper who was completely nude, wearing only high heels and body paint. Nothing was hidden from plain view. She came in dancing through the studio audience which she did many other times throughout the show.

As I said, this was many years ago; back then I wasn't where I am now in God. I would not watch this today. Satan will use this garbage to multiply the natural desires into a desire where our emotions are out of control. Society has made this type of thing commonplace. Satan and the demonic will make you feel like you are missing something if you don't watch it. God says it is sin. It is no coincidence the belt of truth covers the area that it does. Being constant in prayer, communication with God and his Word can give you the strength to resist. If we do not know God's Word as the truth, then we could very easily be deceived by this way of thinking from Satan. This is a very powerful armor the enemy will use to kill, to steal, and to destroy us.

The helmet of salvation protects our minds where we fight many of the battles that we fight. (Matthew 1:21) says: "You shall call his name Jesus for he shall save his people from their sins." The name "Jesus" means savior, from there we get the word salvation. The word salvation is translated throughout the Bible as forgiveness, freedom, deliver, deliverance, save, health, healing, safety, protection, welfare, defend, avenge, rescue, and preservation, whatever we may face, we have the protecting, rescuing, deliverance and healing of God's salvation and the atonement of Jesus. This covers our entire being, including our soul, our mind, our will, and our emotions.

When the temptation is spoken into our minds and our spirits, and we're enticed as in (James 1:14-15): "But every person is tempted when he is drawn away, enticed and baited by his own desire." Some versions use the word "conceived," meaning the temptation has been planted inside you, it feels like it is growing, and has to come out. This is the desire controlling the emotions. Sometimes it is the spirit of error that is in control causing mental and spiritual strongholds of bondage, stubbornness, and believing false teaching. As I have said many times, you have to know God's Word. Having this piece of armor in place guards us against being deceived. You have this protection in your mind, your spirit, your will, and your emotions. David said: "I will hide your word in my heart, so I won't sin against you." When we know God's Word, "God will keep us in perfect and constant peace whose "mind" both inclination and its character is stayed on you." Be of a sound and healthy mind.

The counterfeit is Satan trying to convince us that we don't need salvation and that we have other means to achieve salvation through ourselves and our works. Is your life messed up, then how are your mind and your emotions? What does your mind and emotions constantly dwell on?

The breastplate of integrity and righteousness: Without God's righteousness in our lives we are unprotected from attacks by the enemy, just as an earthy soldier would be without their armor. Being upright, virtuous, moral, and honest and doing the right thing even if you're alone can be hard without God's power and protection. The importance of being a man or woman of integrity, even when you're alone, lays in the fact that you are never alone. The spirit realm is watching what you do. (Hebrews 12:1) says that we are surrounded by a great cloud of witnesses. This is how Satan and the demonic gain information to accuse you to God. Satan teaches us to lie, to steal, and to cheat. As a counterfeit he wants us to feel as if we don't have to be so honest. He wants to set us up for failure. The breastplate protects our hearts from becoming hardened. It keeps us honest in our business dealings with others. The breastplate protects the front of the chest, and God has our backs as well.

The sword of the spirit is also one of our weapons. It is the Word of God. We can't survive without the Word. In (Psalms 119:105) the word is our lamp to our feet. In (John 17:17) the word is what sanctifies us. In (Hebrews 4:12) the Word is quicker and sharper and more powerful than any other weapon that we can have. It can cut through anything that Satan can ever throw against us. We can use the Word in spiritual battle the same as an earthly soldier would use a sharp, steel sword in battle. The Word can find truth and can reveal deceit. In the (4th Chapter of Matthew), Jesus used the Word to defeat Satan, and that is why we have to know it also.

The sword is always used in close combat with the enemy; the Word is used the same way, spoken out of our mouth to the enemy, revealing what is inside of us. The counterfeit here is to make people believe, by the spirit of error, that they don't need God's word. Many false cults such as Modernism, Post Modernism, and Secular Humanism deny the power of the Word, relying instead on man's wisdom, and using everything they can think of to solve any problem, instead of relying on faith in God. Their false religions deny God's Word, or they attempt to replace it with something else like the Human Manifesto. When God is replaced in this way, we see another example of demonic idol worship being adapted to modern times and placing Satan and the demonic in the place of God. Just a hint, God doesn't like that.

Santa Claus or Satan Claus?

The Santa Claus that we have at Christmas time is supposedly taken from the fourteenth century Saint Nicholas, a Roman Catholic bishop who is well known for the gift giving and good works that he did. Or basically another scheme of the church to Christianize a pagan holiday. God told us many times in his Word that we are not to place anyone, anything, or any image before Him or in the place of Him. In (Exodus 20:3), God commanded His people to have no other gods before Him. And in (Exodus 20:5-6) God said to have no graven image before Him. Yet, at Christmas time each year many believers, all around the world, do this with Santa Claus. Most children in the United States know who Santa Claus is, but ask them Who Jesus is. Many would say, "Jesus Who?" Now, I know that we can carry anything to the extremes, but let's examine the facts.

The name Santa is an anagram from the name Satan. He is a replacement for Jesus Christ as the reason for the season. Santa is ascribed to being eternal, with no beginning or end. Jesus is eternal with God from the Alpha and the Omega, the beginning and the end, according to (Revelation 1:8).

Santa lives in the north. God's kingdom where Jesus dwells is in the north according to (Psalms 48:2), "Beautiful for situation, the joy of the whole earth, is mount Zion, on the side of the north."

Santa is always pictured wearing a red suit. According to (Revelation 19:13), Jesus wears a red robe: "And he was clothed with vesture dipped in blood, and his name is called the Word of God."

Santa is always pictured with white hair and a beard and a twinkle in his eye. According to (Revelation 1:14), Jesus has white hair: "His head and his hairs were white like wool, as white as snow; and his eyes as a flame of fire."

Santa flies, defying the laws of gravity, giving gifts to the entire world. According to the book of James every good and every perfect gift comes down to us from God. (Ephesians 4:7-8) says: "But unto every one of us is given grace according to the measure of the gift of Christ….And he gave gifts unto men."

Children all over the world sing "Santa Claus is coming to town." We don't know when, but the story says that he is coming at night. Basically, the hour of his coming is a mystery. In the four gospels, Jesus compares His coming as a thief in the night, as a mystery, even Jesus doesn't know the hour of His coming, only God knows. In (Revelation 22:20) Jesus said: "Surely, I come quickly."

Santa knows everything, where you are always, what you're doing, if you are good or bad, and children are taught to fear and revere him. This is called "omniscient," or all knowing; only God is omniscient. (Proverbs 15:3) says, "The eyes of the Lord are in every place, beholding the evil and the good."

Santa is everywhere at once or omnipresent, because he can visit every home in the world in one night. Jesus is the only omnipresent one, because He said in (Matthew 18:20): "For where two or three are gathered together in my name, there I am in the midst of them."

Santa is thought to be omnipotent or all powerful. (Matthew 28:18) says that ALL power is given to Jesus in heaven and earth, not to Santa.

Every year in malls all around the world Santa sits on a throne. In (Revelation 5:1) and (Hebrews 1:8) Jesus is sitting on a throne.

When Santa is sitting on his throne he calls for children to come to him and tell him what they want. In (Mark 10:14) Jesus calls the little children to Him; and (Hebrews 4:16) says that we are to come boldly to His throne.

Santa is always telling children to obey their parents. In (Ephesians 6:1), children are taught to obey their parents.

Santa is seen as a judge of the good and the bad from a record book that he and the elves keep on every person. In (Romans 14:10) and (Revelation 20:2), Jesus is the judge with the Book of Life.

Santa is known as Father Christmas. In (Isaiah 9:6) and (Hebrews 12:2), God is our everlasting Father.

Santa comes through the clouds. In (Acts 1:9-11), Jesus will come back in the clouds.

Santa is supposed to live in a bright, sparkling city. Revelation says that Jesus is the light of God's city, the New Jerusalem.

Santa is known as a symbol of world peace. In (Isaiah 9:6), Jesus is the Prince of Peace.

Jesus is the "Lord of Host" in (Malachi 3:5; Isaiah 8:13 and Psalms 24:10). Santa is the lord over a host of elves.

Santa has elves that help him with his work. Have you ever wondered what an elf really is?

An "elf" is a small, magical, supernatural being, a fairy, or a witch. They come from German and Norse mythology and folklore. They were believed to be mischievous and have the power to hinder and afflict humans and livestock in a sinister way. The Drow elves were believed to be very evil and chaotic in the lives of humans. In Satan's kingdom these are called demons and evil spirits. In God's kingdom there are angels, who are messengers for God, ministering help to saints in (Psalms 91:11) and to Jesus in (Matthew 4:11).

Santa is taught to be a carpenter, making toys of wood. In (Mark

6:3), Jesus was a carpenter.

Another anagram of the name Satan is Sanat Kumara who is worshipped by New Ager's as God, as the supreme leader, the life and intelligence within our planet. Sanat Kumara is also known as the lord of the world. (2 Corinthians 4:4) says that Satan is the God of this world. In (John 12:31, John 14:30, and in John 16:11) Jesus called Satan the prince of the world.

You can look at these facts and make up your own mind, but I believe that Satan has devised the plan, trick, scheme, and deceit of Santa Claus as another counterfeit to replace Jesus Christ as a lie, and to attempt to place him in the long list of names of gods throughout history, simply to get him lost in the mix.

Many years ago, before I learned the information that I have taught in this book My oldest son and I were talking about the past and he said, "I wish that you had never taught me that Santa was real when I was little, because later when I found out that he was a lie, I wondered if Jesus was also a lie." I'm glad that God helped me to correct that error with the knowledge that he taught me in later years. Now I'm asking you two tough questions: "What have you taught your children? Have you replaced Jesus with Santa Claus?"

The name "Ole Nick," as Santa is often referred to, is an informal name for the Devil.

Chapter 27

Generational Curses

What is a "curse?" The dictionary says, "a prayer, "invocation," which means invoking of a supernatural power, an expression of a wish or calling on God or the gods to bring evil, harm, injury, doom, or misfortune to someone or a group of people; to speak offensive words in anger or annoyance to call upon divine or supernatural power to send injury upon, to bring evil to afflict and to torment someone."

To "afflict" means to strike, seize, to come upon, as in a military attack.

Curses can be a reason for trouble, affliction, and attacks in our lives.

Generational curses are Satan's main control on the human race. If you could see all the generational curses in effect around the planet earth today as a piece of wire, and have a piece of that wire connected to all the people that curses are connected to, I believe there would be so many that all you would see would be a large mass of wire, not able to see through it to the actual earth inside it.

Sometimes generational curses are also called transference, inheritance, or familiar sin. The root word for familiar comes from the word "family" meaning lineage, and descended from a common ancestor's past. All generational curses are demonic. If people understood generational curses better I believe a lot of the sin committed would not occur.

Generational curses can be broken by identifying and confessing the sin of the ancestors as shown in (Nehemiah 1:4-9, 14:20 and Daniel 9:1-21).

(Deuteronomy 28) says sin, disobedience and rebellion will bring curses on us, and the reasons for the curses are to drive us out of inheriting God's promises.

(Exodus 20:5) and (Deuteronomy 5:9) both say: "For I, the lord thy God, am a jealous God visiting the inequity of the fathers upon the children unto the 3rd and 4th generation of them that hate me."

This verse says to the 3rd and 4th generation, but a generational curse can go on indefinitely or for100's or 1000's of years if each generation continues to renew the contract with the demonic spirits behind the curse by giving into the temptation to the sin that brought the curse in the first place through ignorance of what they are doing, until someone learns how to break and end it.

In (Hosea 4:6) God said, "My people are destroyed for a lack of knowledge." The word "destroyed" means to tear down, to demolish, to do away with and to kill. That's why God said in (Isaiah 5:13): "Therefore my people are gone into captivity, because they have no knowledge."

The word "captive" means "to be taken or held as a prisoner."

The word "prisoner" means "one held captive or confined."

"Confine" means to keep within limits, to restrain someone, as in prison or in a sickbed.

The word "knowledge" means a range of information that we must know to be strong so as not to be destroyed.

How generational curses are created is through agreement and covenant. When we obey and do what God tells us to in his Word, when we speak God's Word in faith, when we stand on His promises, when we teach people how to be saved, healed, blessed, delivered and set free by His power, we can say that we have come into agreement and covenant with God and His word.

When we as Christians come together according to (Matthew 18:19) (…if two of you shall agree on earth as touching anything that they shall ask, it shall be done for them of my Father which is in heaven) then we have come into agreement and into covenant not only together but also with God and his Word.

Paul said in (1 Corinthians 10) that if anyone takes part in any pagan feast or festival, or takes part in idolatry, which many believers and unbelievers alike are guilty of, then you become partners with demons. The word "partner" means to "join together." "Join" means to connect and to "unite." "Unite" means to put or join together so as to become "one," as in a marriage contract which is an agreement and covenant, and this creates soul ties, and this takes us to the word generations, which takes us to generational curses.

In the book of Hosea, it says that when the people began to worship the idols which were actual demonic spirits, then the people began to love the same sins that were promoted by the demonic spirits. They were emotionally tied in agreement and covenant through obedience.

People think of sin too lightly. They have the attitude of "Oh well, God will forgive me." And He will if they are truly sorry.

According to (1 John 1:9 and 1 John 2:1), Jesus is faithful and just to forgive us because He is our advocate. But when someone knowingly commits willful, premeditated sin, they are coming into agreement and covenant with a demonic spirit.

Let me show you how it works. Look at (James 1:14-15): "But every man is tempted when he is drawn away of his own lust and enticed." Who draws and entices you? Well, who do you think that it would be? It's the demonic spirit who brings the temptation. Who plants the thoughts in your mind, affecting your will and your emotions which is your soul? Verse 15: "Then when lust hath conceived...," meaning to become pregnant with. The evil desires, the temptation, the lust has been implanted inside of you. The thing is in you wanting to be birthed and burning to get out. "Conceived" also means there has been a union between two, a union that creates a soul and a spirit tie between the two. Therefore, you are coming into agreement and covenant between the demonic spirits. Then James says when the "lust is conceived it brings forth sin. And sin when it is finished, brings forth death." (Isaiah 28:15) says: "We have made a covenant with death, and with hell we are at agreement."

When you obey these demonic spirits, and knowingly and willfully commit these premeditated sins, you open yourself up to generational curses with its bondage taking over your life. The word "bondage" means slavery and to be subject to force.

OK you want more proof? (Romans 6:16) says to whom you yield yourselves servants to you obey. The amplified says "To whom you continually obey then you become slaves of him to whom you obey."

The word "yield" means to surrender, to concede, or to give your right to another, to give way to force.

The word "surrender" means to give up possession of your rights, to give oneself up as a prisoner.

The word "force" means to physically restrain by force against a person, the power to control. Binding power.

The word "give" means to hand over control to another, to devote or sacrifice, to inflict, punishment by force.

The word "servant" means one who endures a term of imprisonment.

The word "slave" means a human being who is owned, or is property of another, one who is dominated by a stronger influence, and one who has lost the right of his or her own free will.

"Obey" means to carry out the orders of another, to guide by another, and to give your alliance over to.

"Alliance" means an agreement of becoming allies for the same common objective, associated with, and united, by a treaty.

The word "treaty" means an agreement.

The word "agrees" means to consent to and to be in accord with.

The word "accord" means to agree, to harmonize and to grant.

The word "grant" means to give or transfer by legal access and procedure and to give legal right.

The word "agreement" means a contract.

The word "contract" means an agreement between 2 or more that is enforceable.

The word "covenant" means an agreement.

And again, the word "slave" means a human being who is owned or is property of another, one dominated by a stronger influence. One who has lost the right of their own will.

That's what a generational curse is and what it does. It is the agreement, covenant, and contract between you and a demonic spirit, where by willfully committing sin and opening a doorway of legal and free access, you have handed over your will and your control to be bound, afflicted, tormented, punished, restrained and to give yourself up as a prisoner to be confined physically, mentally, spiritually and emotionally. And you have become a slave as one who has given away and lost the right of their own will.

Therefore, Satan and the demonic spirits want your will.

(Proverbs 26:2) says: "A curse without a cause shall not come." A curse cannot land on you, or your descendants, unless you or your ancestors have given it an open door of legal access by sin.

We can see this many times in Scripture that these curses come through sin, disobedience, rebellion, pride, lust, witchcraft, perversion, idolatry, unforgiveness, mishandling of money, oaths, pacts, blood covenants, ungodly soul and spirit ties, physical and sexual abuse, and many other ways.

These give the demonic an open door of free legal access into your life to afflict and to torment you.

Have you ever seen a family where the parents or the grandparents have a problem and it seems the same problem or problems have been "handed down" to everyone else or it "runs" in the family?

Even in cases of adopted children, who have never been around their birth parents, but as they became older begin to show the same traits as the birth parents spiritual, mental, and emotional, an attraction to the occult, sexual addictions. This is not learned behavior; it is passed down by the same demonic spirits that are ruling the family blood line.

In (2 Samuel 12-13), the prophet Nathan came to King David and told him that because he had Uriah killed so he could have his wife, his sin of the sword would not depart from his own sin that calamity would come upon his household. David's son Absalon was killed because of this sin.

You could be carrying around a curse that you are not even aware of that was placed on your family line many generations ago. It could be anything from uncontrollable anger problems, drugs, gambling, alcohol problems, to physical or sexual abuse. Physical and sexual abuse seem to be an overwhelming occurrence of both victims and abusers.

Maybe a mother who was abused as a little girl has a daughter who becomes abused by a totally different person, but the same generational curse is still attacking the same family line. I know a woman whose life was destroyed by molestation and sexual abuse from her grandfather from age 5 until about age 16. He would hold knives to her throat, guns to her head, threatening to kill her if she told anyone, forcing her to do all kinds of sexual acts, much more horrible than I can even go into. She was driven by hatred, fear, insecurity, inferiority, and codependency. After this old man finally died in a nursing home while still having a strong mind, the nursing staff said his last few hours were spent in pain and agony. He was screaming that his feet and legs were on fire, and he tried to pull them up out of the fire. He was screaming that "they" (creatures that were very frightening to him) were there to get him. After his death, other now-grown women began to come forward with stories of him abusing them also. It could have been dozens. Many generational curses were created in the lives that live on today because of his sin. I know this is a true story because I personally knew this family and the old man.

Children are vulnerable and defenseless so when this happens to them, and if it is not reversed, they often grow up to pass it on. Four types of abuse that causes generational curses are: 1. Sexual abuse which causes shame, fear, anger and sexual problems in the victims which can lead to wrecked marriages. 2. Physical abuse which causes rage, anger problems, bitterness, unforgiveness, personal relationship problems and becoming an abuser. 3. Psychological abuse which causes a negative self-image, a spirit of rejection, anger, rage and often becoming an abuser. 4. Religious abuse which causes extreme confusion about who God is; His love for you causes a problem with being able to trust God and can very often cause someone to totally lose their salvation. I experienced the last 3 of these as a child. I remember it all too well. It was difficult to get past. You can read about it in my testimony.

But all these are designed to ruin or to curse a child's life beyond repair by Satan, so he can ruin the children and then destroy the adult race in the future because children become adults, parents, and then grandparents. These can set up generational curses that can be passed down.

Often the abused becomes the abuser. Having gone through physical and verbal abuse as a child, it created extreme anger and rage in me. As a child, I wanted to hurt others as I was being hurt. I began brutally torturing and killing animals because it felt good and gave me power. I would hurt other children who were smaller than I was. I had no remorse over it. If God had not delivered me, well, I don't like to think what I could have become. It would have been a curse passed down to others. Thank God, it's dead.

Maybe there is an unusual amount of divorces or adultery that seems to run in a family.

It could be that mental illness seems to run in a family. There was no report in the Bible of King Saul having mental illness, which was probably bipolar disease, until after he had gone to see the witch of Endor which God had clearly commanded him not to do. Saul had also disobeyed God because God had commanded him to kill all the witches. This was the sin, rebellion, and disobedience that allowed his life to be attacked by Satan and the demonic.

Maybe it's heart problems, maybe the same kind of cancer that runs in a family, maybe it's strokes which run in my family. A few years ago, I was having severe neurology problems one day. The doctor told me that my blood pressure was about 200 over 150 and that I was in the first stages of a stroke. He said from what he was seeing

I should have been either dead or in critical condition, but the stroke had mysteriously stopped before it had gotten to that point and was not advancing; he didn't know why. You see if you're a child of God, he can intervene in a generational curse. The reason the stroke had stopped was this: A friend of my brother called him and said, "I was praying, and God spoke to me and said Satan had planned to end Nathan's life today with a stroke, but God put forth his hand and said "No, I will not allow you to do it."

That's why I wasn't dead.

The attack of these curses can cause paranoia, self-pity, phobias, inner turmoil that leads to excessive fears that control your life, knocking you out of many good things because of spiritual and mental strongholds, anxiety, panic attacks, suicide, diseases, infertility, and an uncommon amount of accidents.

These emotional problems can cause time release generational curses that don't show up until later in life. These curses can cause emotional problems like depression, jealously, paranoia, self-pity, phobias, inner turmoil that leads to excessive fears that control your life. These can cause spiritual and mental strongholds, anxiety, panic attacks, suicide, diseases, infertility problems, high blood pressure, chest pain, back pain, extreme fatigue, body pain, joint pain, insomnia, sexual problems, weight loss or gain, chronic financial problems that are constantly stealing your money (this leads to you not being able to support the work of the ministry because you constantly have to cannibalize your seed which is your tithe to pay your way out just to keep your head above water). God said in (Malachi 3:9) that you are cursed with a curse when you do this. But you are blessed when you give it.

Repeated unforgiveness can cause soul and spirit ties that can bring on generational curses from many different directions. In (Matthew 18:34) Jesus said that God would turn the servant that was unwilling to forgive his fellow servant over to the tormenters.

The word "tormenters" means a source of great pain or anguish, a great source of anxiety, to cause great physical, mental, emotional, and spiritual pain, and to annoy and to harass. The word "annoys" means to hate and to irritate by action.

Some demonic spirits work in collusion together. The word "collusion" means a secret agreement between 2 or more for a fraudulent or illegal purpose, "fraud" meaning to trick or to deceive someone out of their legal rights.

Here is how it works, if you have unforgiveness toward someone. They are being oppressed by curses; your unforgiveness is strong enough that a spirit tie is created between you and that person. At that point, you just inherited not only all the demonic oppression and demonic influence (which are two different things), but also all the generational curses that happens to be on that person. But like they say on TV, "But wait there's more, if you act right now, you can also accept all the demonic oppression, depression, influence and generational curses that are on the person who is tied to them. But wait there's more, since you acted right now you can also receive all the demonic oppression, influence and generational curses from everyone that they were tied to, and everyone tied to them, and everyone tied to them and on and on and on."

And it works the same with soul ties created through fornication. But in both cases, it's like a pyramid effect.

This means they work together. But this also means that they all can be defeated together at one time.

Let me show you another way this also works.

Each person on the face on the earth, who does not have the knowledge to break the curses from them, has a minimum of 30 people (not counting themselves) who are affecting their lives now, in the present, and the future but also the future of all your future descendants.

(Exodus 20:5) and (Deuteronomy 5:9) say God will visit the sin of the parents up to the 4th generation: 2 parents, 4 grandparents, 8 great-grandparents, and 16 great-great grandparents. That's a total of 30 people, not counting all the stupid things you've done yourself, who are affecting your present, your future, and the future of all your descendants. But wait, you said your parents got divorced when you were two, your parents both got remarried. You had a bond with them; spirit and soul ties may be created between you and the step parents which also includes their family ancestors. Guess what? The 30 people who are affecting you just doubled to 60.

But you may say there is no way that is possible because step parents, step children and in-laws are not in the family blood line. They don't have to be. In the book of (Ruth chapter 1 the 14th verse) says that Ruth "clave" to Naomi, her mother-in-law. The word clave is used in the King James. The word "clung" is used in the amplified Bible meaning the same as the word "cling" and means to be emotionally attached like glue. The word "attached" means to connect by "ties" of affection. The word "connects" means to join 2 things together. The word "tie" means to "bind" together. The word "bind" means to bind by oath, legal restraint or contract. The long story made short is that, yes, blended families and in-laws can be spiritually tied together emotionally, and any spirit tie will transfer generational curses by free legal access.

But wait there's more: (Deuteronomy 23:2) says some curses can go to 10 generations. That's a minimum of 1024 people who are right now affecting your present, your future, and the futures of all your future descendants. If there were any divorces and remarriages, then add 30 more if each time only one parent got remarried and 60 more each time both parents got remarried. It would not be very likely that all 1024 people would get divorced and remarried, but if they did that would mean that your life, in the present, your future, and the future of your descendants, would now be affected by over 31,000 people.

Or maybe it is that the family is constantly being afflicted by spiritual manifestation problems. I have the story of my family and my house in another chapter.

In the book of Leviticus, God is giving clear instructions "do not have any other Gods before Me," talking about worshipping idols. Now these idols were not just a powerless image someone made from wood, stone, or gold that meant nothing. These represented and were possessed by demonic spirits. That is why worshipping them carried such a strong penalty.

The names of some of these idols were Beliel, Molech, Astroth and others. I have studied demonology; you will find every one of the idols mentioned in the Bible and all the characteristics that the Bible associates with them are the same characteristics given to them in demonology and in the satanic bible.

Many of these characteristics consist of different kinds of sins like murder, sexual abuse, sexual immorality, drunkenness, homosexuality, and Satan worship.

Beliel alone is responsible for every sin and generational curse that is known to the spirit realm and we see it happening every day.

In (Deuteronomy 13:13), the sons of Beliel were responsible for leading people away from God to worship other gods. And they were cursed for it. Today it's done through occult practices, like Satan worship, rebellion, witchcraft, séances, and Ouija boards.

Just playing around with mediums, fortune tellers, hypnosis, mind control, voodoo, palm reading, good luck charms, tarot cards, and many more will open an open door of free access to demonic intervention in the form of generational curses. It can bring spirits of bondage of like perversion and addiction, oppression, demonic influence and even possession.

Beliel is also the demonic strongman that brings generational curses through Halloween. I have found from my study that this started centuries ago, as far back as the book of Deuteronomy. The same sinful acts the sons and daughters of Beliel were involved in are the same sinful acts that are used today by witches and Satanist in the ceremonies. Beliel required gifts and offerings to be brought to him, including human sacrifice. Then it accelerated more about 2000 years ago, when Druid priests would dress in costumes made of animal skins, going from home to home, requiring gifts, offerings and a virgin for a human sacrifice, often of the first born. This offering was made to Samhain.

Remembering that for everything that God has Satan has a counterfeit, the gifts and offerings were a counterfeit for the gifts and offerings that were brought to the priest of God in the temple. The human sacrifice was a counterfeit for the sin offerings that were made leading up to the ultimate sacrifice of Jesus, giving His life, shedding His blood for our total salvation.

After giving the gifts, offerings, and the virgin for sacrifice, there would be a hollowed-out turnip or pumpkin with the face of an evil spirit carved into it. It was set by the door. This was done as an agreement, covenant, or contract between them and the demonic spirit. This was a covenant that was made to appease the evil spirit, so it would not kill or harm them anymore. This was a counterfeit to when God made a covenant with Moses, saying if you apply the blood on the doorpost the death angel will pass by without causing any harm or death to them.

Isn't that what it's all about? When we apply the blood of Jesus our sins are forgiven. When we apply the blood of Jesus we are saved, healed, blessed, delivered and set free by the power of almighty God. When we apply the blood of Jesus we can see the hurts we've experienced from our childhood healed. We can see the bondages that have held us captive to Satan and the demonic broken and destroyed.

But Halloween is a counterfeit of the trinity who is God, Jesus, and the Holy Spirit. In the Satanic world, it is a celebration dedicated to the demonic trinity, with is Satan as the false God, Beliel as the false Son, and the spirit of antichrist as the false Holy Spirit. It's a time of sex with demons, orgies between animals and humans, rape, molestation, murder, sacrifices of babies and adults, séances, conjuring spirits, casting spells and curses, and release of time released generational curses. The same acts that were taking place in the Old Testament worship of Beliel; this was responsible for all of these sins with an army of demonic spirits working in collusion together below his command and authority.

(2 Corinthians 6:15-16) says what concord Christ has with Beliel, and what agreement hath the temple of God with idols?

The word "concord" means agreement, harmony, and peaceful relations.

(Isaiah 28:15) says we have made a covenant with death and with hell, we are at agreement. Another name for Halloween is the "festival of death."

Even if Halloween seems simple and harmless today, even if the agreement or contract is not clearly understood, it doesn't matter; you are still willfully coming into agreement and covenant with the demonic spirit Satan, the spirit of antichrist, and with Beliel. I have an entire chapter dedicated to this subject.

Geographic areas of the earth can come under a generational curse

In the (18th chapter of Leviticus) it mentions many different types of sins that God calls abominations. The word "abomination" means a strong dislike, to hate and to loathe. He says this will bring a curse. The 27th verse says even houses and lands where these sins took place were defiled.

The word "defiled" means "to make filthy or profane;" "filthy" means "obscenity;" "profane" means "disrespect for sacred things."

6666

We see from (Ephesians 1:22, Ephesians 3:10, Ephesians 6:12; Colossians 1:16 and 1 Peter 3:22) that there are different ranks of authority in the Satanic/demonic kingdom. One man said: "Oh, I don't believe in demons and that Satan has a kingdom." Well, Jesus said in (Matthew 12:26): "and if Satan be divided against himself how shall his kingdom stand." Jesus admitted in that verse that Satan does, in fact, have a kingdom. When Jesus was in the wilderness 40 days fasting, Satan came to Him showing Him all the kingdoms and said: "If you will bow down and worship me all these kingdoms I will give to you." He was not just talking about the earthly kingdoms, such as Rome and Jerusalem. Knowing what we see in our earthly realm reflects what is in the spirit realm, Satan was also offering Him the demonic kingdoms.

In (Daniel 10), an angel appears to Daniel telling him that from the first time that Daniel had prayed 21 days ago God had sent him with the answer. But for 21 days, the prince of Persia had withstood him in a spiritual battle. The conflict was so difficult that God had to send Michael, the archangel, to conquer the prince of Persia. Since this took place with angels who could only spiritually fight with other spirit beings in the spirit realm then the prince of Persia had to be a demonic spirit who was over the Persian Empire. But the angel told Daniel that while Michael and the demon were fighting he remained there "with the kings," demonic kings over that geophysical area. This proves that some of them of higher authority are ruling over different geographic regions of the earth.

I believe this shows that when the people of a geographical area, as

318

a majority or as a whole give their wills and their control over to the will and control of the demonic spirits that are in control of that area, the land itself can come under a generational curse.

What drove me to pornography and strip clubs?

Two guys said they were going to force me into a homosexual act with them. One was much larger than I was and was holding my arms behind my back and I could not get away. I was literally willing to die a slow, painful, death, hoping for a quick, sudden and painless death before that happened. Up to this day, I do not know what they saw or heard, but I do believe in angels. Suddenly the big guy let go of me and runs out the door. The other guy is hopping and stumbling as he is trying to run to the door and pull his pants up at the same time. Thank God that the act never happened.

After that, I was so affected, emotionally and physically, that I did not want anything to do with a man. I did not want to shake hands with a man because I did not want to feel a man's hand touching my hand. And there was no way I was going to give a man a manly hug as we do at church. It created something in me that I had to prove to myself and everybody around me that I liked women.

I had the 2nd largest collection of magazines I had ever seen, was addicted to internet porn, strip clubs, and addicted to everything that had to do with women. See the event that happened to me was a setup by Satan and the demonic and was so extreme that along with my not handling the situation correctly, it opened doors to all these things in my life. And these would have been passed down to my sons if God had not delivered me from them.

Inter-vows and word curses:

A good friend of mine said it doesn't matter what you say, the words we speak don't mean anything. But they do. They are very important.

(Proverbs 18:21) says death and life are in the power of the tongue. David said in (Psalms 39:1): "I will take heed to my ways that I sin not with my tongue." The words we speak are spirit and life in (John 6:63). God's words are His thoughts. (Jeremiah 29:11): "God's thoughts for us are for a blessing, peace, prosperity and an unexpected end and not for evil." In (Mark 11:23), Jesus said that "our" word we speak which He gave us authority to speak "will" release power to receive whatever we speak. In (Matthew 23:22), Jesus also said that whatever we ask in prayer, which is speaking words, while believing, then we will receive it.

In (Jeremiah 1:12), God said that He would hasten His word to perform it. The word "hasten" means to cause it to come up faster, to speed up, to act and move swiftly.

Saying things like: you're so stupid, you're as dumb as your father, you're as ugly as your mother, you will never amount to anything, and you're worthless, no good, you can't do anything right…can cause defeated lives and learning disabilities all because of word curses spoken over you that became strongholds mentally and spiritually that you accepted as truth, but were lies and deceptions. I allowed this in my life.

I had been told all my life how dumb and stupid I was. I was told I couldn't do anything right. You don't know how to do anything and if you tried you'd just mess it up and someone else would just have to fix it. So, I didn't try. I gave up basically. I was convinced I was a failure before I even started, so I didn't start anything. I gave up. I had low self-esteem. I thought there was no way people could like me, somebody as stupid as me.

Jesus said as a man thinks in his heart so is he, and from the abundance of the heart your mouth will speak. That's why we need to transform our minds as Paul said in (Romans 12:2) to lift each other up and encourage each other with our words.

When I began going to World Outreach Center in Oneonta, Alabama, in June of 1998, all the people there became as close as family to me and to each other. They saw something in me that I didn't see in myself, including my pastors Frankie and Laura Powell. My pastors, and everyone, were so positive they all encouraged me saying: "You can do it. I know you can. I believe in you. You can do all things through Christ, and that means you, Nathan."

(Proverbs 6:2) says that we are snared with the words of our lips; you are caught by the speech of your mouth. In (Numbers 14:37), we find that the men that brought an evil report about the Promised Land were killed. A curse came on them because of the words they spoke. It's because of God leading me that I have become what I am today. Because of a strong faith, church and great pastors who knew how to encourage with words.

How churches can come under a generational curse:

I believe many churches have come under a generational curse because of word curses against the churches and the pastors, through slander, gossip, strife, and sowing discord. Churches who allow demonic spirits like Jezebel to come in and run the church into the ground are at risk. All this will cause a decrease in souls being saved, a decrease in people receiving what they need from God, and a decrease in tithes and offerings. People will begin to leave the church. The pastor will get burned out and will want to leave or quit the ministry. The church will begin to die because a door of legal access has been opened, allowing a demonic spirit to bring a curse upon the people that make up the church. If you don't believe me just read the (2nd and 3rd chapters of Revelation). You never speak against leadership, God will not bless that, even if the pastor is wrong, you will be blessed for obeying, and let God deal with the pastor if he is wrong.

Stifling the Holy Spirit will bring the people responsible under judgment for anyone they turn away from God. Judgment came upon the children of Israel when they murmured and complained against Moses.

(Matthew 15:18-20) those things which proceed out of the mouth come forth from the heart, and they defile the man. For out of the heart proceed evil thoughts, murders, adulteries, fornication, thefts, false witness, and blasphemies. These are the things which defile a man. All these can form a generational curse.

Satan cannot read your mind, but he can hear what you say, and he can watch how you react.

If you say with your mouth, and accept defeat, sickness, financial ruin, that you will die young of the same thing that your parents did, that nothing ever works out for you, if you speak it then Satan will be more than glad to put it on you.

And it forms a word curse on your life that can be passed down your family blood line.

Making Judgments and Inner Vows Can Bring Curses:

A person often has a defensive attitude when making an inner vow or judgment.

THAT WILL NEVER HAPPEN TO ME.
WELL, MY KIDS WILL NEVER ACT LIKE THAT.
I WILL NEVER GET DIVORCED.
MY DAUGHTER WILL NEVER GET PREGNANT BEFORE MARRIAGE.

Satan and the demonic cannot read your mind, but they can hear what you say, and they can watch your reactions to the situations they create. Your words can give them plans on where and how to attack you.

An inner-vow statement is usually spoken out of the fear that a person has in his heart. Job said, "The thing I have greatly feared is come upon me." He spoke it with his mouth, out loud.

Acting on fear enables Satan and the demonic to have an open door of legal access into your life. Fear is a paralyzing force that stops God from working in our lives because fear gives Satan access to work in your life.

Fear contaminates faith. (1 John 4:18) says fear has torment.

Fear is a spiritual force that WILL bring about negative spiritual manifestations in your life, just as faith will bring a positive spiritual effect in your life. Where there is no fear Satan has no access to your life. Fear comes from doubting God's words because fear believes that God will not do what He has promised in His Word to do for us. God did not create fear, Satan did. Fear is not the nature of God, so it shouldn't be ours. Fear expects bad things to happen because fear believes the word of Satan instead of believing the Word of God. This means you attack fear with God's Word, the Bible, and with prayer, praise, and thanksgiving.

(2 Timothy 1:7): "For God hath not given us the spirit of fear, but of power, and of love, and of a sound mind."

The word "Power" here means the ability to get results, the legal authority, force, strength to supply with a source of power given to do great things.

A few years ago, in a town next to where I lived, a man's daughter was diagnosed with cancer. The father made the statement that if the cancer would leave his daughter that he would gladly take it upon himself. Miraculously, his daughter was found to be cancer free. Shortly after that the father was diagnosed with the same type of cancer his daughter had and died about a year later. Because he spoke it and he accepted it.

I was watching a show on TV; scientists were watching the birth of a new solar system. I thought, wow, in the beginning God spoke creation into existence. It's never recorded where He ever told it to stop, so His Word is still doing what He told it to do. He has given us the power of our words. (Mark 11:23): "But shall not doubt in his heart, but believe that those things that he saith shall come to pass, he shall have whatsoever he saith." This does not only work in prayer but also in our daily lives if we speak it.

But let me tell you the good news: (Galatians 3:13) says that Christ has redeemed us from the curse.

(John 10:10) says the thief has come to kill, to steal and to destroy, but Jesus said I have come that you may have life and that more abundantly.

(Philippians 2:8-9) says God has highly exalted Him and given Him a name which is above every name, above generational curses, above bondages, above what any demon of hell is trying to pass down to my future generations. It also says that at the name of Jesus every knee of every principality, every power, every ruler of darkness, spiritual wickedness in high places, every might, every dominion and Satan himself shall bow before Jesus.

And since (Ephesians 1:22) says that all these things are under the feet of Jesus, and Jesus said in (Luke 10:19) that I give you power over all the power of the enemy and nothing shall by any means harm you.

And (Romans 8:17) says that I am an heir of God and a joint heir with Jesus Himself then all these things are under my feet too.

To break the curses, you have to:

1. Recognize that it's there.
2. You have to repent of the action that caused the curse.
3. You have to renounce the curse by falling out of agreement with it. (Leviticus 26:40): "If they shall confess their iniquity, and the iniquity of their fathers with their trespass against me," then God says he will remember His covenant with us and forgive us.
4. And once delivered you have to resist the temptations that will come to re-trap you after the curse has been broken.

Summary:

Generational curses are real; they are caused by disobedience, sin, involvement with the occult, sexual immorality, withholding tithes, speaking negative words, they can be inherited, or you start one yourself; they will be passed down your family blood line. They can affect you physically, mentally, emotionally and spiritually; can cause family trouble, divorce, adultery, sexual addictions, financial problems, suicides, and deaths.

Pray:

In the name of Jesus, I renounce and break all generational curses of lust, perversion, rebellion, any curses from soul and spirit ties, unforgiveness, disobedience, Satan worship, casting spells, witchcraft, any use of Ouija boards, and any other demonic objects, of taking part in Halloween, watching and allowing in my home demonic movies and video games, of familiar spirits, séances, idolatry, poverty, rejection, fear, confusion, of all spoken curses and negative words spoken over me myself, other people, and spirit beings, any disease, sickness, hatred, anger, any curses on my finances, any curse of misuse of money by my ancestors, I renounce and break any binding oaths, pledges, pacts, blood covenants, any thoughts, wishes of harm and written curses that would affect my life in a negative way, every time release the curse that would activate in my life as I grow older.

I renounce all false beliefs, religions and philosophies inherited by my ancestors; I renounce any curse of death, defeat, failure, spoken by people in authority over me. In the name and authority of Jesus Christ, I renounce, I break agreement with, all these curses, agreements, and covenants from my life from this moment, all the way back through my family line to Adam.

God, I ask you to close any door I or my ancestors have opened, all the way back to Adam. I accept from this moment on a generational blessing in my life and for the lives of my future generations. I and my descendants will serve God in ministry. We will bring people into the kingdom of God. We will teach future generations how to be saved, healed, blessed and delivered, and how to defeat Satan and his demonic forces. In the name of Jesus, I and my future descendants are now free.

Chapter 28

Agreement and Covenant

Now that you understand how generational curses work and some of the ways they are created, also understand that all generational curses begin with agreement and covenant. Let's go deeper into understanding how this binding contract works.

Just to review what we've already studied before:

"Agree" means to consent to, to be in accord with.

"Accord" means to agree, to be at harmony with, and to grant.

"Grant" means to give or transfer by legal procedure.

The word "agreement" means a contract.

The word "contract" means an agreement between 2 or more, by law.

The words "covenant, concord and compact" all mean an agreement.

There are always terms and conditions that apply in the agreement. When covenants are agreed upon, the general idea is that it will never be broken. Although contracts between 2 or more can be enforced by law, they can still be broken or terminated by the agreement of both or all individuals involved (which some say proves that a contract is not a covenant). Anytime one side breaks the agreement there will always be consequences to pay.

God always takes covenants very seriously. With God, a covenant is a personal relationship.

(Deuteronomy 4:31) says that God will not forget the covenant that He had made with their fathers. God said in (Psalms 89:34), "My covenant I will not break, not will I alter the thing that is gone out of my mouth." When God gives us His word in promises He will not take it back. Both (Deuteronomy 4:31) and (Titus 1:2) say that God cannot lie, that He will not change His mind from what He has promised, and that He will do what He says He will do, and there is no time limit for it to expire.

Satan and the demonic are deceivers and liars. They bring people unknowingly and ignorantly into covenant relationship with them through disagreement of what God says about us, and the situations we are going through, and that they are just little sins or maybe not sins at all, after all you deserve it. These thoughts are continually planted into our mind and spirit and are played over and over by Satan and the demonic.

After they are listened to and obeyed, the person becomes programmed to operate off this as if it were normal operation. By doing this, they conform to the Satanic/demonic strongholds.

The word "conform" means to bring into agreement, to be in agreement, and to act in accordance with what someone else says. When we say what Satan and the demonic say about us in defeat, fear, failure, lack and etc., then we are confirming what Satan's word says, or coming into an agreement relationship with Satan and the demonic instead of what God's Word says about us. When someone does this they are surrendering their will and their control to Satan. But just as God will uphold the covenant that he has made, so will Satan, because it gives him the legal right to enforce that covenant. That is why Paul told us in (Romans 12:2): "And be not conformed to this world: but be transformed by the renewing of your mind, that you may prove what is the good and acceptable will of God."

The original Greek word in this verse for conform means to conform to another's example. Why would we want to conform to Satan's example by repeating his word over us? The original Greek word for "transformed" in this verse means to be transfigured by a supernatural change. The word "transfigured" in the Webster Dictionary means to change so as to GLORIFY someone. Who are you going to glorify God or Satan? You do it by whose word you agree and obey. This creates a covenant with the one you obey. How can we do as this verse says and present ourselves as a living sacrifice, making our bodies holy, being acceptable to God in his service, if we're not transformed and transfigured by His Word?

When understanding spiritual agreements and covenants there are some simple rules to always remember.

1. For whatever God has Satan always has a counterfeit. A good example is the Holy Spirit speaking to believers and unbelievers, demonic spirits operating under the spirit of antichrist also speaks to believers and unbelievers alike. The chapter that deals with Halloween also has many of these examples.

2. For whatever happens in the spirit realm on one side there is always an opposite, counter offensive launched to combat it from the other side. Just remember God is all powerful, Satan is not. A good example is the chapter on the great outpouring of the spirit of God in the last days. I believe from dreams God has given me this is to counter the great outpouring of the demonic spirit in the last days, in the form of the spirit of antichrist, the new age cult, secular humanism, witchcraft and Satanic cults all these are on an increase now because of this demonic outpouring.

3. What we see in the physical realm where we live reflects what is going on in the spirit realm. A good example of this is what the Bibles description of the Satanic/demonic kingdom and how it is set up in rank of delegated power and authority; we see the same type of set up from the beginning of recorded history in earthly kingdoms.

4. There are laws and covenants that exist in the spirit realm, and we see them operating on the same level in the physical realm and they can also cross between the two realms to create a spiritual legal binding covenant, binding the physical you to the demonic.

(Matthew 18:34) is a good example of this where the wicked servant was turned over to the demonic torments because of the spirit tie of unforgiveness. Another example (Romans 6:23): "For the wages of sin is death." This combines both physical and spiritual realms of death, combining both realms being governed by one law or covenant. (Isaiah 28:15) says, "We have made a covenant with death, and with hell are we at agreement." And it does not matter whether you know or understand the terms or not, they still apply, because by accepting the temptation you came into agreement with a demonic spirit and the law that God set forth is in force to punish sin.
In other words, when demonic spirits are obeyed by yielding to their temptations, it is usually something that we greatly desire and have an intense lust for, then we are worshipping them in obedience, and that is coming into agreement and covenant with them.

5. Watch the words you speak, they can bring a curse upon your life. Jesus said in (Matthew 12:37) that we will be either condemned or justified by the words that we speak. (Proverbs 21:18) says that life and death is in the power of your tongue. Satan and the demonic watch and listen and will use it as accusations to God against you to obtain legal grounds to attack you.

A good example of this: I had migraine headaches most of my life. I had been prayed for many times for this and in the last year I have not had one. Well, I mentioned this to someone, and knowing better, I failed to cover what I had said with prayer and praise, and knowing better, I failed to use the authority that I have been given by Jesus in (Luke 10:19) to bind the enemy from an attack of my words. It was not six hours later I awoke with a severe migraine that lasted for two days.

6. According to (Deuteronomy 28), every covenant that is broken and violated will have consequences on you personally; physically, mentally, emotionally, financially, spiritually, and all of this will be passed down to your children.

7. There will be a change of ownership of your soul.

8. According to (Exodus 20:5) and (Deuteronomy 23:2), your ancestors can be affecting your life because of the covenants that they made.

9. According to (Exodus 23:32) every covenant made outside of God is condemned by God.

10. Every demonic covenant, agreement, generational curse, every word curse, and every bondage can be broken by the blood of Jesus.

When you understand these principles you better understand not only how the demonic works but also how spiritual agreements and covenants work. The Bible is full of covenants that God made with different people. God makes us a promise in (Psalms 89:34): "My covenant will I not break, nor will I alter the thing that is gone out of my lips." In (Titus 1:3), lying is one of the 30 things the Bible says God cannot do.

(1 John 5:18) Amplified: "We know that whosoever is born of God does not deliberately and knowingly practice committing sin, but the One Who was begotten of God carefully watches over and protects him and Christ's divine presence within him preserves him against the evil and the wicked one does not lay hold or get a grip on him or touches him."

The Greek word for "touch" here means to fasten, cling, or attach oneself to. This verse tells us that if we are not practicing sin then

Satan and the demonic do not have the legal right to touch us, or has no legal right to attack us. But coming into agreement and covenant with them gives them that free legal right. We have to learn what we do that causes this agreement and stop doing it. We have to learn the rules of warfare in this area.

Things that we have said can bring us into an ungodly covenant with Satan and the demonic. When we speak things against God's Word, like: "Well, if anybody is going to get sick it will be me;" or, "I will never get ahead financially; I'll always be flat broke" we set ourselves up. This is often done with a defeated or a defensive attitude for example.

"WELL, THAT WILL NEVER HAPPEN TO ME."
"WELL, MY KIDS WILL NEVER ACT LIKE THAT."
"I WILL NEVER GET DIVORCED."
"MY DAUGHTER WILL NEVER GET PREGNANT BEFORE MARRIAGE."

(Proverbs 18:21) says that "Death and life are in the power of your tongue."

You, like Satan, can agree to steal, to kill and to destroy someone's life through the words you speak. Word curses can bring a Church under a generational curse through slander, gossip, strife and sowing discord through spoken words, speaking against leadership, which will also bring judgment. A good example is when Israel in the desert spoke against Moses.

Speaking these word curses can cause defeated lives and learning disabilities in children because words get into the person's spirit and steals, kills, and destroys them. And all this is achieved by people coming into agreement with the demonic spirit who is providing the temptation to you, and agreement and covenant is made when the temptation is spoken into your spirit, you're enticed, without realizing what you're doing, and you obey.

Satan and the demonic cannot read your mind, but they can hear what you say, and they can watch your reactions to the situations they create. Your words can give them plans on where and how to attack you, and when you accept this from them you are coming into covenant and agreement, giving them legal access to attack you instead of attacking them with prayer, praise and God's Word. One of the meanings of the word "agree" is to say the same thing as someone else. In this case, saying what God has said in His Word concerning our situation and Satan's defeat.

Sometimes statements can be made from the fear a person has in their heart. Job said, "the thing I have greatly feared is come upon me;" he spoke it with his mouth, out loud. Acting on fear enables Satan and the demonic to have an open door of free legal access into your life.

Fear is a paralyzing force that stops God from working in our lives because fear gives Satan access to work in your life. Fear also contaminates and weakens faith. (1 John.4:18) says fear has torment. Fear is a spiritual force that WILL bring about negative spiritual manifestations in your life, just as faith will bring a positive spiritual affect in your life.

Where there is no fear Satan has no access to your life. Fear comes from doubting God's words because fear believes that God will not do what He has promised He would do for us. God did not create fear Satan did. Fear is not the nature of God and as His children who believe His Word it shouldn't be our nature either.

Fear expects bad things to happen, because fear believes the word of Satan instead of believing the Word of God which means you attack fear with God's Word, the Bible, and prayer, praise, and thanksgiving. Paul said in (2 Timothy 1:7): "For God hath not given us the spirit of fear, but of power, and of love, and of a sound mind." The word "power" here means the ability to get results, the legal authority, force, strength to supply with a source of power given to do great things.

Every believer should agree that we are coming into agreement and covenant with God and His Word. When we speak what He says and believe it, saying the same things that God has said, we have His power. On the flip side, when you do not believe it, and you speak doubt, and operate off of fear from Satan and the demonic, saying what they have spoken into your spirit man, then you are listening to them, you are accepting what they say, you are obeying them, you are being guided by them, you are carrying out their orders, which is coming into agreement and covenant with them putting you into captivity where you are limited and restricted physically, mentally, emotionally, and spiritually, making you as a prisoner to them. And as Jesus said we are being condemned by our words.

Jesus said in (Matthew 18:19): "Again I say unto you, That, if two of you shall AGREE on earth as touching anything that they shall ask, it shall be done for them of my father which is in heaven."

Now Jesus said "again." Today we would say, "Look, I've already told you this one time, now listen to what I'm saying. I said ask in my name and I will do it. And expect to see what you ask come to pass then I'll make it happen and give you what you ask for."

Simple, case stated, and case closed. If we agree together with these verses, then we agree and covenant with each other and with God.

But what most people do not realize when dealing with the spirit realm is that whatever God has Satan has the opposite as a counterfeit. God has His Word of life for us and Satan has his own word of death for us. If we agree with, or say the same thing as what God says, then we speak life, faith, and power, and according to (Matthew 12:37) we are justified. But if we agree with Satan, or say the same thing as what Satan's word says, then according to the same verse we speak death, destruction, and condemnation to ourselves. This happens by listening to what the demonic is speaking into your spirit man and operating off it as if it was normal operation. When this happens, you are coming into agreement with them. This is one way that mental and spiritual strongholds of bondage are built that controls the mind, the will, and the emotions.

When you obey these demonic spirits and knowingly and willfully commit these premeditated sins, you open yourself up to these generational curses as bondages taking over your life by coming into agreement and covenant with them. The word "bondage" means slavery and to be subject to force.

(Romans 6:16) says whoever continually commits and yields to sin becomes a slave and a servant to sin and to the one who brought the temptation. Who else is it but Satan and the demonic?

Amplified Bible says to whom you continually obey, you become slaves.

That's what a generational curse is and what it does. It is the agreement, covenant and a contract between you and a demonic spirit, where by willfully committing sin and opening a doorway of legal and free access, you have handed over your will and your control to be bound, afflicted, tormented, punished, restrained and to give yourself up as a prisoner to be confined physically, mentally, spiritually and emotionally and have become a slave as one who has given away and lost the right of their own will.

That is why Satan and the demonic spirits want your will.

(2 Corinthians 6:14): "Be not unequally "yoked" together with unbelievers." The word "yoked" is a military term meaning do not leave your rank, referring to not leaving your Christian's ranks. Being yoked also means "bondage," something that binds and unites, to harness and to come together. Going even deeper, it also means to be obligatory bound and being compelled by an oath, legal

restraint and a contract. In other words, you are in agreement. Now remember at the beginning of this chapter the word "agreement" also means a contract.

In verse 15 Paul asked what concord (which is a contract), does Christ have with Beliel? And what do we have in common with the infidel? In verse 16, Paul said that we are the temple of the God. Remember the balance of both spiritual sides of the spirit realm; if we are the temple of God then the unbelievers would be the temple of Satan.

One night I was watching a sitcom on TV, one of the most hilarious shows I've ever seen. The Holy Spirit said, "Do you agree with what they are saying?" I said, "What do you mean?" I thought for a moment and realized the main point of the show was about sex outside of marriage, but portrayed in such a subtle way that I had not picked up on it as I should have. I said, "No, I do not agree with it." The Holy Spirit said, "You are by watching it faithfully; you are feeding your spirit on that." OUCH!!! I stopped watching that sitcom, and began paying more attention to what else I was watching.

Terms and Conditions of Coming Into Agreement and Covenant with Satan

I'm reminded of the famous verse, (Romans 6:23): "For the wages of sin is death."

Spiritual death, not just a physical death and then it's over, but eternity in hell, without God, where the Bible says is extreme fire, heat, pain and remembrance of the opportunities for salvation that you had during your life. The rich man in (Luke 12) made it all very clear when he remembered his life on earth and his family he had left behind whom he knew would end up with him if they did not change their ways. He begged Lazarus to just dip his finger in water to cool his tongue because he said he was tormented in the flame he was in. Some people want to say that Jesus was just using another parable here, but he wasn't, because Jesus said, "There WAS a certain rich man who died and lifted up his eyes in hell."

Remember that for whatever God has Satan has a counterfeit, or the spiritually opposite in operation. Understanding this principal of spiritual warfare, let's look again at (1 John 5:18) Amplified: "We know that whosoever is born of God does not deliberately and knowingly practice committing sin, but the One Who was begotten of God carefully watches over and protects him and Christ's divine presence within him preserves him against the evil and the wicked one does not lay hold or get a grip on him or touches him."

The Greek word for "touch" here means to fasten, cling, or attach oneself to. This verse tells us that if we are not practicing sin then Satan and the demonic don't have the legal right to touch us, or has no legal right to attack us as long as we do not knowingly and willfully commit sin.

So, what is the spiritually opposite here where Satan and the demonic has the control?

It would be read like this, "We know that whoever is not born of God and obeys Satan and deliberately and knowingly and willfully practices committing sin in rebellion, and disobedience against God is not under God's hand of protection, and Satan and the demonic has the free legal right to attack him with physical, mental, emotional and spiritual pain and anguish."

You may say, "But I didn't understand there were terms and conditions." It doesn't matter whether you did or not. The contract was there in God's Word and you just chose not to read it. You have accepted them in many different forms by default.

As I stated, you open up to physical, mental, spiritual and emotional sickliness, pain, anguish, anxiety, and depression, oppression, possession, bondage, captivity, death, spiritual domination, addiction to habits, drugs, alcohol, sexual bondages, pornography, being tormented mentally, destroyed relationships and families, lost jobs, soul and spirit ties, and the list goes on and on, all because you opened the door to Satan and the demonic giving them free legal rights to attack you.

All these are demonically influenced, the temptation having been spoken into your spirit, you accept the temptation into your soul which is your mind, your will, and your emotions, and then obeying it, thus coming into agreement and covenant with Satan and the demonic. And this has the potential of creating curses and generational curses that can be passed down to your future descendants, which can lead to continuing bondages in their lives with the same terms and conditions of the agreement and covenant renewed by them. For this reason, (Leviticus 26:40) tells us that we are to repent for the sins of our forefathers in order for these curses to be broken from us and from our descendants. I do not want my family line going through distress because of my actions. I prefer that they have a heritage of God's power as in (Isaiah 54:17) where no weapon of Satan shall prosper against us.

In (Deuteronomy 28) we find how many curses came upon Israel if they did not obey God's commandments, or if they were not in covenant with him. Jesus said if you're not with Him then you're against Him.

Different Ways Covenants Can Be Made Sexual and Emotional Covenants

In (Matthew 5:28), Jesus taught us against having lustful thoughts about the opposite sex.

Paul taught us all through his writings not to commit fornication, or have sex outside of marriage. Now Jesus said in (Matthew 5:28) that just to have the thought is the same as committing the act itself. The

Bible says in (1 Corinthians 6:16) that whoever lies with a prostitute or harlot, as Paul calls her, becomes one in spirit with her. This is quoted from (Genesis 2:24) where God said a man shall leave his father and mother and cleave to his wife and they shall be one. The word "cleave" means to adhere to, cling to, and to be faithful to. The word "cling" means to be emotionally attached to. Your soul is made up of your mind, your will, and your emotions. This act takes control of you by thoughts in your mind; your will gives in and then you're emotionally bonded in the spirit. The word "attach" means to be connected by ties of affection. The word "tie" means to bind and connect. Now this also refers to any sexual intercourse between any two people, married or not. This is an agreement and a covenant affecting your soul. Read the chapter on soul wounds.

We also find the same covenant in the story of Ruth and her mother-in-law Naomi. In (Ruth 1:14), the King James says that Ruth "clave" unto Naomi; the amplified Bible uses the word "clung." The Hebrew word for "clung" is dabaq and is like the word glue. Both clave and clung have the same meaning, which is "to be tied in the spirit emotionally to each other." A spirit and soul tie which is a form of a covenant.

All through the Old Testament God warns against leaving Him to walk for the idolatries and ungodly nations. We find the word "cleave to the Lord" again in Scripture. "Cleave unto the Lord as you have done this day... take heed that you love the Lord your God. Else if you do turn back and CLEAVE unto these ungodly nations, then they will be snares and traps to you, scourges in your side and thorns in your eyes, until you perish from off this good land which the lord has given you." This describes spirit and soul ties with the demonic and ungodly people. Once you make this conscious free will choice the ties are created, and you have come into agreement and covenant with them.

Dreams

Spiritual covenants can be made through dreams. This is a demonic spiritual attack on your subconscious and spirit and is often represented as a sexual encounter in a dream. This is an oppressive attack, of a demonic tyrannical spiritual authority, and it can cause mental anguish, spiritual and physical distress, and discomfort.

I have talked with people who have experienced this. While asleep, these spirits come in through the dream, sometimes in the form of someone they know, or sometimes in the form of a beautiful person they desire. The dream is so real the person can feel the fondling, caressing, and the kisses that get them aroused and that stimulates sexual feelings ending with an orgasm. This will often cause great shame and guilt in the victim. This can cause a bondage to lust and pornography, causing them to be physically, sexually active. This can open a door in their minds to continual lustful thoughts that will end up controlling the victim.

One youth opened up to me and shared this story. For a long period of time a girl about his age would appear to him at night, sometimes in his dreams, sometimes he said he would see her as a real solid looking person when he was awake. He said she was very nice looking and very appealing to him. She would never say anything, but she would always try to get into bed with him and fondle him; he said he could feel her touching him. He said the bed would even sink down when she would lie down next to him. Many times, he would almost give in to her and wanted to, but because of his being brought up in church, he understood what was going on, and he would resist it. Had he given into it, it would have opened doors of legal access for the demonic to work in him. I have also talked to women who have had a similar experience.

Two kinds of spirits who work in this way are "Incubus" spirits, and "Succubus" spirits.

The Latin word for "incubus" means to "lie upon;" it also means a nightmare, and an oppressive burden. This is a male spirit and is sometimes encountered by women. The "succubus" spirit in Latin means to "lie under" and is representative of a female spirit often coming to men. I believe this can lead to demonic influence, oppression, and, in rare cases, possession, depending on how much control the person allows it to have over them.

This is coming into agreement and covenant with the demonic spirit. Some people would say that you have no control of your will in a dream or its outcome because it's just that—a dream. But God showed me in a dream once, that when it is a spiritual warfare dream, you have the same free will as when you are awake, and you have the same authority given to you from God over Satan and the demonic in (Luke 10:19). You CAN defeat Satan in a dream, sometimes even better than when you are awake, because then your mind is out of the way, and your spirit man can operate off of the word of God that is in you and you can be led directly by the Holy Spirit. I have actually seen this happen for myself; it works.

The Sneak Attack

Many Christians have mistakenly come into an ungodly covenant by Satan sneaking an attack on them through deceptions of seemly innocent things and objects. Sometimes objects given to us in ungodly intimate relationships can produce and allow a soul or spirit tie in our lives that will allow demonic influence to be there. You may not understand why you are going through a particular battle that seems to occur over and over; one that you can't get free from. It may be lustful thoughts about some person or many people; it may be an opened door to ungodly dreams. It could be caused by an object given to you from a person you bonded with who was under strong demonic influence or oppression, and now you are linked to them spiritually through that object.

Many people who have bought objects while traveling on vacations, such as charms, little idols, or artifacts may encounter this problem. Concert music CD's or video games that go deeply into the occult may have evil, demonic origins. Some of these items use Satanic and demonic chants, or spells, to welcome demonic spirits into lives and homes. Movies dealing with sexual content, fornication, and infidelity are popular, and we wonder why our minds are consumed by these thoughts. It's what you are coming into agreement with, thus allowing your soul, your mind, your will and your emotions to be controlled by this. And, again, it does not matter if you understand what you are doing, whether you understand the terms of agreement or not, you can still welcome it in and give it free, legal access in your life.

Objects sitting on the mantle that, unknown to you, have been dedicated to demons can open doors. Objects used in witchcraft or Satanic ceremonies, Ouija boards, tarot cards, charms, crystals used in New Age healing, anything connected with astrology, horoscopes, fortune telling, metaphysics, and books on the occult for its promotion can open doors. These objects can open the door to a demonic presence that can and will affect you, your family, and your home with chaos. Maybe family home trouble started all the sudden and you don't know why. Think back to what came into your home about that time that may have opened a door to it. These objects can do that.

A good example of this: I, my wife, and another sister prayed for a family who was having this kind of trouble in their home. For a short period of time after we prayed they experienced a peace they had not had in some time, but then it all came back, multiplied. They had tarot cards, pornography, and illegal drugs in the house. Also, an Ouija board had been used there. They were not ready to let go of these items, so this opened the door for the demonic spirits to return sevenfold as Jesus taught in (Matthew 12: 44-45). By this they were in agreement and not ready to come out of that agreement because of the bondage the demonic had on them.

Another good example of this happened one morning when I got up to go to work and heard very sinister sounding music but was unable to tell where it was coming from. I first thought it was coming from my son's room, but when I got to his door I could not hear it. Then it sounded like it was coming from another son's room, and again at his door, I could not hear it. No matter where I thought it was coming from it wasn't there. Finally, I went upstairs and found a demonic video game that one of my sons had brought in and uploaded into my computer. This game named many demonic spirits whom I had been studying and was familiar with. Had I not studied them I might not have realized the danger that was there. I thought: how dare Satan try to sneak this into my home. If I, as the high priest of my home, and the head spiritual authority in my home, had allowed the game to stay there, it would have been the same as welcoming it into my home. Then I would have been opening a door of attack to my home and my family. I would have also been coming into agreement and covenant with it.

My son knows I do not allow this in my house. When I found it, and commanded any spirit attached to it to leave and rendered them powerless against us in the name and authority of Jesus Christ the music stopped. I found out he had had it for about a month. About a month before this, our dog began barking and growling one night about 2 a.m. He doesn't do that unless there is something there. I found out the next day that my oldest son, and the one who had brought the game in, had experienced an encounter where he was being held down in the bed by an invisible force, hearing low, mumbling voices that he could not understand. As the oldest son began to rebuke it in the name of Jesus it began losing power against him. All of this happened at 2 a.m. the same morning.

What you watch on TV can do it also. Always remember if you welcome anything into your home that is cursed in this way then you, your family, and your home becomes cursed by God. Keep in mind that any prayers or worship offered to anyone or anything other than God the Father, Jesus His son, or the Holy Spirit are prayers and worship that are being offered to demons, and God condemned that in His Word. These prayers and worship, whether from you, your children, in music, movies or games that you have allowed into your home, can be answered by demons in the form of curses, sickness and spiritual warfare attacks as long as you have the door legally opened to them they will flourish in your life, and you will not walk in victory.

But you say: "I am not worshipping demons when I do this." The word "worship" means an intense love or admiration for a deity, feeling, or offering a great devotion of time or service.

God tells us in (Exodus 23:32): "Thou shalt make no covenant with them, nor with their Gods. Do not let them live in your land or they will cause you to sin against me, because the worship of their Gods will certainly be a snare to you." You may not have any control over whether they live in your land or not, but you do have control whether they live in your house or not. When you make a covenant outside of God you are shifting your alliance from God to another god.

Many people have made covenants, oaths, pledges, and even covenants with secret organizations such as witches, Ku Klux Klan, Free Masons, etc. These secret agreements, oaths, and pledges are made and intended to be covenants for life. Let me say here God CAN BREAK ALL THESE. They bring bondage with them because you are now making a spirit tie with the entire group and whatever (witchcraft, murder, idolatry, etc.) they are involved in. You are opening the door for legal access to whatever spirit are oppressing them to now oppress you, and bringing every generational curse affecting their lives in upon you and your descendants.

Here's what happens in the spirit realm when this happens. The person agreeing and coming into the covenant is guilty of IDOLATRY. Because they are pledging their obedience, trust, and loyalty, to the demonic spirits behind the human being, instead of to God; he is pledging his human will to become a human slave. This is worshipping the person or group as an idol. Paul said in (Romans

6:16): "Do you not know that when you offer yourselves to someone as obedient slaves you are slaves of the one you obey, whether you are slaves to sin, which leads to death, or to obedience, which leads to righteousness."

In (Exodus 20), God gave the 10 Commandments and on through to the 28th chapter with blessings. God wanted to make a covenant with His people, Israel. He promised them blessings if they would only love and obey Him. He wanted them to have a real and eternal relationship with HIM, not an idol. He offered to show mercy, kindness, favor and pity to thousands if they would only love Him and keep His commandments. He offered them a long life, blessing, peace and prosperity, rest, divine guidance and protection from enemies, famine and plague, health, healing, supernatural and miraculous help, blessings to their crops, animals, and children and to their business ventures. Wow, sounds like a pretty good deal, doesn't it? But Israel couldn't even do their part to receive it.

Religious and Inherited Covenants

In (1 Corinthians 10:14-22), Paul was teaching us that we should not be partakers of feasts or ceremonies of pagan, heathen or idolatry. We are to avoid saint or demon worship, eating food that has been sacrificed to idols which are demons, cult churches that deny Jesus as the only son of God and faith in His shed blood. And if we do partake, then we become partners with demons. If you study into this you find that soul and spirit ties can come into play here, even as an emotional bond.

The Bible teaches against swearing oaths of allegiance to Satan, Satanism, witchcraft, sorcery, the occult, readings, blood covenants, fortune tellers, palm readers, star gazers, drugs, pornography, séances, and the list goes on and on. I have prayed for people and their homes where these things have been involved, either in the past or sometimes in the present, and have seen lives in bondage, with demonic manifestations occurring in the home. When we have ancestors, who have been involved in these things, the spiritual bondage is passed on down the blood line to the descendants. These are inherited covenants or, better known as, generational curses. Be sure to read the chapter on generational curses for more information.

Even some Christian churches who believe Jesus is God's son and have faith in His shed blood for our atonement are sometimes guilty of putting people into religious bondage. Yes, we believe you have to live a holy life according to (Hebrews 14:12) "that without holiness no man shall see God." Peter tells us to be holy as God is holy. But these well-meaning saints put people, especially new Christians, under such strict requirements that even they themselves could not live up to. They bring these young Christians under an extensive list of do's and don'ts. They bring them under so much condemnation that these young Christians never know if they are saved or not. They are taught if you even get tempted but still don't sin, it doesn't matter; you are evil for even having the temptation to start with. They are taught that God is an evil taskmaster just waiting for the joyful moment that He can crush you and erase your name from the Book of Life and you probably won't have the chance to ever be forgiven. This causes them to live under a constant mental and spiritual stronghold of a fear of losing their salvation and not seeing God as a loving father who wants the best for them, so much so that He gave His only son to die for our sins. In (Jeremiah 29:11) God said: "For I know the thoughts and plans that I have for you, says the Lord, thoughts and plans for welfare and peace and not for evil, to give you hope in your final outcome." Now, does this sound like a mean God? No, it doesn't.

This kind of teaching is a lie from Satan to keep people from ever becoming what God wants them to become; it leaves them defeated. It keeps their faith torn down. But this kind of bondage of ignorance can cause spirit ties of agreement to the enemy, allowing him to control their thoughts and beliefs. I'm not saying they are not saved; they are, but they are deceived and need to break free from this agreement and covenant. This also can be passed down the religious bloodline or be "inherited."

You Have to Take Action to Get Free

You have to:

1. Recognize it's there.

2. You have to repent of the sin that caused the curse to be in effect. (Leviticus 26:40) tells us to even ask forgiveness of sins for our ancestors.

3. You have to renounce the curse by falling out of agreement with it.

4. You must cover yourself, your children and your property, physically, mentally, emotionally, and spiritually with the blood of Jesus.

5. Bind every demonic principality assigned to attack you through any demonic covenant, blood covenant, and oath, word curse spoken by you or others, in the name of Jesus.

6. Once delivered, you must not allow it back again. You must ask God to forgive the sins and any action by you, your family members, or your ancestors that have opened doors of agreement to the demonic. You must break soul and spirit ties of past relationships and ancestors by asking God in prayer, and renounce it. You must be led by the Holy Spirit and do a search and clean out your house of any objects in question by physically removing the objects from the home. If you know the demonic prayers that have been prayed in your home, or over you and your family, renounce them and break them in Jesus' name. You must anoint the house with oil and get others if you need them to come in and pray for the removal of any spirits that may be there, letting them know they are no longer welcome because there is now a change of ownership. I would

suggest first for the group praying to begin by filling the house with nothing but praise to God, inviting in the presence of Jesus and the Holy Spirit to fill every room, the studs inside the walls, the space in between the flooring and ceiling joist, the foundation, the entire structure. Then listen for the Holy Spirit to say, "It's time." Then begin to take authority verbally over the enemy, casting it out of the house and off the property in the name and authority of Jesus Christ. Remember there is power in God's Word spoken through you. If it is a two-story house start with the lowest floor and follow this method all the way to the top floor and attic leaving no room for them to hide.

7. Verbally denounce Satan and any demonic spirits working under him, and claim the blood.

Prayer:

In the name of Jesus, I renounce and break the very foundation of all generational curses affecting my life at this moment. Of lust, perversion, immorality, rebellion, any curses from soul and spirit ties, unforgiveness, disobedience, Satan worship, casting spells, witchcraft, any use of any occult and demonic objects, charms, Ouija boards, watching and allowing into my home demonic movies and video games, familiar spirits, séances, idolatry and the curses of Halloween. I renounce and break any curses of poverty, curses on my finances from misuse of money by myself or my ancestors, curses of rejection, fear, strife, confusion. All spoken word curses, negative words spoken against me by myself, by others, and by any demonic spirits. Of any disease, sickness, hatred, anger. I renounce and break any binding oaths, pledges, pacts, blood covenants, any thoughts, wishes or desires of harm against myself and others, any written or spoken curses by myself or others against me that affect my life in a negative way, every time released generational curse that would activate, as I grow older, and any curse that would negatively affect my advancement in blessings from God.

I renounce and break all false beliefs, false religions, and philosophies inherited from my ancestors. I renounce and break any curse of untimely death, defeat, failure, spoken by myself or others over me. I break all these agreements, contracts, and covenants that I or my ancestors may have made with demonic spirits from myself all the way back through my family blood to Adam. God, I ask You to forgive any of mine and my ancestor's wrong doing. God, I ask You now to close any doors I or my ancestors have opened all the way back to Adam. In the name and the authority of Jesus Christ, I accept from this moment a generational blessing on mine and my descendant's lives. I and my descendants will serve God in ministry. We will bring people into the kingdom of God. We will teach the present and the future generations how to be saved, healed, blessed, delivered, set free by the power of God and how to defeat Satan and the demonic forces. In the name of Jesus, Amen.

Chapter 29

Your Spiritual Authority

(Luke 10:19): Behold I give unto you power over all the power of the enemy. And nothing shall by any means hurt you.

(Philippians 2:9-10): God has highly exalted him, and given him a name which is above every name: That at the name of Jesus every knee should bow, in Heaven and in earth.

(Ephesians 1:21-22): Far above all principality, and power, and might and dominion, and every name that is named and has put all things under his feet.

(Ephesians 6:12): For we are not wrestling against flesh and blood, but against principalities, against powers, against the master spirits who are the rulers of this present darkness, against the spirit forces of wickedness in the heavenly places.

The Satanic-demonic kingdom is set up in a military type of rank, authority, and power.

In (Matthew 12:26) Jesus said if Satan be divided against himself how shall his kingdom stand?

In (1 Samuel 17:8-9), Goliath was in command of the entire army of the enemy. They had David surrounded. So, we can say that Goliath represents the head demonic principality and the troops who are working under him, carrying out the attack against us. Goliath told David if you can find a man who can fight against me and win, then I and my entire army will surrender and bow down to you and we will be your servants. Meaning that Goliath and his entire army would obey David.

Verse 45, David said to Goliath: "You have come to me with a sword," or in other words, you have invaded my turf with your attack on me and my family. "But I come to you in the name of the Lord." In verse 46, David said, "This day will the Lord deliver you into my hand; and I will smite you and take your head from you." Verse 49, David killed Goliath with the stone to his forehead.

Verse 51 David ran up and stood on top of Goliath's dead body, and with Goliath's own sword, or we could say the thing that he meant to be his weapon against us, David cut off Goliath's head. And when the Philistines saw that their champion was dead, they fled. Israel chased them away and spoiled their tents.

In (Matthew 12:29) Jesus said, "How can one enter the strongman's house, and spoil his goods, except he first BIND the strongman? Then he will spoil his house?"

You fight Satan and the demonic from the top down, not the bottom up. You go to the head principality who originated the attack against you, take out "that" strongman, and then you take out all the ones working under his authority.

(1 Samuel 17:47) David told Goliath, "The battle is the Lord's."

You have to rid and keep your life and home from sin or evil objects or the spirit can have legal access to come back. (Matthew 12:43-45) and (Deuteronomy 7:25) tell us to burn these things with fire.

Take spiritual inventory of your life and the contents of your home constantly to keep it free.

Commit yourself, your family, and your home and your property to God. (Proverbs 16:3).

Praise and worship have won many battles in the Old Testament, like Joshua at Jericho.

Deliverance prayer:

In the name of Jesus, I repent of and ask forgiveness of any open or hidden sin that I've ever committed and ask you to destroy all personal and generational sin from my ancestors of rebellion, stubbornness and disobedience, jealousy, envy, for allowing cursed or occultic objects, idols, movies, video games, materials, and anything else that I or my ancestors have knowingly or unknowingly done to open doors in our lives and our home that has given demonic spirits free legal access to attack us in any way.

In the name and authority of Jesus Christ, we reject, renounce, and break every evil, Satanic, occultic and demonic covenant that we or any of our ancestors have made, and every word curse that has ever been spoken over us by someone else.

In the name and authority of Jesus Christ, we destroy every altar in our lives that have been erected from these covenants and curses from Handling cursed objects, contact with Satanic agents, living in or on a previously cursed home or land, receiving cursed gifts, involvement in a demonic ritual, witchcraft, or festivals. We ask in the name and authority of Jesus Christ that any demonic spirits affecting us causing failure, defeat, depression, oppression, affliction, sickliness, delayed blessings, limitations, confusion, strife, frustration, rejection; any soul and spirit ties, and any other weapon formed against us be destroyed now and lose all power against us in the name of Jesus.

In the name and the authority of Jesus Christ, we bind all powers of witches, wizards, familiar spirits, and all the demonic ranks that would try to fight against us and loose the freedom and peace of God in my life, my family's life and our home.

In the name and authority of Jesus Christ, I close any doorway, entrances and exits the demonic have into my home and my life. WE forbid any demonic spirit, any reinforcement of power from the outside to enter this place for any reason. We bind every evil spirit in this place and forbid any violence, manifestation, and any kind of physical, mental or spiritual torment in the name and authority of Jesus Christ.

Now, I am speaking to the demonic principality that is responsible of ordering this attack against us. This is my home, my family, and my property and we belong to God and you are not welcome here. In the name and authority of Jesus Christ, get out of my home, get out of my family, and get off my property and don't come back.

Chapter 30

Words are Important

Words are very important, and what we speak can have a great impact on the authority of God that we walk in. This is why Paul told us in (Romans 12:2): "And be not conformed to this world: but be transformed by the renewing of your mind, that you may prove what is that good and acceptable will of God." The only way that we can do that is to speak God's Word. The original Greek word in this verse for "conform" means to conform to another's example. Why would we want to conform to Satan's example by repeating his word over us? The original Greek word for "transformed" in this verse means to be transfigured by a supernatural change. The word "transfigured" in the Webster Dictionary means to change so as to GLORIFY someone. Who are you going to glorify God or Satan? You do it by whose word you agree with and obey. This creates a covenant and a stronghold with the one you obey. How can we do as this verse says and present ourselves as a living sacrifice, making our bodies holy, being acceptable to God in his service, if we're not transformed and transfigured by our words agreeing with God's Word?

(Psalms 50:23): He who brings an offering of praise honors and glorifies me: and he who orders his way or conversation aright [who prepares the way that I may show him] to "him" I will demonstrate the salvation of God."

The word "salvation" means having forgiveness, healing, deliverance, protection, safety, being rescued, being avenged, and much more.

Whose word are you going to glorify? God or Satan? You do this by whose word you agree with and obey. This creates a covenant and a stronghold of power with the one you obey. How can we do this?

(Romans 12:1-2) says and to present ourselves as a living sacrifice, making our bodies holy, being acceptable to God in His service. How can we do this if we're not transformed and transfigured by His Word?

If your children hear you speaking negative words all their lives, they will be programmed with the wrong thinking that will be difficult to deprogram them of later. That is a stronghold.

Jesus said in (Matthew 12:37) that by our words we are either justified or condemned. In (Matthew 12:34) Jesus said that from the abundance of your heart your mouth will speak. In (Romans 10:8), Paul says that God's word is in our mouth and our hearts. There is a definite connection between our hearts and our mouths. Our faith is released through our mouth when we speak His Word. God said in Jeremiah: "I am alert and active, watching over My word to perform it." (Proverbs 18:21) says death and life are in the power of the tongue. The tongue can produce death because (Proverbs 6:2) tells us to not be snared by our words. (Matthew 8:16) says he cast out the spirits with his word and healed all that were sick by his word and that's what he has given us to fight with. The book of Revelation says they overcame Satan by the blood of the lamb and the word of their testimony. Our words that we speak will either give praise to God or Satan about the situation that we are in. The only way that we can give praise to God is to say what Gods words say. (Amos 3:3) says: "Can two walk together except they be agreed." The word "agree" means to be in accord, to be of the same opinion, to confess the same thing. (Romans 10:10) says with the mouth confession is made unto salvation. (Hebrews 4:23) tells us to hold fast the confession of our faith without wavering, for He is faithful as promised.

If we do not agree with what God says, then we are agreeing with Satan. (Ephesians 4:29) says "let not corrupt communication proceed out your mouth, but that which is good for the use of edifying." In (Mark 11:23) says: "...and shall doubt in his heart but shall believe that those things which he says shall come to pass he shall have whatsoever he says." This not only works in prayer but Jesus said, "as a man "thinks" in his heart so is he," or as we see ourselves and begin to believe that, that is what we are. We have to agree with what God's Word says about us, not what Satan and our situation says about us.

I knew a woman who had a daughter-in-law who had cancer. She said, "I'm praying God will heal her, but I doubt He will." Well, let me tell it how it is. You might as well quit praying, kick back in the recliner, grab the remote and watch TV. Because if you say you doubt that God will do what you are praying for because the situation just looks so bad, then you are giving praise to the power of Satan instead of the power of God. In mathematics if you add a positive 5 and a negative 5 you get ZERO. It's the same result with faith and prayer.

Jesus said in (Matthew 12:34): "Out of the abundance of the heart the mouth speaketh." So, what are you speaking over your situation.

In (Psalms 39:1), David said: "I will take heed to my ways that I sin not with my tongue."

Wrong words can cause your spiritual and physical life to be in chaos or in blessing.

(Proverbs 18:21) says: "Death and life are in the power of the tongue." (Job 6:25): Words are forcible. In (Mark 11:23): Our faith is released by our words. In (Matthew 21:22): Whatever we ask in prayer believing we will receive. In (Jeremiah 1:12): God watches over his word to perform it. (Jeremiah 33:3): God answers us mightily when we call on him with our word of prayer. (Psalms 65:2): God hears our prayers. (Psalms 18:3): God will bring salvation and deliverance when we call on him. (Matthew 16): God gives us the right to bind and to loose. (John 14:13): He will answer what we ask of him.

All of this is done by our words. God hears everything that we say, and since He keeps an account of every word that we say whether good or bad, and then what does God hear you saying? When you pray does He hear you say? Are you speaking blessings or are you speaking doubt and denial into your life? We need to say as God's Word says, and tell Satan (as Jesus did in (Matthew 4)) what God says about you. "I can do all things through Christ that strengthens me." "With his stripes we ARE healed," (Isaiah 53:5).

When God hears you confessing His Word instead of what your situation says then He knows you believe Him and He will honor your faith because that is what faith is when you speak the verses (like what you just read) and stand on them.

You have to find the verses in the Bible referring to all of the subjects and the areas that you are facing and memorize (or in my case write down) the verses. Then begin to use them in prayer and in praise and confess them over your life, hold on to the promises because they are YOURS. And tell Satan what God's Word says about you; rebuke him with the Word as Jesus did in (Matthew 4), and tell him that you will not accept his defeat upon your life.

Don't ever say that you're defeated or a failure because:

"God...Always causeth us to triumph in Christ," (2 Corinthians 2:14).
"God, I thank you that through you that I have victory and that I triumph in everything that I do."
(Romans 8:37), "In all these things we are MORE than conquerors through him that loved us."
(Philippians 4:130, "I can do all things through Christ that strengtheneth me."
(Isaiah 54:17), "No weapon formed against thee shall prosper."
(Luke 10:19), "Behold, I have given you authority to tread upon serpents and scorpions, and over all the power of the enemy: and

nothing shall in any way hurt you."

God, through you I am victorious and a conqueror over every attack that is planned for me. I ask you to destroy any weapon that comes against me. And I walk in your authority and power that you've given me. Everything that I do is blessed because I trust you and your word.

Don't ever say you have no strength because:

"The Lord is the strength of my life," (Psalms 27:1).
(Psalms 9:9) says, the LORD will be a refuge for the oppressed, a refuge, and a refuge in the times of trouble.
(Psalms 46:1), God is our refuge and strength a very present help in the time of trouble.
(Psalms 18:2), The LORD is my rock and my fortress and my deliverer, my God, my strength.
(Isaiah 40:29), He gives strength to the weary and increases the power of the weak.
(1 John 4:4), Greater is he that is within us than he that is in the world.

God, I thank you that I have your strength and power in my life today, right now because you are my rock and my fortress and my deliverer. God, I run to you to deliver me. Satan cannot overcome me because I walk in your strength and your promises for me, and he cannot overcome your word. God, you know no defeat and neither should I because I trust you and your word.

Don't ever say Satan has power over you because:

"Greater is he (God) that is in you than he that is in the world." (1 John 4:4)
"Behold I unto you power....and over all the power of the enemy" (Luke 10:19)
"God hath highly exalted him and given him a name above every

358

name" (Philippians 2:8).

"Which he wrought in Christ, when he raised him from the dead and set him at his own right hand in the heavenly places. Far above all principality, and power, and might and every dominion and every name that is named. And hath put all things under his feet," (Ephesians 1:20-22).

"And if Children, then heirs; heirs of God, and joint-heirs with Christ." (Romans 8:17).

In the name of Jesus, which is above every name, God, I thank you and I accept the power that you have given me over all the power of Satan. Because of that God is great and powerful in me. I have power over all the ranks of Satan, above all principality, power, might and dominions. I am an heir and a joint heir of Jesus and all power has been given to me including the power to use his name. And all things that are not from God are under my feet also.

Don't ever say I can never get my healing because:

(1 Peter 2:24): By His stripes we are healed.

Chapter 31

Try Prayer, Praise and Worship Instead of Word Curses

Prayer, praise, and worship are great ways to keep your home clean from invading forces. As a believer, you have to rid and keep your life and home from sin and evil objects or the demonic spirits can have legal access to come and attack. Take spiritual inventory of your life and the contents of your home constantly to keep it free. Commit yourself, your family, and your home and property to God. Keep a close watch on what you and your family are allowing into your home, on television, video games, and music. These are just a few of the ways the enemy can cause tension, strife, confusion, and discord to tear the family apart.

Praise and worship won many battles in the Old Testament, like Joshua at Jericho.

Deliverance prayer:

In the name of Jesus, I repent of, and ask forgiveness for, any open or hidden sin that I've ever committed and ask you to destroy all personal and generational sins from my ancestors, rebellion, stubbornness, disobedience, jealousy, envy, for allowing cursed or occult objects, idols, movies, video games, materials, and anything else that I or my ancestors have knowingly or unknowingly done to open doors in our lives and our home that has given demonic spirits free legal access to attack us in any way.

In the name and authority of Jesus Christ, we reject, renounce, and break every evil, Satanic, occultic and demonic covenant that we or any of our ancestors have made, and every word curse that has ever been spoken over us by someone else.

In the name and authority of Jesus Christ, we destroy every altar in our lives that have been erected from these covenants and curses from handling cursed objects, contact with Satanic agents, living in, or on, a previously cursed home or land, receiving cursed gifts, involvement in a demonic ritual, witchcraft, or festivals.

We ask in the name and authority of Jesus Christ that any demonic spirits affecting us causing failure, defeat, depression, oppression, affliction, sickliness, delayed blessings, limitations, confusion, strife, frustration, rejection, any soul and spirit ties, and any other weapon formed against us be destroyed now and lose all power against us in the name of Jesus.

In the name and the authority of Jesus Christ, I bind all powers of witches, wizards, familiar spirits, and all the demonic ranks that would try to fight against us and loose the freedom and peace of God in my life, my family's life and our home.

In the name and authority of Jesus Christ, I ask to close any doorway, entrances and exits the demonic has into my home and my life. We forbid any demonic spirit, any reinforcement of power from the outside to enter this place for any reason. We bind every evil spirit in this place and forbid any violence, manifestation, and any kind of physical, mental or spiritual torment in the name and authority of Jesus Christ.

Now, I am speaking to the demonic principality that is responsible for ordering this attack against us. This is my home, my family, and my property and we belong to God and you are not welcome here. In the name and authority of Jesus Christ, get out of my home, get out of my family, and get off my property and don't come back.

I've heard many people say "I just can't think of all that much to pray, I pray everything I think of and I'm through in 3 minutes. Jesus said in (Luke 18:1) "men ought ALWAYS to pray" Paul said in (1

Thessalonians 5:17) "pray WITHOUT ceasing." Ok so how do I do that, I know we can't go 24 hours a day in nothing but prayer, but there is a way that I hope to teach you that you can increase your prayer life, where you can spend much more time in prayer, and at the same time tear down strongholds in your life, building up a life of praise that, will have you walking in victory. Giving YOU power over the power of Satan and his ranks. Jesus said in (Luke 10:19) "I give you power over ALL the power the power of the enemy." It will change your whole outlook on life from negative to positive building your faith level where you believe and trust God and his word. What am I talking about, learning to use God's word in prayer and praise and learning the promises of his word?

The way God first showed this to me was in a dream. I had been going through a spiritual battle; I won't go into all the details, but God showed me the demonic spirit that I was fighting. He explained to me that it was a mid-ranking spirit that was sent to carry a plan against me that was orchestrated by Satan. As I looked at this spirit I saw deep gashing scars covering its body that had been there so long they were healed over. I thought, "What are those scars from?" The Holy Spirit answered me and said, "THOSE ARE BATTLE SCARS WHERE HE HAS BEEN DEFEATED IN CONFLICTS OF SPIRITUAL WARFARE BY ANGELS AND THE DEFEAT WAS DUE TO THE PRAYERS OF THE SAINTS PRAYING THE WORD OF GOD."

I felt a power of anointing rise inside me like I've never felt before in my life. Scripture began to flow out of me toward the demonic spirit in the form of prayer with a force that I've never experienced before or since. The spirit would not look at me, nor would it turn its back to me, but it began to back away and run in fear, due to God's Word. As I awoke I was praying out loud with the same force as in my dream. The authority that God has given us in His Word, to use His name, will work in the physical realm and in the spiritual realm when God gives you a spiritual dream.

Chapter 32

Armor of God

(Ephesians 6:11): "Put on the whole armor of God that ye may be able to stand against the wiles of the devil." As Christians, we are in a battle for our very existence. Satan and the demonic are trying to kill, steal and destroy us physically, mentally, emotionally, and spiritually. Jesus gained dominion over Satan and the demonic not only on the cross but also in (Matthew 4) during the 40 days of fasting, and he has given us the same full dominion over them. Our main defense is having the full armor in place in our lives.

Paul said in (2 Corinthians 10:4), "For the weapons of our warfare are not carnal." "Carnal" meaning not of the flesh, not material, worldly, sensual or sexual, but mighty through God's power to pull down strongholds. Verse 5 says, "Casting down imaginations, and every high thing that exalted itself against the knowledge of God and bringing into captivity every thought to the obedience of Christ. The battles that we fight are in the spirit realm, so our weapons have to be spiritual weapons."

This verse tells us that we are to destroy all false religions, doctrines, mythology, evil desires, thoughts and temptations, attacks of low self-esteem, attacks of word curses spoken against us. We are to destroy this by knowing the Word of God and being fully clad with God's armor.

Spiritual battles can be obstacles, temptations, or conflicts that we face. Satan and the demonic can come against your family to cause divorce; and can come against your finances to keep you from being able to support your family and the ministry; through physical attacks on your body, keeping you from being physically able to do any work for God.

(Ephesians 6:10-18): Finally, my brethren, be strong in the Lord, and in the power of HIS might. Put on the whole armor of God that ye may be able to stand against the wiles of the devil.

For we wrestle not against flesh and blood, but against principalities, against powers, against the rulers of the darkness of this world, against spiritual wickedness in high places.

Wherefore take unto you the whole armor of God that ye may be able to stand in the evil day, and having done all to stand.

Stand therefore, having your loins girt about with truth, and having on the breast plate of righteousness, and your feet shod with the preparation of the gospel of peace, above all taking the shield of faith, wherewith ye shall be able to quench all the fiery darts of the wicked.

And take the helmet of salvation, and the sword of the spirit, which is the word of God: praying always with prayer and supplication in the spirit, and watching thereunto with all perseverance and supplication for all saints.

The word "wiles" in the 11th verse means a sly and beguiling trick, to lure away. Paul tells us to not be ignorant of Satan's devices, his plans and schemes to trap us and to make us become his slaves to sin.

Verse 12 says "wrestle" is "pale" and means one-on-one combat to the death. Not our death but theirs. This warfare is between saints of God and Satan and the demonic spirits.

The last part of this verse says, "in high places;" the Greek word here is "epouranois" which means in the "heavenlies."

The word "principality" means a prince that rules over a territory. The Greek word for principalities is "archas" which refers to the top-ranking demonic positions over geographic regions of the earth. (Ephesians 6:12) in the amplified Bible says "despotisms," which are basically the same but explains it a little deeper. "Despotism" means a system or government with a ruler having absolute authority; a form of government system ruled by a tyrant dictator, and a master of slaves.

The word "powers" means one with influence over other nations, a person or thing having influence, force or authority, legal authority and vigor, force and strength. Here it is referring to demonic spirits who are second in command below the principality. Who would still be over geographic regions, broken down to smaller areas, with others under their authority to carry out commands and strategies against the saints? The word "powers" in Greek is "exousia" and means delegated authority. The word "delegate" means a person authorized to act under the rule of another's representation, to entrust power and authority to another of higher authority. These are given orders to be carried out for all kinds of evil.

"The rulers of the darkness of this world;" in this, the word "ruler" means one who governs. It is taken from the Greek word "kosokrateros" and is made up of 2 other words "kosmos" and "kratos." The word "kosmos" means "order" or "arrangement". "Kratos" means "raw power," this means raw power that has been harnessed to put into an order. The word was also used by the Greek military to describe certain aspects of the military.

Remember that what we see in the physical realm where we exist reflects what is going on in the spirit realm where the demonic kingdom exists. The Greek army had a lot of young, strong soldiers who had a lot of natural fighting ability, strength and energy—or raw power. For that raw power to be harnessed and effectively used in battle, it had to be harnessed, trained, and organized by top-ranking officers, providing a strong military instead of confusion and weakness.

We are on a battlefield also. The war that we're in does not have cease fires. Even if you're not directly under fire at this moment you are still a target and are on the battlefield. Because you are a threat to the enemy. That's why we must stay constantly in prayer and in God's Word, learning and knowing how to use it. We are an army and we need to join and fight as an army.

Satan (and the demonic) is the adversary that we're fighting. Jesus said that they are thieves here to "steal, to kill and to destroy." (1 Peter 5:8) Amplified says, "be well balanced (temperate, sober of mind), be vigilant and cautious at all times; for that enemy of yours the devil, roams around like a lion roaring, in fierce hunger, seeking someone to seize upon and devour."

The Armor

(Ephesians 6:14): "Stand therefore, having your loins girt about with TRUTH." I like the way the amplified Bible says it: "Stand therefore, [HOLD YOUR GROUND] having tightened the belt of truth around your loins." In (John 14:6) Jesus said: "I am the way, the TRUTH and the life." When Jesus was praying for the disciples in (John 17:17), He prayed to God to: "Sanctify them through thy truth: thy WORD in truth." Jesus also said in (John 8:32): "And ye know the truth and the truth shall make you free." Verse 36: "If the Son therefore shall make you free, ye shall be free indeed." The secret to truly having freedom from the hurts, habits and bondages that we face is knowing Jesus as the living word and knowing God's written word. Knowing this will bring faith to you when facing these battles. (Romans 10:17): "So then faith comes by hearing, and hearing by the word of God."

Let me explain how this can work when you're facing a problem. First, "DON'T PANIC," no matter how the situation looks; realize that God is in control. Take care of whatever steps you need to; for instance, if it's a medical emergency then of course call 911, call an ambulance, call people to be praying, use common sense. Then do

366

not automatically look at the situation as being something that can automatically defeat you.

Learn to STAND YOUR GROUND. Then pray and give God total control of the situation as (1 Peter 5:7) tells us to "cast all our cares on him." I learned this when I had a problem and after praying for the answer, I figured out what I needed, and did things my way. That only made the situation worse. I did this three times. Finally, I said, "God, I give up. Here take it." Then I visualized in my mind God reaching down and myself raising the problem up to Him and Him taking it out of my hands. The problem disappeared the next day. I thought, wow, that was easy.

Then say: "All right God this is just another chance for you to work a miracle." Find scriptures that relate to your situation, God's healing promises, God's faithfulness, and His overcoming power, and the authority Jesus has given you over Satan in (Luke 10:19). "Behold I give you power over all the power of the enemy and nothing shall by any means shall hurt you."

It's all in His Word; you just have to find it. Memorize or write down these scriptures and begin to use them in prayer, praise, worship and thanksgiving over your situation. Remind God that you are standing right here; you refuse to accept anything else except His victory because His Word promises it and quote it to Him.

Begin to tell Satan that he has lost, that you refuse to accept his defeat because God's Word says (quote your verses) to him. Do this over and over and over and DO NOT waver in what you're doing or believing. When you do this, you are STANDING YOUR GROUND in faith. Then you will see God work a miracle in what you're facing, and your faith level will go up a few points.

You will get another chance (sooner or later) to do it all over again because you are Satan's target. Each time you see God work miracle after miracle your faith level will go up. It is just like lifting weights:

it takes constant working out over and over to become a body builder. And it is the same way with building faith.

Chapter 33

My Testimony

When I was very young I had a physical handicap. To start with my legs were twisted and I had to wear braces on them. Also, I was not capable of speaking anything audible enough to be understood. The specialist at UAB medical center in Birmingham, Alabama said I would never be able to be any better and there was nothing they could do for me. Just before I went into the first grade after much prayer I could walk and contrary to medical science my speech had greatly recovered. That is something that was never supposed to happen.

Growing up we were a very dysfunctional family. A friend of mine said she was raised by Ozzie and Harriet. My brother and I were raised in a totally different atmosphere. Our mother was diagnosed as being severe bipolar, paranoia delusional, schizophrenia, severe anger issues, and psychosis. In her head "THEY" were always watching her. "THEY" were always tapping her phone and recording her conversations. "THEY" could even see her through the telephone. This was in the 1970's and 80's before there were cordless, cell phones and camera phones. "THEY" were always spying on her. "THEY" were always hovering in I'm not sure what maybe the mother ship over our house at night. She would see and hear "THEM" in the television watching her even when it was unplugged from the wall. She would hear a voice that she thought was God telling her some of the most bazaar things. I know God very well and he doesn't say the things she accused him of saying, nor does he lie. She thought everyone was out to get her and didn't like her. We tried to keep this secret hid from everyone out of shame. We weren't in denial we just didn't want to admit it was happening. Come on and laugh that's a joke.

My mother having been severely physically abused and we believe sexually abused as a child for several years ended up being an abuser. For years she would be locked in an outside wood shed. I went through years of being physically abused because of this being passed on as a generational curse. Many, many times, I did not know why I was being hit with no explanation. More times than I can count for many years I remember being held down on the floor while being beaten with whatever item she could get her hands on. She would go into fits of anger and extreme rage and I would get the brunt of it. She would break things in the house out of anger and rage and I would get the blame. I wasn't codependent I just tried every way I could to make her happy so she wouldn't have a reason to yell, scream and hit. I would even hide but it didn't work. I was told my entire childhood how stupid, worthless, and ugly I was. No girl would ever want to go out with someone as ugly as I was. I was told that I would never amount to anything. I didn't have enough brains to do anything right. That I would fail at everything I would ever try to do. I had no confidence and very low self-esteem. I believed this lie of Satan until I was 36 years old. I was forced to wear out of date clothes to school, clothes that sometimes-looked like girl's clothes. Naturally I endured much torment by the other kids at school. I dreamed of doing the first school shooting in the 1960's and 70's because of this torment. More than once as a child she stripped me to my underwear in public as I stood there in front of people. Sometimes as an older child she would make me wear cloth diapers and expect me to go outside and play in them.

She constantly said she was going to walk out and leave some day and never come back and I had hoped she would. My father would never do anything to stop the abuse. He would sit and read the newspaper or watch sports while this was going on. He told someone once that he knew she was mean to my brother and me but that kept her off his back. Naturally I begin to see God as a mean tyrant who hated me, eagerly waiting to beat me up over the slightest mistake. As a child I lived in constant fear that they would carry me off and abandon me in the woods.

It was so bad at about the age of 13 or 14 I had a 22 caliber pistol pointed at her. I wanted to kill her because I hated her so much. I would often envision her suffering a slow painful death from a brain tumor or cancer. Or maybe a horrific car crash where she suffered, screaming in agony as the rescue workers had to cut her out of the car. The only reason I didn't shoot her is I didn't want to go to jail. I did not realize it at the time as a child, because of mother abusing me, being smaller and defenseless against her created anger in me. It gave me the power to turn on those who were smaller and defenseless against me. I caused them pain as she caused me pain. I would hurt smaller children because I wanted to see them cry. I wanted them to feel the pain of what I could do. I wanted them to look in my eyes and know that it was me causing them pain. I wanted to see the fear in their eyes. It gave me power and a sense of fulfillment. For years I tortured and killed animals as a child because I also felt like it gave me power. I did not feel bad about it. I had no remorse. It fed something in me and made me feel good. As I got bored with torturing animals I begin to wonder how it would be to abduct and torture a human being. For years I thought in detail about how I could do this when I got older with the entire plan thought out. As I would be carrying on a conversation with someone, I would see a vision of taking whatever weapon I could get my hands on, maybe a brick or claw hammer and at an unexpected moment beating their head into a bloody, gory mess. Or tying them down as a hostage and slowly dismembering their body while they were alive. And of course, I would have to kill them, I couldn't release them after all that.

I know what Satan's plan was for my life. It was to be a psychopathic serial killer. I had been trained and cultured for this my entire childhood. But I thank God that he had a plan for my life. It was to give and to speak life into people, not to take it. It was teaching and preaching his word to a world who doesn't know he cares. And I praise God that his plan won.

The words "I LOVE YOU" were never said in our home. This made it very difficult for me to be able to tell anyone else "I love you." When my older son was born I held him in my arms and after a long time I was finally able to force the words out 'I love you." I was 45 years old before I accidently not meaning to say the words "love you too" to my mother one day. I said, "Oh no what did I just do, and how can I take it back, I didn't mean to say that." Although she still had the same mental problems she in her own way was trying to make amends at that time for what she had done years earlier. I had to forgive her for it which was hard to do.

On top of this I was raised in a church that taught us that everything was a sin. When I say everything, I mean everything. There was even a way to literally justify how picking your nose was a sin. After studying the bible for many years now I can say there is no scripture that says "thou shalt not picketh thy nose." And that you had to live in constant fear of God leaving you and withdrawing his spirit from you forever. Never to EVER have any chance of him taking you back and you could NEVER have repentance again if you just "accidently" messed up and sinned. The church leaders basically believed that you could never be as holy and perfect as they were. Most of them had not faced temptation in probably 36 years. They believed that you were evil if you were even tempted, although you never yielded to it. You would not be tempted if you were not evil already. We were taught as 14 and 15-year-old boys that if you noticed girls that meant that you were a sex maniac and were probably very close to being demon possessed. We were also taught that we could be demon possessed at any moment. I envisioned walking down the street one day and all of a sudden falling to the ground slithering around like a snake, foaming at the mouth, speaking in a deep demonic voice. After all, understand that I do not believe the hyper grace teaching. I believe that if we sin, we have to repent and ask God to forgive us. But we were NOT taught that God was a loving, forgiving, and merciful Heavenly Father. We were taught he was ONLY a mean God of judgment and he was just waiting for the moment for you to make a mistake just, so he could kick you out of his presence, and he would enjoy doing it because you deserved it. I believed it because this is what I had seen my entire childhood. Basically we always had to wonder if we were saved or not. Because we were taught that we could try to live right our entire lives and still not make it to Heaven and bust Hell wide open. And they really enjoyed talking about busting Hell wide open. Satan used this to build another stronghold of bondage in my life. In this church I was not taught how to build a spiritual foundation.

But I did experience a mighty move of God there from the age of 16 to 18 that put something within me where I could never give up on God. In this church the young people became hungry for a move of God. They began to pray for God to use them to reach the world. We began to pray before each service in the back room and we saw God move mightily. Soon that wasn't enough, we had to have more. We became Holy Ghost addicts. We began having prayer meetings on Friday nights, Saturday nights, on camping trips, sleepovers, riding down the highway, basically anywhere, anytime. We would see young people so drunk in the Holy Ghost that they could not stand by themselves. We saw young people slain in the Spirit. We saw broken bones healed instantly. We saw cancer healed. We saw people get up out of wheelchairs. Soon it caught on in the rest of the congregation and the church was on fire spiritually.

So, as I became a young adult this revival subsided after about 3 years. I did not know how to stand and endure and when the winds of temptation began to blow my spiritual house was built on sand and I fell big-time. I quickly fell into pornography going to bars, strip clubs, ungodly relationships, and many other things, and I could not stop. Lust controlled my life. That's all that was on my mind. I stole money, stole things and sold them. I did things that I would have gone to jail for if I had been caught. I burned a house down. Ran from the police several times and never got caught. Five times God spared my life. A car chase 2 times. Once 2 guys were holding me in the basement of a building and they had plans for a sexual encounter. I said that I would die before that happened. Suddenly, they took off running out of the building putting their pants on as they ran, as if they had seen something there besides me. I think maybe an angel appeared to them to rescue me. A man tried to kidnap me in Birmingham and I began to run as he was chasing me. When he got about 5 foot from me he stopped running and was no longer looking at me it was as if I was invisible. I hid behind a car as he passed right by 2 times and never saw me. Another time a guy with a gun was going to kill me. Long story short I got away.

I did other things that I will never be able to tell about. I had a severe anger problem. Things were destroyed by my hands due to my anger. I've ran people off the highway more than once because they made me mad. One day going to Clanton Alabama I ran a girl off the road into the medium. She ran thru a road construction sign, came back up on the road did a 360, ran off the road on the right and ran thru a big green sign on the side of the highway. She was just one of many people I did that to. I did a lot of really bad things to people for revenge. I've put water in gas tanks and sugar in the oil in engines and I've never got caught.

I did things that would make you sick to your stomach and literally theirs also, if they had known what they had eaten. I did Vandalism to people's property. There are people still wondering today who did some of those things, just because they made me angry. I've cost people a lot of money in revenge. Some things I will never be able to tell about.

Because of what I had been taught and the way that I saw God because of the stronghold Satan had over me I was 99.9% convinced because of the things I had been doing that God had left me forever. That I would never have a chance to come back to him. I believed that he would never take me back. I was almost convinced that I was a spiritual outcast from God forever and that he now hated me for what I had done. But I had a .01% chance of hope in me that maybe; just maybe what I had been taught was wrong. I can't describe the agony and despair I felt believing that God had left forever. I tried to pray for almost 3 years and felt like I wasn't getting anywhere. Because at that time I didn't believe that God would touch me. I basically believed that he wouldn't. I had no one I could turn to. Sometimes I would take so many pain pills I would just get stoned and go to sleep. That way I could forget everything. I sure couldn't go to the church people I knew. If I did they'd shoot me with their spiritual shotguns and kill me for coming into their holy presence with a spiritual problem. So, I cried, I begged, I pleaded, I prayed and although God was there all the time, the stronghold was so strong I didn't know it. I couldn't feel him. One day after praying I said God even if I never feel your spirit again, and even if you never forgive me and even if you never take me back I will never give up trying, and you will never get rid of me and you will never get me off your back and that's a promise.

One really bad day I felt like I couldn't take much more of this agony. I picked up my pistol and as I looked it, I heard a voice say all it will take is just one shot and all of this will be over. It was really starting to sound very temping. I just couldn't take any more and as I picked the pistol up and had it half way to my head I remembered my promise to God and I said "NO," I PROMISED GOD I'm NOT GIVING UP."

Later on, sometime after that I was driving down the interstate on a really bad day when once again the emotional pain and agony got the best of me. I heard the same voice again, "YOU SEE THAT CONCRETE PILLAR HOLDING UP THE OVERPASS, STOMP IT TO THE FLOOR HIT IT AT 100 MPH AND ALL OF THIS WILL BE OVER." Once again, I remembered my promise to God. "I SAID NO, I PROMISED GOD I'M NOT GIVING UP."

Another day all the pressure of believing God had left me forever had become more than I could take. I had a bottle of pain pills that was narcotics, the voice said just take the whole bottle you'll just go to sleep; you'll feel no pain, and all this will be over. But this time something was different, this time I felt anger. And with a loud angry voice I yelled, "I SAID NO, I PROMISED GOD I'm NOT GIVING UP AND I'M NOT NOW SHUT UP." (I was always a little hard headed)

One night shortly after that I met Jesus one on one. I don't know if it was a dream, a vision, or if it actually happened in person. All I can tell you is that I was there when it happened. At first, I saw myself kneeling and praying in a dark room. I saw a tall broad-shouldered man dressed in white from the shoulders down to the floor enter the room. The room lit up as he walked over to me. All of a sudden, I was not watching from across the room, now I was there kneeling. He never said a single word as he knelt beside me and put his arms around me. As he did he totally engulfed me. I knew this was Jesus.

At that moment something in me broke. I felt God's love like I'd never felt it before, like an open flood gate after a deluge. That one stronghold of seeing God as a mean God that hated me, being convinced I was a spiritual outcast from his presence was instantly destroyed. It no longer existed. I now knew God loved me and that he was with me and I was convinced of that. But I still had all the other bondages to overcome.

For some reason I thought I had to make a deal with God. So, after that I would say ok God its Monday I will not give in to any of those things I've been doing between now and Friday. By Monday night I was all messed up again. So, I'd cry and cry and pray and say God I'm sorry if you forgive me I won't ever do it again. I won't give in between now and the end of the week, I promise. The next day I'd be right back there again. The bondages were so strong I couldn't stop by myself. This went on with this same routine for what seemed to be a million times. But I was really trying and very sincere. After a while I figured out this wasn't going to work. I said God with your help I think I can make it 60 seconds at a time. And that's about it. And I said Satan listen up from now on when you tempt me I'm going to pray and read the bible. If you don't stop then I'll memorize some bible verses and THEN if you don't stop, I'll find some way to witness to somebody. Well over the next few years or so I did a lot of fighting. I did a LOT of praying. I did a LOT of bible reading and memorized a LOT of scripture. And even found a few people to witness to.

What I didn't realize was this was building a spiritual foundation which was something I never had. One day I realized that it had been a long-time since I had a battle with the old things I used to fight. Matter of fact I now hated those things and found them to be very repulsive. Then God gave me another dream.

I was walking down a long dirt road. There was a very deep drop off on the right side of the road and I could not see the bottom. On the left side of the road was a swamp that came all the way up to the road. In front of me was an extremely steep road that seemed to go almost straight up to the top of a mountain. I climbed for some time with great effort and finally reached the top. As I stood there on top of the mountain I looked back down from where I had come. I saw a huge dead snake about the size of a house coiled up under the water of the swamp at foot of the mountain. God gave me a message as I stood there.

He said "AS LONG AS YOU CHOOSE TO REMAIN ON TOP OF THE MOUNTAIN YOU ARE DELIVERED. BUT IF YOU EVER CHOOSE TO GO BACK DOWN THE MOUNTAIN FROM WHERE YOU CAME THE SNAKE WILL COME BACK ALIVE AND WILL TRY TO CONSUME YOU". I have chosen to stay on top of the mountain. God helped me to work through all the issues from my childhood. The relationship with my mother and dad was restored. Both my parents have passed away now. I have forgiven them. My wife and I had taken over my dad's health care 24/7 for 9 months before he died. My self-esteem and confidence are restored. Now some people think that I am over confident because I really think a lot of myself. I'm not passive aggressive. I'm no longer vengeful. I'm delivered from all the other bondages that once hold me captive for so long. The self-guilt is gone, the mental torment is gone, and the strongholds are destroyed. I don't have visions of killing anyone anymore. I love animals. I love helping people. The depression is destroyed. I never had anyone to talk to for help, just God. That's a miracle.

During the time all of this was going on I later went thru 13 years of a bad marriage. She told me if I didn't stop going to church and start drinking, partying, and going to clubs with her she would find her someone who would. Knowing what that meant, I said well go ahead and find you someone who will because I made God a promise that "I'M NOT GIVING UP." I had just come out of that lifestyle; I wasn't going back into it. Even if that meant losing my family.

She did find someone who would join her, she divorced me in June of '98 for the one who would. I didn't leave her; she left me by her own free will choice. I lost everything I had, my home, my sons, my money, my automobiles, my everything. I was living in a Chevrolet van for about a year wherever I could find to park at night. It was hot in the summer and cold in the winter. She later died due to her life style.

I walked into a church service during this time where no one knew me. The minister pointed at me and said he had a word from God for me.

He said, "God said that Satan has tried many things to destroy your life and he has failed.
But God says that I will restore back to you ALL the things that have been stolen from you.
As long as you seek me first, you won't have to seek to obtain all these other things. Because
I will freely give the desires of your heart. I will give you a family and I will give your sons back to you as you have asked me to do."

God restored everything that had been stolen from me. I now have more than I did back then. God sent me a good wife, cars, a home and I even ended up with custody of both my sons.

Satan tried to end my life one day long after this with a stroke. The doctor said from what he was seeing I should have either been dead or in critical condition. He said it had just stopped progressing for some strange reason before it got to that point. He did not know why. I do know why.

At the time this was going on, my brother received a phone call from a friend. She relayed a story that she was praying, and the Holy Spirit spoke to her that Satan had planned to end my life that day with a stroke, but God put forth his hand and said, "NO, I WILL NOT ALLOW YOU TO DO IT."

I co-pastored for some years which was the most life-giving thing I've ever done. I pray to be in a pastoral position again soon.

I've worked in Celebrate Recovery where God uses me in changing lives. My wife and I have taught Encounter Ministries in different churches. That consist in the teaching of this book plus more information on healing, deliverance and the strategies of Satan and the demonic. It also teaches how to walk that freedom daily. In this type of ministry, we can go into other churches conducting teaching seminars.

Nathan Vaughn

To schedule teaching and ministry engagements
Contact: Nathan Vaughn with Kingdom Exposed Ministries
Phone: 205-427-4414, 205-222-2231
E-mail: nathanv61@hotmail.com